The Baptist Faith and Message 2000

The Baptist Faith and Message 2000

Critical Issues in America's Largest Protestant Denomination

Edited by
Douglas K. Blount
and
Joseph D. Wooddell

ROWMAN & LITTLEFIELD PUBLISHERS, INC.
Lanham • Boulder • New York • Toronto • Plymouth, UK

ROWMAN & LITTLEFIELD PUBLISHERS, INC.

Published in the United States of America
by Rowman & Littlefield Publishers, Inc.
A wholly owned subsidary of The Rowman & Littlefield Publishing Group, Inc.
4501 Forbes Boulevard, Suite 200, Lanham, Maryland 20706
www.rowmanlittlefield.com

Estover Road
Plymouth PL6 7PY
United Kingdom

British Library Cataloguing in Publication Information Available

Library of Congress Cataloging-in-Publication Data:

The Baptist faith and message 2000 : critical issues in America's largest Protestant
denomination / edited by Douglas K. Blount and Joseph D. Wooddell.
    p.   cm.
Includes bibliographical references and index.
ISBN-13: 978-0-7425-5102-2 (cloth : alk. paper)
ISBN-13: 978-0-7425-5103-9 (cloth : alk. paper)
ISBN-10: 0-7425-5102-4 (pbk. : alk. paper)
ISBN-10: 0-7425-5103-2 (pbk. : alk. paper)
    1. Baptists—United States.   I. Blount, Douglas K., 1965–   II. Wooddell, Joseph D.,
1968–   III. Title.
BX6461.7.B37 2007
286'.132—dc22   2007010348

Printed in the United States of America

The paper used in this publication meets the minimum requirements of American National
Standard for Information Sciences—Permanence of Paper for Printed Library Materials,
ANSI/NISO Z39.48-1992.

Contents

Foreword

Always be ready to give a defense to anyone who asks you for a reason
for the hope that is in you.

—1 Peter 3:15, Holman Christian Standard Bible

*W*ith the above directive in mind, the 1999 Southern Baptist Convention
voted for then-president Paige Patterson to appoint a committee to review the
Baptist Faith and Message and bring any recommendations for its revision to the
next annual meeting. Facing a new century, messengers to the convention voted
overwhelmingly for a reexamination of our confessional statement. It was widely
recognized that, in a culture hostile to the idea of absolute truth, this generation
of Southern Baptists must set forth and clarify the veracity of Scripture as they
understand it. This was especially true in light of the conservative resurgence
within our denomination and the need to address specific issues that had arisen
since the adoption of the 1963 version of the *Baptist Faith and Message*.

Given this charge, the *Baptist Faith and Message 2000* study committee was
formed. It was my privilege to be a part of this committee and to be present for
all of its meetings. Dr. Patterson appointed a committee representative of
Southern Baptist life. It was diverse not only in gender but also in ethnicity,
representing the African-American, Hispanic, and Asian communities. It
included theologians, pastors, a Baptist Student Union director, a state convention's Woman's Missionary Union and Women's Ministry director, seminary
presidents, an agency head, and laypersons. Only persons committed to the
inerrancy of Scripture were appointed to the committee.

The chair of the committee was the gracious and irreplaceable Adrian
Rogers, who conducted each meeting with efficiency, humility, and humor. At
its first meeting Dr. Rogers challenged the committee to consider the various
questions that had arisen regarding the 1963 version of the *Baptist Faith and
Message*. We were then encouraged to discuss and examine carefully each issue
raised by these questions and its relation to Baptist beliefs. Dr. Rogers was quite
firm that there be no discrepancy or ambiguity in our language, since words
communicate the essence of our faith. We also wanted to retain as much language from the 1925 and 1963 versions as possible.

With the input of theologians, pastors, and laypersons, the statement was carefully crafted. We all believed it important not to use technical theological terms that would be unintelligible to the average Baptist. Rather, we worked diligently to choose language that best and most simply conveyed our beliefs. As women on the committee, Heather King Moore and I believed, along with the other committee members, that Article VI on the church needed to speak to the issue of women in the pastorate, as this is an issue within both Baptist life and the broader culture of evangelicalism.

Our committee was honored to be given this assignment and serve in this historic task. When presented on the floor of the convention in Orlando, messengers adopted the *Baptist Faith and Message 2000* as it was presented with a near unanimous vote. In so doing, Southern Baptists embraced their rich Baptist heritage and bore witness to the holy and inerrant Scriptures. While future generations will be called upon to give their own defense, I believe that our committee fulfilled the charge given to us for our day and hour.

In light of the historical importance of this document to Southern Baptists, I enthusiastically welcome this book edited by Drs. Blount and Wooddell. I believe it will be extremely helpful in articulating why certain changes were necessary and why certain language was chosen. The contributors bring expertise to their chapters and each affirms the truth of our long held convictions. I pray that the Holy Spirit will use this book and our doctrinal confession to enable us to continue giving "a defense for the hope that is in us"!

Susie Hawkins
4 September 2006

Baptist Faith and Message 2000 Committee Members:
Max Barnett (OK)
Steve Gaines (AL)
Rudy A. Hernandez (TX) (deceased)
Charles S. Kelley Jr. (LA)
Heather King Moore (IN)
Richard D. Land (TN)
Fred Luter (LA)
R. Albert Mohler Jr. (KY)
T. C. Pinckney (VA)
Nelson Price (GA)
Adrian Rogers (TN), Chairman (deceased)
Roger Spradlin (CA)
Simon Tsoi (AZ)
Jerry Vines (FL)

Preface

Douglas K. Blount and Joseph D. Wooddell

$\mathscr{B}$ aptists are a confessional people. Like most Christians throughout the church's long history, they believe it important to summarize their doctrinal beliefs and commitments. Among Southern Baptists, this belief has given rise to the *Baptist Faith and Message,* now in its third edition. This statement of confessional commitment first appeared in 1925, with a second edition in 1963, and the most recent one in 2000. In this volume's introductory chapter, Tom Nettles discusses the history and purpose of the *Baptist Faith and Message,* so we shall not treat them here. A brief word on the committee charged with bringing recommendations to the 2000 annual meeting of the Southern Baptist Convention regarding the revision of the document is, however, in order.

In 1999, "T. C. Pinckney of Virginia made the motion that the incoming president [Paige Patterson] appoint a committee to revisit the statement," which he did.[1] A broad spectrum of Southern Baptist life was represented. The committee was multi-ethnic, with four ethnicities—African-Americans, Anglos, Asians, and Hispanics—represented. Women were represented by Heather King Moore and Susie Hawkins. Baptist Student Ministries were represented by Max Barnett. SBC agencies (as well as theologians) were represented by Albert Mohler, Richard Land, and Charles Kelley. Pastors and evangelists on the committee included Adrian Rogers (who served as its chair), Steve Gaines, Rudy Hernandez, Fred Luter, Nelson Price, Roger Spradlin, Simon Tsoi, and Jerry Vines. Finally, T. C. Pinckney, Susie Hawkins, and Heather King Moore represented SBC laity.

We should also say a word about the purpose of this volume of essays—*both* what it is *and* what it is *not* intended to be. As the reader will no doubt discover in the following pages, the *Baptist Faith and Message 2000* has given rise to much controversy. In 2001, the Southern Baptist Theological Seminary published a relatively brief (though quite helpful) exposition of the document.[2] Until now, however, a one-volume explanation and defense of the *Baptist Faith and Message 2000* has not appeared in more extensive, book form. We felt that such a volume was needed. It is intended to be used in college and seminary classes in such disciplines as theology, church history, and Baptist distinctives as well as in churches and denominational settings. It aims at educating both Baptists and non-Baptists on the *Baptist Faith and Message 2000,* explaining what the confession actually says and defending it against criticisms that have been directed against it.

Some of the confession's eighteen articles have changed little or not at all over the years and require little defense. However, even some unchanged articles are nonetheless controversial within and without Baptist life and thus do require defense. Still other articles have changed substantially over the years and require extensive discussion. Of course, all articles require *some* explanation. Given these factors, the authors of the various chapters were at liberty to use their allotted pages to deal with their articles as they saw fit.

It goes without saying that not all Baptists will agree with everything in this volume. And, of course, the volume itself is not intended to be a once-for-all, definitive explanation or defense of the *Baptist Faith and Message 2000.* In fact, *we* do not necessarily agree with all that's said in this volume. Had we written the entire book, we would have treated some of the articles differently. But such is the nature of the people called Baptist (and, by God's grace, of the larger body of Christ). We do think, however, that the essays presented here accomplish their end and we recommend them heartily. Before reading any particular essay in this volume, we also recommend first reading the article of the confession that it addresses. Our hope and prayer is that the body of Christ be stronger, purer, and more effective as a result of this study, that the Kingdom of God would be advanced, and that Baptists and non-Baptists alike would clearly understand and appreciate the *Baptist Faith and Message 2000.*

Many thanks to former Rowman & Littlefield editor Jeremy Langford for taking on this project, and to R&L's Ross Miller, Ruth Gilbert, Kat Macdonald, Heather Carreiro, and Coghill Composition for seeing it to completion. Thanks also to all of the contributors; we are blessed to have such competent scholars give much time and effort to what we pray is a worthy cause. The contributors themselves are grateful to colleagues and students who read their manuscripts and provided valuable insight. We appreciate Morris Chapman, Augie Boto, and the SBC executive committee for permission to reprint all three versions of the *Baptist Faith and Message.* Doug dedicates this work to his parents, Bill and Judy Blount, whose home gave faith wings; Joe dedicates this work to his father, John Wooddell, who taught him to think critically and Christianly, and to his mother, Brenda Ruffner, who has sacrificed so much for

her children. We both wish to acknowledge publicly our love and gratitude to
our families for their sacrificial love and support, and especially to the Lord
Jesus Christ, who allows us the privilege of laboring for Him.

NOTES

1. Paige Patterson, personal correspondence, 7 March 2006.

2. The publication can be found at www.sbts.edu/pdf/bfmexposition.pdf. The copyright information states, " 'An Exposition from the Faculty of the Southern Baptist Theological Seminary on *The Baptist Faith and Message* 2000' was produced by The Southern
Baptist Theological Seminary. The articles included in the publication initially appeared in
the 'Issue Insight' column of *Towers*, the campus publication for Southern Seminary. Executive Editor: Bryan Cribb. Design and Layout: John Rogers. Copyright 2001, The Southern
Baptist Theological Seminary."

· *Introduction* ·

How to Lose Your Way:
A History Lesson in Confessions

Tom J. Nettles

A PATH DIVIDES

*W*hen E. Y. Mullins said "Amen" at the 1922 annual meeting of the Northern Baptist Convention in Indianapolis, Indiana, he knew that the adoption of
a confession of faith was inevitable for the Southern Baptist Convention.
Although they had become organizationally distinct in 1845, the first real split
between Baptists in the North and Baptists in the South came at this 1922
convention. Mullins had just witnessed a theological coup on the part of the
liberal wing of the Northern Baptists.

Quite aware of the liberal hegemony in the educational institutions and
the resultant encroachment of liberalism even into the mission field, conservative leadership in the North sought to stem the tide of this "unquestioned
defection from the faith that now endangers the good name and the greater
progress of our holy cause." The Minnesota pastor W. B. Riley believed that
Baptists worldwide expected and hoped for "a declaration from us concerning
the 'faith once delivered to the saints' " to remedy this serious doctrinal permu-
tation. He then moved that the Convention adopt the New Hampshire Confession and recommend it to the local churches.[1]

Immediately subsequent to his recommendation, Cornelius Woelfkin
offered a substitute motion. Woelfkin served as pastor of the famous Park Ave-
nue Baptist Church from 1912 to 1926 and prepared the way for his successor,
Harry Emerson Fosdick. Fosdick, who moved the church out of the Baptist
fold, renamed it Riverside Church, and made it the prow of liberal ministry.
Woelfkin served churches in New York and New Jersey from 1885 except for
the years 1906 to 1912 when he taught homiletics at Rochester Divinity
School and helped facilitate the final stages of its weary journey into liberalism.

His motion said simply, "The Northern Baptist Convention affirms that the New Testament is the all-sufficient ground of our faith and practise [sic], and we need no other statement."[2]

Mullins doubtless was chagrined and perplexed by this development. He was seeking to mend fences with his brethren in the North since he had discovered they were "abnormally sensitive" due to a misperception of Southern Baptists' intentions in the *Fraternal Address* of 1919. The *Address* presented to Baptists worldwide a statement of faith that they might have a means by which to "identify their oneness" with Southern Baptists. It ended with an invitation for "those in every land who find themselves in agreement with the above articles of faith and who crave fellowship with others who hold them" to correspond with the Foreign Mission Board of the Southern Baptist Convention. E. B. Pollard, a Northern Baptist, thought this appeal to unity "on the basis of a creed" was a "wedge to divide Northern Baptists" and an attempt to draw conservative Northern Baptists "into cooperative relations with the Southern Baptist Convention." Mullins defended the doctrinal statement on the basis of much broader needs, asserting, "I think there are times when such statements are justifiable and may be of great value." He viewed the "present one of those occasions."[3]

Prior to the confessionally fatal Northern Baptist Convention of 1922, Northern and Southern Baptists contemplated a jointly issued confession. In January, James M. Wood, president of Stephens College at Columbia, Missouri, invited certain leaders of both Conventions to an "informal conference" that included their respective presidents, E. Y. Mullins and Helen Barrett Montgomery. Participants hoped that such a fraternal meeting would mollify suspicions aroused earlier by the *Fraternal Address*. Both addressed the question, "What is the proper purpose of a Baptist confession of faith, and should Baptists have one?" The discussion showed "approximate and substantial" agreement on a variety of issues. The unofficial conference decided, therefore, to appeal to the respective conventions to cooperate on the adoption of a "statement of Baptist doctrine and polity, setting forth briefly the fundamentals of our faith and the peculiar beliefs and observances which characterize and distinguish us."[4]

Accordingly, the Southern Baptist Convention, meeting in May 1922, adopted a resolution proposing that a committee of twenty, including the presidents as *ex officio* members, be charged "with the duty of preparing a statement of faith and polity."[5] Less than two months later the goal of a jointly issued confession ended abruptly with Woelfkin's motion. When Mullins prayed immediately following that debate, he no doubt saw visions of alarmed Southern Baptists pressing toward a declaration of doctrine. They would not be ashamed to set forth their jointly held view of the gospel nor would they shy away from letting the world know their distinctively Baptist doctrines.

AN OBJECT LESSON IN
NON-CONFESSIONALISM

If any wanted to use the Northern Baptist Convention as an object lesson as to why confessions should be used they would not have long to wait. Since A. H. Strong's visit to the mission field and his sounding of the alarm of the dangers of liberal education to missions in 1918, complaints of liberalism on the mission field had increased.[6] A special committee appointed to investigate these allegations made its report in 1925. They were particularly concerned with the policy of the Board of Managers in the appointment and retention of "missionaries who do not accept or have repudiated or abandoned the evangelical faith as held historically by Baptists."

One can see the difficulties the Board faced in trying to sort out the doctrinal fitness of missionaries without having a confessional standard. "Liberty must be limited," they averred, "and it must be limited by loyalty, loyalty to Christ as risen Saviour and Lord, loyalty to the gospel of divine grace, loyalty to the great Baptist principles which bind us together." These words beg for a statement of faith to enunciate these "great Baptist principles." And again, "Liberty must never degenerate into license or into indifference to dangerous error," implying consensus as to what constitutes dangerous error. Then adding with painfully undefined words, liberty "must always be exercised in our denominational sphere within the bounds of the Christian and Baptist faith." But what Baptist faith do they mean? As a Convention they had decided not to define it. The investigation committee quoted the Board's representation as to how they sought to maintain doctrinal equilibrium.

> Guided by the facts that Baptists have always been known as evangelicals, and that the gospel is the most important message of the Scriptures, we have demanded that all our officers and missionaries be loyal to the gospel. We will appoint only suitable evangelical men and women; we will appoint evangelicals and we will not appoint non-evangelicals. And by the gospel we mean *the good news of the free forgiveness of sin and eternal life (beginning now and going on forever) through a vital union with the crucified and risen Christ, which brings men into union and fellowship with God. This salvation is graciously offered on the sole condition of repentance and faith in Christ and has in it the divine power of regeneration and sanctification through the Spirit. The only reason we have for accepting this gospel is our belief in the deity of Christ in whom we see the Father, a faith founded on the trustworthiness of the Scriptures and the fact that we have experienced this salvation in our own hearts.*[7]

While a historic evangelical might respond positively to the doctrinal abstract given as a definition of the gospel and the body of truth implied in it, its historical context engenders questions. What is a "suitable evangelical"? By what standard does the Board define one? Through what denominational warrant did they gain the right to offer a set of criteria for the appointment of missionaries? When they state, "By the gospel *we mean*," was the Convention to understand that the Board had an independent authority to establish an epitomized doctrinal standard irrespective of the Convention's vote to have none except the New Testament? Their candid admission that they had an "inclusive policy" that ranged widely to retain personnel of "varying theological beliefs" gave way to "certain limits which the Board regarded as 'the limits of the gospel'." It seems that the only limiting authority in the Convention was the Board of Managers and its own vision of theological parameters.

The context shows that deeply imbedded concerns about doctrine prompted the investigation. At the same time, the confession in the heads of the members of the Convention had no final leverage on the Board's policies. They could only hope that the Board shared their outlook and that a commonly held standard would be sufficient to repel error and recover from decline. Officially, however, theological expectation was empty and eventually must give way to latitude of theological expression. They had to work and cooperate in light of the reality that lack of confessional definition meant virtual unlimited acceptance of the personal theologies of any that called themselves Baptists. Certain facts had to be taken into account.

1. That the denomination, itself, is constituted of individuals who are allowed a wide degree of theological difference.
2. That a test of membership in the Convention is not put on theological grounds.
3. That representatives of widely differing theological views are members, occupy the platform and take part in the deliberations of the Convention without a theological test being applied.
4. That the denomination appeals to all for support, accepts money from all, thus implying that in some fair way representation should be given to these various groups in the work of the denomination.[8]

In spite of such latitude, the committee's investigation did yield some cases of doctrinal divergence "so extreme that in our judgment they do not come within the limits laid down by the Board." One missionary believed that "many a poem of our day [is] as God-inspired and as God-filled and helpful as many of the Books of the Bible and more so than some." Another believed that the doctrine of an atonement for the forgiveness of sins "could not possibly be acceptable to our Father" and the idea violated "the perfect quality of God's fatherliness." Another affirmed, "There is no man, no matter how vile, without some solid good, some of the stuff of God in him," and that there is some "invitation of God to which he will respond, although he may have to hear it in the next world." Another doubted the reality of eternal life, disagreed with Paul's "philosophy" of centering so much hope in the resurrection, and said the "Christ life" is best even if there is no eternity. Others believed that the doctrine of Christ's unique and particular deity could not be sustained and, in fact, was an insult to the beauty of his sacrificial human life and death.[9]

This alarming sprinkling of missionaries with such anti-evangelical ideas prompted the investigation committee to remind the schools to "recognize their responsibility," so the report reads, "to train and send forth men and women who fulfil these requirements and who will consequently go out having a warmhearted, positive, and evangelical Christian message."[10] None would now, however, be able to recognize an "evangelical Christian message," for the Convention had poked out its eyes while urging itself to see.

Upon hearing the report, conservatives seized the opportunity to bring in a confession of faith by the back door. They wanted to give substance to this undefined "evangelical Christian message." Rev. W. B. Hinson of Oregon moved the adoption of the following resolution.

> Whereas, The report of our committee appointed a year ago to investigate the work on our foreign fields reveals both a careful and extensive survey of the same; and
>
> Whereas, According to its report there are at present upon some of the stations men and women who do not hold to the fundamentals of the Christian faith as historically interpreted by Baptists, and
>
> Whereas, The Northern Baptist Convention in its sessions in Indianapolis adopted the New Testament as our basis of faith; and
>
> Whereas, The New Testament clearly teaches the divine and direct creation of man in the image of God, the supernatural inspiration of the Scriptures of both the Old and New Testaments, the certain Deity of Jesus Christ, involving his virgin birth, his sinless life, his sacrificial death, his bodily resurrection and ascension to the right hand of God, and his return; and
>
> Whereas, The same Scriptures clearly declare the necessity of the sinful soul's regeneration in order to redemption; the baptism of believers as a condition of church-membership; and involves for all the saved a commission to preach the gospel, baptize into the name of the Lord Jesus, and teach the observance of all things which he has commanded. . . .

The resolution then commended the Commission for its careful work, commended theologically orthodox missionaries, and asked the convention to instruct the Mission Boards to "recall immediately every representative, whether in evangelistic or educational work, who is found on investigation to deny any of the great fundamentals of our faith aforementioned." These should be replaced with "competent men and women whose evangelical faith and fervor cannot be questioned." Further, no one "should accept place on our mission boards who cannot, with whole heart, believe and advocate the historic Baptist and evangelical faith."[11]

To adopt such a resolution would be to adopt a confession of faith—greatly truncated, but a confession nevertheless. The consideration of the resolution was postponed and brought to the floor later reduced greatly. The first three "whereas" statements remained as stated. All the rest was omitted and replaced with "*Resolved*, That we urge upon our Foreign Mission Board such action, in light of the facts reported by the Commission, as seems to them will best conserve our denominational interests and best advance the kingdom of Christ."[12] The convention again avoided the danger of expressing and adopting a confession and left doctrinal matters purely and exclusively at the Board's discretion.[13]

ENOUGH OF THE FOOLISHNESS

Southern Baptists were in no mood for such nonsense as a refusal to state clearly their theology under feint of reverence for Scripture. Their hackles had been raised in World War I by the nondenominational character of much of the religious ministry to the troops. Southern Baptist colleges were under siege with the intrusion of evolution into the textbooks, raising the broader question of whether distinctively Christian education was even a possibility. A report at the 1922 meeting of the Convention cautioned strongly, "In our effort to raise the academic standards for our schools to the highest demand of the secular schools, we must not sacrifice or suffer to be eclipsed our moral and spiritual and doctrinal standards."[14]

The Seventy-Five Million Campaign had put a halt in the step of many Baptists who suspected that an expanded denominational program of financial support that created interdependent institutional life would necessarily produce doctrinal disintegration. Those that followed the progression of conflict in the Northern Baptist Convention had good reason for their suspicions. Due to such suspicions, indoctrination received special attention during the campaign. In 1920, the committee expressed confidence that Southern Baptists had been through the first year of the campaign "without the impairment of their conscience or the embarrassment of their doctrines." They achieved a "victory without doctrinal regret and they face the future with the heart-joy of having kept the faith while they obeyed the Saviour's command to go forward."[15]

By 1923 agitation over the evolution question in the public generally and in Baptist schools in particular boiled at fever pitch. The increasing interdependence of Convention institutions, a "situation not contemplated by the founders of this body," called for reaffirmation of "certain great truths, such as creation by divine fiat as set forth in the word of God; the incarnation, involving the virgin birth of our Saviour and His atoning death."[16] The Convention, however, in the judgment of the Committee on Resolutions, must take care not to violate the "sovereignty of the churches" or give the appearance of intermeddling in institutions over which it has no jurisdiction. They expressed particular concern over a resolution presented by Brother Brownlow of Tennessee who called for a "death bomb" approach to correct those who are "insane on the phantom of higher education."[17]

While Brownlow's resolution failed to reach the floor for a vote, much sympathy had already been indicated for rigorous doctrinal affirmation. Mullins had addressed the Convention on the subject "Present Dangers and Duties." His address included a statement on "Science and Religion." On the motion of E. D. Cameron of Oklahoma, Mullins's statement was adopted "as the belief of this body." Mullins had cautiously protested against the imposition of evolution theory as fact, though it would probably continue to be a working hypothesis of science. The facts of religion in no way contradict the facts of science, Mullins insisted, and Southern Baptists must "record our unwavering adherence to the supernatural elements in the Christian religion."

> The Bible is God's revelation of Himself through man moved by the Holy Spirit, and is our sufficient certain and authoritative guide in religion. Jesus Christ was born of the Virgin Mary through the power of the Holy Spirit. He was the Divine and eternal Son of God. He wrought miracles, healing the sick, casting out demons, raising the dead. He died as the vicarious atoning Saviour of the world and was buried. He arose from the dead. The tomb was emptied of its contents. In His risen body He appeared many times to His disciples. He ascended to the right hand of the Father. He will come again in person, the same Jesus who ascended from the Mount Olives.

Mullins went on to declare that adherence to those "facts" was a "necessary condition of service for teachers in our Baptist schools" and that all should "be careful to free themselves from any suspicion of disloyalty on this point."[18]

The next year, 1924, sympathy for a confession of faith intensified. John E. White, chairing the Committee on Resolutions, rejected two resolutions proposing doctrinal statements by C. P. Stealey of Oklahoma and R. K. Maiden of Missouri. Instead they pointed to the fraternal message of 1919 and Mullins's statement of 1923 as "sufficiently comprehensive and definite." The issue, however, cropped up again as C. P. Stealey continued his campaign for a confession by issuing another resolution for the adoption of a confession. Again the committee refused to submit it to the Convention. Given the atmosphere of concern about doctrinal purity, however, the Committee on Resolutions presented a supplementary recommendation that an ad hoc committee be formed "to consider the advisability of issuing another statement of the Baptist faith and message and to report at the next Convention." Those suggested for the committee were: E. Y. Mullins (Chair), L. R. Scarborough, C. P. Stealey, W. J. McGlothlin, S. M. Brown, E. C. Dargan, R. H. Pitt. The next year the *Baptist Faith and Message* was presented. After some discussion and an attempt to amend the article on creation, the recommendation of the committee passed.

"AN AVERSION TO ALL CREEDS"

If it were not clear to the Convention from his activities of the two previous years as a member and Chair of the Committee on Resolutions, 1925 showed unmistakably that John E. White had no sympathy with the movement toward the adoption of a confession of faith. White, President of the College for Women in Anderson, South Carolina, warned that Baptists were in danger of abandoning their time-honored position of having an "aversion to all creeds but the Bible." "It is beyond all dispute," so assuredly he opined, "that this aversion has been a constant and dominant sentiment with American Baptists, and in no section of them more so than among the Baptists of the South."[19]

White's viewpoint had several questionable assumptions. He referred to W. B. Johnson's famous remark, "We have constructed for our basis no new creed, acting in this matter upon a Baptist aversion to all creeds but the Bible." White took this as summarizing the position of all the Augusta delegates as well as Baptists through the centuries. Those "fathers and founders" have the right, according to White, to "speak with high appeal to every Baptist conscience upon" the question of creeds. Should the 1925 Memphis Convention adopt a confession, it must do so, White averred, in the face of a full knowledge that it departs from "the former and long established conception of its functions and of its traditional attitude toward creedal authority."[20]

Although White has found soul mates in the present, many of his contemporaries disagreed. V. I. Masters, editor of the *Western Recorder,* claimed that "No new creed," simply affirmed doctrinal unity, in 1845, between Baptists of the North and the South. No doctrinal explanation was needed for the division. "The only thing that was at stake was our planning for conducting mission work. What differences were there were hinged around slavery." The confession to be proposed in Memphis, Masters continued, could not be made compulsive for a single local church but certainly "could and should be binding upon the Convention's own Boards and agencies."[21]

Mullins, though expressing ambivalent ideas about prescriptive confessions, at this time considered it a good idea for Southern Baptists. He crystallized several points in an article entitled "Baptists and Creeds." Mullins identified four fallacies concerning creeds and answered four reasons for opposing a restatement of beliefs. On three occasions in the short article he answered the misimpression that creeds oppose Baptist views of liberty. He believed that some interpreted liberty as license and others misapplied liberty as "an exaggerated individualism." Mullins spoke of the "group right of self-protection." As Baptists are trustees of certain truths "they have an inalienable right to conserve and propagate those truths unmolested by others inside the denomination who oppose those truths." Mullins believed that the adoption of a new confession—and by this he had in mind the 1925 *Baptist Faith and Message*—would correct some "deadly tendencies at work—deadly." A confession would help "clear the atmosphere and learn where we are drifting."[22]

L. R. Scarborough, president of Southwestern Baptist Theological Seminary and member of the committee on the confession, agreed. Such a confession as was to be proposed would "guard our young people from the teachings and the poisonous inoculation of error contrary to Christ and His Word." He could guarantee that "the Southwestern Seminary, for one, will adopt it and require the hearty endorsement of all of its teachers to its doctrinal content."[23] His advocacy of the confession went even further.

> Why should not the trustees of all our schools make the same requirement of their teachers? We must guard all the foundations of our faith, if we are to be faithful stewards and trustees of the Gospel and deserve and hold the confidence of our people. I do not believe that Southern Baptists will approve or finally allow any of our schools to hold their confidence and support if we school men do not guard with sacred care the vital essentials of the faith of the New Testament. I am sure they ought not to do it.

White held his ground, however, and insisted that confessional conformity violated a sacred Baptist trust. The Baptist "aversion to all creeds" was no private opinion of one man, W. B. Johnson, but the resolute conviction of the whole body of Baptists, not only in 1845, but in all the years prior to that. White issued a challenge: "If any scrap of proof that the founders of the Convention had joined as individuals in the adoption of the New Hampshire confession or other formal creed by any Baptist general body, or did afterwards do so, I will humbly apologize for my ignorance and error."[24]

IGNORANCE AND ERROR

Indeed, White's position involved both ignorance and error. The latter would have been fatal. The Northern Baptist Convention, now American Baptist Churches USA, failed to recover from their dilemma. If White had had his way, the same decline would have enervated Southern Baptist denominational life. The adoption of the *Baptist Faith and Message* in 1925, bringing to fruition the confessional propensities of Southern Baptists, established a sense of doctrinal responsibility that has generated substantial reform in times of doctrinal crisis.

White's ignorance arose from a failure of both historical knowledge and context. In context, Johnson already had affirmed, "Northern and Southern Baptists are still brethren. They differ in no article of the faith."[25] Additionally, Johnson made no reference to articles of faith in the comments under question, but spoke metaphorically of the constitution for the new convention. The Northern Board had imposed a new article, "No slaveholders," on the previous constitution. The South remained on the original "ground from which it has been so unconstitutionally and unjustly attempted to eject us." Southerners adopted a constitution "precisely that of the original union" using the "very terms" and upholding the "true spirit and great object" of the late General Convention. In that sense they "constructed . . . no new creed" (i.e., no innovative article in the Constitution) demonstrating a "Baptist aversion for all creeds but the Bible" (i.e., rejection of slavery on moral grounds had no biblical warrant).[26]

Historical knowledge of the more comprehensive witness of Baptists would have demonstrated unequivocally the fallacy of White's erroneous but confident claim. Surely Timothy George is right when he writes, "Each of the 293 'delegates,' . . . who gathered in Augusta to organize the Southern Baptist Convention in 1845, belonged to congregations and associations which had adopted the *Philadelphia/Charleston Confession of Faith* as their own."[27] The pastor of the first Particular Baptist church in London, John Spilsbery, believed that a confession of faith was essential for the being of the church. Benjamin Keach, Thomas Grantham, John Gill, Andrew Fuller, Abraham Booth, William Screven, Oliver Hart, Richard Furman, Adoniram Judson, Luther Rice, Basil Manly, the Philadelphia Association, the Charleston Association, James P. Boyce, J. B. Gambrell, B. H. Carroll and a host of others could be added to the list of Baptists who accepted the obvious reality that the adoption of a doctrinal standard was "only requiring that a man appear to be a Christian before he can have a right to be treated as such."[28]

Even those most vocal about the Baptist non-use of confessions as terms of "union and communion"—declaring that the Bible alone served that purpose—during the Campbell controversy, nevertheless affirmed that nothing "requires that the churches be gagged, to prevent their proclaiming to the world, in this way [i.e., via creeds] what they believe to be the great truths of our religion." In fact, publishing creeds has "stayed the injurious influences of slander and misinterpretation." As a matter of faithful stewardship of truth, "unless a church is ashamed of her doctrine, we can see no good reason for her shrinking from its publication. Truth needs no concealment and seeks none."[29]

In 1868, the editor of the *Christian Index and Southwestern Baptist* gave an account of trouble within Unitarianism which had driven them to make a "Statement of Christian Faith." The writer observed that their fifty year noncreedal experiment had demonstrated the "folly of the war against creeds." Unitarians earlier rejected the creed because of their antipathy to its trinitarianism; their reversal of practice came because "without them original Unitarianism cannot save itself." Given these realities, the author concluded, "Baptists, as friends of creeds, will not be likely to abandon them."[30]

Clearly, John E. White, to use his suggested nomenclature, was ignorant on the issue of Baptist confessions. Following in his steps would bypass many candles that light a way to truth and make us stumble into a sure path to lose our way.

NOTES

1. *Annual of the Northern Baptist Convention* (American Baptist Publication Society, 1922), 129.

2. Ibid., 133.

3. This material comes from correspondence and personal papers of E. Y. Mullins located in the archives of Boyce Memorial Library at the Southern Baptist Theological Seminary, Box 39, folder 5.

4. *Annual of the Southern Baptist Convention* (1922), 20–21. This precise wording appears as part of the introductory section to the articles of faith in the *Fraternal Address*.

5. *Annual of the SBC* (1922), 20–21.

6. See A. H. Strong, *A Tour of the Missions: Observations and Conclusions* (Philadelphia: Griffith and Rowland, 1918), 165, 193–94, 211.

7. *Annual of the Northern Baptist Convention* (1925), 86.

8. *Annual of the NBC* (1925), 85–86.

9. *Annual of the NBC* (1925), 88–91.

10. *Annual of the NBC* (1925), 93.

11. *Annual of the NBC* (1925), 95.

12. *Annual of the NBC* (1925), 174.

13. Due to the concerns expressed by conservatives, the Foreign Mission Board restated its set of criteria for the appointment of missionaries that had been included in the report of the investigative committee. *Annual of the NBC* (1925), 241.

14. *Annual of the Southern Baptist Convention* (1922), 34.

15. *Annual of the SBC* (1920), 55.

16. *Annual of the SBC* (1923), 62

17. *Annual of the SBC* (1923), 62–63.

18. *Annual of the SBC* (1923), 19–20.

19. John E. White, "A Baptist Aversion to All Creeds," *Western Recorder* (March 19, 1925), 4.

20. White's attitude and viewpoint gained a new group of advocates near the end of the twentieth century. Fisher Humphreys has argued that Baptists have used confessions only as descriptive of faith and not as prescriptive. "Creeds that are used prescriptively are wrong" [*The Way We Were* (Macon: Smyth & Helwys, 2002), 124]. Although he affirms that a denomination cannot allow just any type of teaching in its institutions without restraint, he laments that such care is necessary for it "falls below the Baptist ideal." E. Glenn Hinson—in *Are Southern Baptists "Evangelicals"?*—notes: "All observers of Southern Baptists can discern a radical tilt from an anti-creedal toward a creedal stance in theological matters" [(Macon: Mercer University Press, 1983), 187]. Bill Leonard, writing in 1990, argues that the adoption of a convention-wide confession in 1925 increased confessionalism throughout the century: "Once a confession was written down and officially approved, however, the scene was set for its more arbitrary use in defining the doctrinal parameters of the SBC"; the difference between a confession and a creed is, in Leonard's view, a moot point practically [*God's Last and Only Hope* (Grand Rapids: Eerdmans, 1990), 79]. E. Luther Copeland, in *The Southern Baptist Convention and the Judgment of History*, represents Southern Baptists as moving from "non-creedal beginnings to the present highly restrictive creedalism" [(Lanham: University Press of America, 1995), 113]. Walter Shurden states, "It is a near unanimous opinion among Baptist Historians that Baptists have historically been anti-creedal people." They have shunned the adoption of creeds as "theologically restrictive statements" designed to curtail "freedom of inquiry" ["Major Issues in the SBC Controversy" in *Amidst Babel, Speak the Truth*, ed. Robert U. Ferguson (Macon: Smyth & Helwys, 1993), 8]. Shurden slightly nuances Leonard, observing that the SBC managed to ignore the 1925 and 1963 Confessions [*Baptist Studies Bulletin*, June 2002], but since 1979 has allowed fundamentalists to turn a non-binding confession into a "creed that straps the conscience." Grady Cothen fears a "creeping creedalism" among Southern Baptists who began as people who declared they had "no creed but the Scriptures" [*Whatever Happened to the Southern Baptist Convention?* (Macon: Smyth & Helwys, 1993), 157]. Chauncy Daley writes, "Creedalism is the death blow to freedom and the priesthood of every believer" ["A New and Different Convention" in *The Religious Herald* (August 9, 1990), cited in Cothen, 163].

21. V. I. Masters, "For a Baptist Confession of Faith," *Western Recorder* (March 19, 1925), 12.

22. E. Y. Mullins, "Baptists and Creeds," in *Axioms of Religion*, comp. R. Albert Mohler Jr., ed. Timothy and Denise George (Nashville: Broadman & Holman, 1997), 186–91.

23. L. R. Scarborough, *Western Recorder* (April 2, 1925), 5.

24. John E. White, "Dr. John White Objects to Baptist Confession of Faith," *Western Recorder* (April 2, 1925), 16.

25. W. B. Johnson, "The Southern Baptist Convention, To the Brethren in the United

States; to the congregations connected with the respective Churches; and to all candid men" in Hortense C. Woodson, *Giant in the Land: The Life of William B. Johnson* (Springfield: Particular Baptist, 2005), 205.

26. Woodson, *Giant in the Land*, 206–7. There can be no doubt that Johnson had personal reservations about the usefulness of creeds and confessions. See Greg Wills, *The First Baptist Church of Columbia, South Carolina, 1809–2002* (Nashville: Baptist History and Heritage Society, 2003), 17–19. Few, if any, of the other delegates shared his views and would never have consented to a straightforward disavowal of creeds, definitive articles of faith, or prescriptive confessions.

27. Timothy George, *Baptist Confessions, Covenants, and Catechisms* (Nashville: Broadman & Holman, 1996), 11.

28. *The Complete Works of the Rev. Andrew Fuller*, ed. Joseph Belcher, 3 vols. (Philadelphia: American Baptist Publication Society, 1845), 3:449. For Boyce's strong commendation of subscriptive confessionalism, see James P. Boyce, *Three Changes in Theological Institutions* (Greenville: C. J. Elford's Book and Job Press, 1856), 34–44. For B. H. Carroll's strongly expressed affirmation of "creeds," see B. H. Carroll, *An Interpretation of the English Bible: Colossians, Ephesians, and Hebrews* (Cape Coral: Founders, 2001) 6:139–50. See also J. B. Gambrell, "Concerning the Uses of Creedal Statements," in *Baptist Standard* (January 22, 1914), 1; idem, "The Uses and Abuses of Creedal Statements," in *Baptist Standard* (June 18, 1914), 1, 32.

29. *The Western Baptist Review* (Frankfort, 1845), 1:140.

30. *The Christian Index and Southwestern Baptist* (April 30, 1868).

· Article I ·

The Scriptures

Joseph D. Wooddell

$\mathcal{T}$he writings that constitute the Bible are, and always have been, authoritative for Christians.[1] Converts to Christianity, however, don't normally attempt to establish the veracity of Scripture and then, on that basis, embrace Christianity. Rather, they normally find the great truths of the gospel compelling, and then "sign on" to Christianity, accepting Scripture as authoritative. My essay, therefore, is not an attempt to convince unbelievers of the veracity of Scripture (or the veracity of the Southern Baptist position on Scripture), although I do hope to show that Southern Baptists are not unreasonable in holding their view of Scripture as expressed in the *Baptist Faith and Message 2000*. The explanation and defense are directed primarily toward *Christians*, and particularly Southern Baptists, who object to the new statement.

The Bible is *a* book of books (i.e., a book comprising many books), and *the* Book of books (i.e., the most important of all books). The *Baptist Faith and Message 2000* rightly refers to Scripture as holy, inspired, perfect, divine, true, trustworthy, the supreme standard; it also strongly implies that Scripture is inerrant ("truth, without any mixture of error"). The *Baptist Faith and Message 1963* referred to the Bible as "the *record* of" God's self-revelation to man (emphasis added). Throughout this chapter, I shall refer to the phrase "the record of" as (R). The *Baptist Faith and Message 2000* refers to Scripture simply as "God's revelation." The 1963 version also includes a phrase, known as the criterion statement, which I shall refer to as (C). It goes as follows: "The criterion by which the Bible is to be interpreted is Jesus Christ." The *Baptist Faith and Message 2000* deletes (C), instead stating, "All Scripture is a testimony to Christ, who is Himself the focus of divine revelation." All three versions of the *Baptist Faith and Message* state that the Bible has "truth, without any mixture

1

of error, for its matter," but the 2000 version alone concludes from this that "all Scripture is totally true and trustworthy."

(C) and (R) have given rise to the main controversies concerning the new document, and so are worth treating here. One's view of inspiration and inerrancy, however, will affect one's view of both (C) and (R), so I shall treat these doctrines as well. If biblical inspiration and inerrancy are accepted, then biblical authority (according to which Scripture is the "supreme standard") ought also to be accepted. The following discussion thus moves from the inspiration of Scripture to its inerrancy, then to (R), and finally to (C). In so doing, it seeks to explain and defend Article I as it currently stands.[2]

INSPIRATION

Historically, the Church normally has taken biblical inspiration to involve more than mere human intuition or illumination. The Church Fathers, Medievals, and Reformers generally shared a robust view of inspiration.[3] While opinions differed about whether the human agent was more passive (per dictation and verbal theories of inspiration) or active (per dynamic theories, according to which the human author freely chose words, style, etc.) in writing Scripture, almost none would say divine inspiration was *merely* some "higher development of man's natural insight" (per intuition theory), or "an intensifying and elevating" of man's "religious perceptions" (per illumination theory).[4] As David Dockery maintains, "In the history of the church, the divine character of Scripture has been the great presupposition for the whole of Christian preaching and theology."[5] Referring to Scripture as inspired is not like referring, for example, to a work of art as inspired, for works of art come from merely human effort or genius, while Scripture comes only by divine agency. Indeed, God is its primary author, the human agent being an instrument through whom He produces it. Traditionally, then, the Church has understood the doctrine of biblical inspiration to affirm that God, having chosen to write the texts of Scripture through human agents, is the ultimate author of Scripture.[6]

Critics might ask whether it's even possible for God to speak to man. For Christians, however, the answer is obvious—we know that He can because He has in fact done so. If something is actual, then obviously it's possible. But for those needing a stronger argument, perhaps the following will suffice. If God exists, is maximally perfect (that is, is perfect with respect to such attributes as power, knowledge, and goodness) and the creator of everything apart from Himself, then He is able to speak so that man may understand and record what He says. God, being maximally perfect, is able to accommodate Himself to man. It is also reasonable to think of God as the primary author of such writings. For, if God is able to create and sustain the human mind and body, then He can direct both mind and body to produce a written document of which He is the primary author.

So, God is *able* to speak to man, but *would* He do so? Again, Christians believe He would, for in fact He has. If God is maximally perfect (and thus perfectly good), it seems reasonable to suppose that He wants the best for man, and that what's best for man involves some sort of relationship with (or, at least, recognition of) God. Since then God is both able and willing to communicate with man, it is reasonable to believe that He has done so, perhaps by inspiring human authors to write inspired words.[7]

Biblical writers *were* inspired; the biblical writings *are* inspired. There is no need to choose between the two—neither is unreasonable, and Christians have generally held both to be true. According to all three versions of the *Baptist Faith and Message*, the Bible "was written by men divinely inspired" and "has God for its author." If God is its primary author, it seems unlikely that Scripture makes any false—not to mention contradictory—claims. And this point leads to the topic of biblical inerrancy.[8]

INERRANCY

The first thing to note about the doctrine of inerrancy—call it (DI)—is that discussion of it, like so many other Christian doctrines, is in-house discussion.[9] The Church has no need to prove (DI) to unbelievers. As mentioned earlier, people generally embrace the great truths of the gospel before struggling with such in-house doctrinal issues as biblical inerrancy. The following discussion, therefore, has to do with whether the Church's historic affirmation of (DI) is reasonable, relevant, and right.

All three versions of the *Baptist Faith and Message* state that the Bible has "truth, without any mixture of error, for its matter." The *Baptist Faith and Message 2000* then adds, "Therefore, all Scripture is totally true and trustworthy."[10] That the Bible is inerrant simply means that it makes no false—and thus no contradictory—claims; if the Bible makes an affirmation, then that affirmation is true. If an inerrantist sees what looks like a false statement in Scripture, he gives the text the benefit of the doubt, assuming that he either does not have all the information necessary to judge the claim at issue or has failed to read the text correctly. Affirming biblical inerrancy thus involves giving Scripture the benefit of the doubt over any would-be competitors.

The question of whether (DI) is reasonable seems easy enough to answer. If God is maximally perfect and has written a book, then that book probably would be inerrant. It certainly seems reasonable that a maximally perfect person could write such a book. This assumes that such a person would have the character, knowledge, and power necessary for doing so. But, of course, this is precisely what orthodox Christians believe about God. So, on an orthodox construal of God, it seems reasonable to believe Scripture to be inerrant.

Normally, inerrancy is thought to characterize only the original documents penned by the human author.[11] But, as far as we know, we possess no such documents. How then is the doctrine of biblical inerrancy helpful, practical, or relevant? After all, if the doctrine applies only to documents, which for all we know we don't possess, what use is it? Here again the answer is not far to seek. If the original documents speak falsely, there seems no way to determine which of their claims are true and which false. However, if the original documents were wholly truthful, then at those points on which our current manuscripts agree, we may be confident that what the text affirms is in fact true. In cases where those manuscripts do not agree, moreover, textual criticism can in nearly all such cases determine the probable reading of the original documents. And where textual criticism cannot determine the probable reading, the textual disagreements threaten no fundamental Baptist—or even orthodox Christian—doctrine. So (DI) is *both* reasonable *and* relevant. But is it right?

While I cannot prove its truthfulness, (DI) seems more probable than its denial; one who affirms it therefore seems right to do so. For if God, who is perfect, were to write a book, would that book not be wholly truthful? So if the texts of Scripture speak falsely, why believe it to be divinely authored?[12] Denying (DI), then, amounts to placing human reason above Scripture. It involves giving oneself rather than Scripture the benefit of the doubt. Endorsing inerrancy, however, gives Scripture rather than its reader the final, authoritative word.

RECORD OR REVELATION?

General revelation (which is available to all men) is found both in creation and conscience. Special revelation is found foremost in Christ and Scripture. The *Baptist Faith and Message 2000* states that the Bible "is God's revelation" of Himself to man, while the 1963 version states that it is "the record of" God's revelation.[13] As mentioned above, I shall refer to the phrase appearing in the 1963 version as (R). I oppose (R) not because I think it untrue, but because I think it inadequate. For, while the Bible records God's revelation to man, it is more than a mere record of that revelation. It is itself revelation. Why then would anyone wish to endorse (R) rather than to say simply that the Bible *is*

God's revelation? There are at least three possible reasons—call them (R1) through (R3)—why someone would endorse (R) and yet deny that the Bible *is* God's revelation. According to (R1), revelation refers *only* to God's acts in salvation history; according to (R2), revelation is found primarily in one's personal experience with Christ and not in mere words; according to (R3), Scripture contains errors and should thus *not* be counted itself as revelation. I shall address each of these putative reasons in turn, arguing that none is ultimately convincing.

In the spirit of (R1), one commentator states that deleting (R) from the *Baptist Faith and Message* is unfortunate because it "has the effect of centering the revelation of God in God's mighty acts, i.e., in the *events* of salvation history, rather than in the *words* which describe these events. . . . Deleting this phrase has the unfortunate effect of elevating the Bible above Christ."[14] But this simply mischaracterizes the matter. Deleting (R) does *not* elevate the Bible above Christ. In fact, Scripture itself attests that Christ is God the Son become human (cf. John 1:1–4; Col. 1:13–20; Heb. 1:1–10). Taking revelation to be "God's mighty acts" but not the product of those acts seems dubious at best. For to distinguish between the activity by which God produces, say, the biblical texts and those texts themselves in such a way that the former count as revelation but the latter do not undermines the historic Christian commitment to viewing the whole of creation as revelation. For, of course, if such a distinction thus holds in the case of Scripture, it must likewise hold in the case of creation. And in that case God's creative activity, but *not* the creation itself, rightly counts as revelation. But this flies in the face of Scripture which clearly teaches that creation itself is revelation (cf. Rom. 1:20). As Millard Erickson states, then, "If revelation is defined as only the actual occurrence, the process of the *revealing*, then the Bible is not revelation. Revelation is something that occurred long ago. If, however, it is also the product, the result or the *revealed*, then the Bible may also be termed revelation."[15] (R1), therefore, becomes moot.

(R2), according to which "revelation is found primarily in one's personal experience with Christ, and should not apply to mere words," implies that "revelation is not propositional but personal."[16] Let this interpretation of (R2) be (R2'). Now (R2') sets up a false dichotomy, for revelation is *both* propositional *and* personal. What's more, (R2') presupposes that personal experience can be wholly divorced from propositional awareness, but this strikes me as impossible. One well-meaning proponent of (R2') has said to me, "I just want to love God and win people to Christ." But when I asked him to tell me a little about God and Christ, and what it means to win someone, each answer he gave was propositional in nature: Christ is God's Son, He died to atone for our sins, in order to be saved one must repent and submit to His lordship, and so on. These propositions often require further explanation, impossible apart from more propositions.[17] In short, it is impossible to separate revelation from propositional expression. So God's use of propositional language should be neither surprising nor problematic. Nothing said here, however, is meant to deny the personal nature of revelation. God's self-disclosure is revelation by persons to persons.

Another interpretation of (R2)—call it (R2″)—claims that Scripture becomes revelation as one reads and interprets it through one's relationship with the living Christ. Of course, the problem with this understanding is that two or more Christians might arrive at mutually exclusive interpretations of the same passage of Scripture. (R2″) leaves us no way of adjudicating between such competing interpretations. Such criticism should be sufficient for discounting (R2″).

Yet another reason one might have for endorsing (R) but denying that Scripture itself is revelation is (R3), according to which Scripture contains errors. If we affirm Scripture as revelation, the reasoning goes, we open ourselves to the suggestion that God's revelation contains errors. But, of course, such a suggestion is untenable. Now if Scripture contains errors, then obviously enough one who views it as revelation ought also to view revelation as containing errors. Such reasoning, however, simply assumes that Scripture *does* speak falsely. Since Christians have historically endorsed the total truthfulness—that is, the inerrancy—of Scripture, proponents of (R3) will have to demonstrate that Scripture errs; otherwise, their argument will be unconvincing. So far as I know, no such demonstration has been put forward.

Finally, one might ask why (R)—given its truth—should be deleted from the *Baptist Faith and Message*. The reason for deleting it is that retaining it implies that Scripture is *merely* a "record of God's revelation" rather than revelation itself. As I have attempted to show, however, there seems to be no good reason for supposing that Scripture itself is not revelation. To say that Scripture is *both* the record of revelation *and* itself revelation seems unnecessarily awkward. Better simply to state that Scripture *is* revelation—which implies that it is also an accurate record.

THE CRITERION STATEMENT

The most contentious revision in the *Baptist Faith and Message 2000* is the deletion of the criterion statement (C), which states, "The criterion by which the Bible is to be interpreted is Jesus Christ." (C) itself can be interpreted and applied in numerous ways, and so proves problematic. This section discusses just two ways of understanding (C) and considers whether to retain, abandon, or modify (C).

Let (C1) be the notion that Christians should focus on the living Christ rather than on the words of Scripture. One publication—call it the "Comparison"—states that deleting (C) reinforces *"words of scripture rather than the living Christ."*[18] The "Comparison" sees the difference between the living Christ and the words of Scripture as a distinction between "Jesus Christ" and "eternal truths," between "two distinct foundations for faith and practice," between "a person in whom we believe" and "a set of truths which we believe," between "relational" and "propositional" foundations. "In describing Baptist faith and practice," it asks, "where do we start—with Jesus Christ or with eternal truths?"[19] It might just as easily ask, "Where do we start—with Jesus Christ or with Scripture?" But with whose Jesus do we start? And how do we know of Him? Presumably, of course, it is the Jesus *of the Scriptures* whom we know *by the Scriptures.*[20] So (C1) turns out to be problematic. It attempts to force one to choose between Scripture and Christ, between the Word of God written and the Word of God made flesh. It thus sets up a false dichotomy—presenting one with a choice one need not make. We know the words and actions of Christ via Scripture. Moreover, a high view of Scripture ensures that a Christian will focus on *both* the sacred texts *and* the living Christ to whom they bear witness. So the "Comparison" fails to establish (C1).

(C2) is the notion that "the only vantage point for interpreting Scripture is Jesus Christ." Regarding (C2), the "Comparison" states, *"For traditional Baptists there is no alternate vantage point for interpreting scripture than Jesus."*[21] (C2) is the most apparent way of understanding (C). Most whom I have found either for or against (C) have held their position primarily based on (C2). Commenting on (C), Herschel Hobbs writes that "any interpretation of a given passage must be made in the light of God's revelation in Jesus Christ and his teachings and redemptive work."[22] Given these remarks, Hobbs seems committed to (C2) or something similar to it. Such a view could be construed as saying that the red letters are the interpretive grid for the rest of Scripture. For reasons I shall discuss presently, however, Christians should not adopt this standard.

One proponent of the "Comparison" with whom I spoke—call him Smith—believes that OT prophecies as well as NT teachings are rightly understood only through Christological lenses. When pressed for an example, he said that Paul and Jesus had different notions of pastoral leadership and authority and he would rather side with Jesus than Paul on the issue.[23] This perspective fits well with the "Comparison," which states, "Where scripture seems unclear, we rely on Jesus to provide clarity. Wherever scripture seems to be in tension with itself, we affirm that Jesus is the interpretive key to resolving these tensions. Wherever scripture is subject to contradictory and incongruent interpretations, we look to Jesus for guidance."[24] This view pits Scripture (and perhaps personal experience) against Scripture, and what serves as arbiter are the words of Christ (or perhaps one's personal experience). But if Hobbs is correct that the "Bible is the written Word about the living Word"[25]—then, in some sense, *all* Scripture meets this Christological criterion! How does one affirm that Scripture may be "contradictory" and "incongruent," and yet also affirm that all Scripture is Christological—i.e., that it accurately attests to Jesus? I cannot see how one can make sense of such an affirmation.

So (C2) is problematic in a way which has shown up already. It states that the only vantage point for interpreting Scripture is Jesus Christ. But, of course, we need Scripture (either directly or indirectly) in order to have any knowledge of Jesus. So in vying for Jesus as the interpretive key, we are in reality pitting some Scriptures against others, claiming that some are more authoritative than others. How can Jesus be the interpretive key to Scripture when everything we know about Jesus comes from Scripture? Interestingly, Hobbs suggests a better way. "Indeed," he writes, "the Bible is its own best interpreter as one discovers its meaning in any particular in the light of the whole."[26]

One cannot interpret biblical texts about Jesus without some preconceived notion of who God is in the first place. In the end, then, the "Comparison" falls prey to the very thing it seeks to repudiate. Its starting point turns out to be an assumed set of propositions—a set of eternal truths—rather than the initially attractive but ultimately elusive relational or personal foundation which they claim.[27] Not even the disciples could have begun where the "Comparison" hopes to begin. For even they began with certain presuppositions regarding the nature of God.[28] So (C2) fails because it ends up asserting the very thing its advocates hope to avoid; it begins with certain propositions about God (and reality in general).[29] It also pits Scripture against Scripture (or perhaps subordinates it to experience). So, while (C2) is the most obvious and popular understanding of (C), it is not an understanding which Christians should embrace.

CONCLUSION

Denying inspiration and inerrancy places man above God, making divine revelation subject to human reason and experience. Furthermore, the Bible is not *merely* a record of revelation but rather *is* revelation. Finally, the criterion statement is problematic and unhelpful. Article I of the *Baptist Faith and Message 2000* is, therefore, more helpful and accurate on these matters than either of the earlier versions. More can and should be said regarding Article I and its history, particularly regarding other putative interpretations of the criterion statement as well as the Barthian or neo-orthodox influence on that statement. Limitations of space, however, preclude such discussion here. While we should not worship Scripture, and while mere intellectual assent to scriptural propositions is not salvific, we come to know God by His Spirit's work through Scripture, by which revelation we must always guide and interpret our own experience.

NOTES

1. Incidentally, it was not until 1546 at the Council of Trent that the Roman Catholic Church officially canonized the Apocrypha (which comprises several extra-biblical books *not* included in the Protestant Bible).

2. While other issues relevant to Article I would be worthy of attention, limitations of space preclude attending to them here.

3. See James Leo Garrett, *Systematic Theology: Biblical, Historical, and Evangelical*, vol. 1 (Grand Rapids: Eerdmans, 1996), 120–21. Garrett states, "For most of the centuries of Christian history the concept of the divine inspiration of the Bible was largely unchallenged through major objections, if not always clearly interpreted or precisely defined. Its major challenge has come in the modern period through the impact of literary and historical criticism. . . ."

4. Herschel H. Hobbs, *The Baptist Faith and Message* (Nashville: Convention Press, 1971), 22. See also Millard J. Erickson, *Christian Theology*, 2d ed. (Grand Rapids: Baker, 1998), 231–33.

5. David S. Dockery, *Christian Scripture: An Evangelical Perspective on Inspiration, Authority and Interpretation* (Nashville: Broadman and Holman, 1995), 39.

6. Dockery thinks it important to eschew mechanical dictation theories of inspiration in favor of some theory of inspiration which accounts for both the divine and human authors' roles. See his *Christian Scripture*, 37–55. I agree with Dockery in holding to a verbal, plenary view of inspiration (according to which Scripture is inspired *in its entirety, down to the very words*). However, while I do not hold a dictation theory of inspiration, I see no problem with such a view.

7. Much has been written in recent years raising doubts about man's ability to interpret language well enough to understand truth, about whether language is even able to refer to anything beyond itself—i.e., to nonlinguistic entities such as rivers, rocks, and trees. However, claims that language cannot refer to anything beyond itself are ultimately self-refuting. Proponents of such a view undercut their own arguments, making claims which purport to describe—and thus to *refer to*—reality. For a helpful discussion of religious language, see Alvin Plantinga, *Warranted Christian Belief* (New York: Oxford, 2000), chapter 2.

8. One colleague suggested that, in discussing inspiration, I exegete 2 Tim. 3:16. While doing so might prove helpful to some, I have chosen not to for three reasons. First, several excellent studies on this text already exist. Second, due to limitations of space, I have had to leave out much potentially helpful information. Third, while it is interesting and instruc-

tive to see what Scripture says about itself, using Scripture to argue for its own inspiration seems to beg the question.

9. For an excellent discussion of inerrancy, see Douglas Blount's "The Authority of Scripture," in Michael J. Murray, ed., *Reason for the Hope Within* (Grand Rapids: Eerdmans, 1999), 399–422.

10. "Totally true and trustworthy" echoes *The Chicago Statement on Biblical Inerrancy*, which states, "Recognition of the total truth and trustworthiness of Holy Scripture is essential to a full grasp and adequate confession of its authority." The *Chicago Statement* may be found in its entirety in Norman L. Geisler, ed., *Inerrancy* (Grand Rapids: Zondervan, 1980), 493–502.

11. See Article X of *The Chicago Statement on Biblical Inerrancy* as well as "Transmission and Translation" in the section of that document entitled "Exposition," in Geisler, *Inerrancy*, 496 and 501–2 respectively.

12. Of course, one need not hold to inerrancy in order to hold generally to biblical authority. For a good discussion of this issue, see Douglas Blount's "The Authority of Scripture," in Murray, *Reason for the Hope Within*, 404.

13. Neither phrase appears in the 1925 version.

14. "1963 and 2000 Baptist Faith and Message Statement: Comparison and Commentary," www.bgct.org/bgctroot/bfm/bfmcomp.pdf (accessed 26 November 2002), emphases in original. This document is hereafter referred to as "Comparison."

15. Erickson, 222, emphases in original.

16. Where "proposition" refers to a statement or truth claim, as distinguished from a command, question, exclamation, proposal, suggestion, and the like.

17. And, as mentioned earlier, since all such claims assume a reference to reality, we cannot claim that the words refer merely to other words.

18. "Comparison," 11, emphases in original.

19. "Comparison," 8. According to the "Comparison," these distinctions, as well as the "omission of the 1963 sentence which disavows creedalism," make the *Baptist Faith and Message 2000* creedal rather than confessional (9).

20. In fairness, at least two other means of learning about Jesus seem possible—namely, personal experience (presumably with Christ Himself) or other authorities (either oral or written, including, say, creeds, papal edicts, and the like). Given their aversion to creeds and human authorities, however, I assume that the writers of the "Comparison" would reject other authorities. As for personal experience, I assume that those writers would agree that even personal experience must be measured against Scripture—at least by the words of or about Jesus.

21. "Comparison," 12, emphasis in original.

22. Hobbs, 30. Hobbs then seems to contradict himself when he immediately adds, "Indeed, the Bible is its own best interpreter as one discovers its meaning in any particular in the light of the whole." First, Jesus is the interpretive key; then, Scripture as a whole is that key. The reader is left wondering which view Hobbs endorses.

23. To treat the example in more detail, Smith contended that Paul had an authoritarian view of pastoral leadership, while Jesus viewed the pastor primarily as a servant. Moreover, Smith sees these two views as opposed so that one must be chosen over the other.

24. "Comparison," 12.

25. Hobbs, 30.

26. Hobbs, 30. Another solution might be to see how the Church has traditionally understood certain Scriptures or doctrines.

27. "Comparison," 8–9.

28. E.g., that God may relate to humanity in an understandable way, that God is good, that it is possible for a divine-human person to exist.

29. In fact, every view on biblical authority or hermeneutics rests on certain presuppositions. There is no "view from nowhere," no neutral, objective ground from which to work. Of course, this in no way implies that objective truth—or knowledge of such truth—is not possible.

· *Article II* ·

God

Douglas K. Blount

$\mathcal{N}$ot surprisingly, perhaps, the longest article in the *Baptist Faith and Message* deals with the doctrine of God—what theologians refer to as "theology proper." Of course, the article on the Scriptures comes before it. But even that article must take a backseat to Article II in terms of importance. For, while the first article establishes the primary means by which God makes Himself known, the second article concerns the divine nature itself. So, while the first article deals with the primary means by which we know God's nature and activity, the second article deals directly with that nature and activity.[1]

Given the significance of Article II, then, it comes as no surprise that it contains some of the most significant changes made to the confession. To be sure, some of the changes in it simply update the article's language. So, for instance, in §C—the section of Article II dealing with the Holy Spirit—the 1963 edition's affirmation that the Spirit's "presence in the Christian is the *assurance* of God to bring the believer into the *fulness* of the stature of Christ" becomes the 2000 edition's affirmation that the Spirit's "presence in the Christian is the *guarantee* that God will bring the believer into the *fullness* of the stature of Christ" (emphases added).

Other changes, however, involve more than a mere modernization of language. Indeed, three are particularly significant. For while they do not alter the faith Baptists have traditionally embraced, these changes do highlight and make explicit certain aspects of it. For example, the *Baptist Faith and Message 2000* inserts the word "triune" between "eternal" and "God" in the last sentence of the first paragraph of Article II, making explicit the confession's commitment to orthodox Trinitarianism. In this case, the size of the change belies its significance.

That same paragraph, however, includes an entire sentence that does not appear in the confession's earlier versions. "God is," that sentence states, "all powerful and all knowing; and His perfect knowledge extends to all things, past, present, and future, including the future decisions of His free creatures." Here the size of the addition *does* signal the significance of the change. For that sentence signals the rejection of a popular theological paradigm which seeks to overturn the traditional Christian understanding of divine knowledge. In rejecting that paradigm, the confession explicitly commits its adherents to an orthodox view of omniscience.

In §B, the 2000 edition describes Christ as taking upon Himself not, as the 1963 edition puts it, "the demands and necessities of human nature," but rather "human nature with its demands and necessities." At first glance, this change might appear insignificant, a mere rearrangement of words. Together with another change in the section, however, it makes explicit the Baptist commitment to an orthodox Christology. That other change replaces the 1963 edition's statement that Christ partakes "of the nature of God and of man" with the statement that He is "fully God, fully man." These two changes thus make explicit the Baptist conviction that the Christ of Chalcedon *is* the Christ of Scripture. In what follows, I discuss further the *Baptist Faith and Message 2000*'s explicit commitment to orthodox understandings of Trinity and Incarnation; first, however, I discuss its commitment to a traditional understanding of divine knowledge.[2] I conclude from these discussions that Southern Baptists' most recent confession situates them unequivocally within the mainstream of historic, orthodox Christianity.

THAT GOD EXHAUSTIVELY
KNOWS THE FUTURE

The most obvious change in Article II of the *Baptist Faith and Message 2000* concerns a recent theological paradigm. This paradigm, which has renewed evangelical—especially Baptist—interest in theology proper, is known as open theism because it sees the future as open for God. Its advocates have put it forward as an alternative to the traditional view dominant in Christian thinking since the patristic era.[3] By affirming that God's "perfect knowledge extends to all things, past, present, and future, including the future decisions of His free creatures," the confession positions itself in clear opposition to this paradigm.

As the above indicates, open theism derives its name from its view of the relationship between God and the future. On that view, God lacks exhaustive foreknowledge; the future is thus "open" to Him. So, while God might have a fairly good idea of how things will go, He does not know *precisely* what will happen. According to Gregory Boyd, for instance, the future is "*partly* determined and foreknown by God, but also partly *open* and known by God as such."[4] This stands at odds with traditional, orthodox Christianity, according to which God enjoys exhaustive foreknowledge.

According to open theists, divine uncertainty about the future results from God's decision to grant freedom to some of His creatures.[5] On this, the authors of *The Openness of God* state,

> God, in grace, grants humans significant freedom to cooperate with or work against God's will for their lives, and he enters into dynamic, give-and-take relationships with us. The Christian life involves a genuine interaction between God and human beings. We respond to God's gracious initiatives and God responds to our responses . . . and on it goes.[6]

That God genuinely interacts with His creatures fits perfectly well with orthodox Christianity. In characterizing divine interaction with creatures, however, open theists part company with such Christianity. For, on their view,

> God takes risks in this give-and-take relationship, yet he is endlessly resourceful and competent in working toward his ultimate goals. Sometimes God alone decides how to accomplish these goals. On other occasions, God works with human decisions, adapting his own plans to fit the changing situation. God does not control everything that happens. Rather, he is open to receiving input from his creatures. In loving dialogue, God invites us to participate with him to bring the future into being.[7]

So, according to open theists, God *takes risks* and *adapts His plans to changing situations*. His doing so results from the fact that He has created free creatures together with the assumption that He cannot know in advance what these creatures will freely do.

Now the suggestion that God lacks exhaustive foreknowledge is the most prominent feature of open theism, but it is not the view's most significant feature. For open theism involves not only an understanding of *what* God knows, but also an understanding of *how* He knows. "Instead of perceiving the entire course of human existence in one timeless moment," Richard Rice states, "God comes to know events as they take place. He learns something from what transpires."[8] Obviously, if He comes to know events *as they take place*, God is *temporal*, existing *in time*. And, of course, in *coming to know* what takes place, God experiences changes internal to Himself. But, in that case, He turns out to be mutable. Moreover, since the changes God experiences result from creaturely activity whose occurrence he does not foresee, His creatures affect Him. God thus turns out to be passible. Thus, according to open theism, not only does God lack the knowledge traditionally ascribed to Him but He is also temporal rather than timeless, mutable rather than immutable, and passible rather than impassible.

Such an understanding of the divine nature stands in marked contrast to the orthodox Christian understanding, according to which God not only exhaustively knows the future but is also timeless, immutable, and impassible. Moreover, while both open theism and orthodox Christianity affirm divine eternality, omnipresence, and omniscience, they understand these divine attributes in radically different ways. Orthodoxy understands God's knowledge to extend to *all* events, even those which are future; open theism, which sees it as impossible for anyone—even God—to foreknow what free creatures will freely do, denies that divine knowledge extends to all events. As already mentioned, orthodoxy has traditionally understood divine eternality in terms of God's existing timelessly ("outside of time," so to speak); open theists understand it in terms of God's existing everlastingly ("within time").

These differing understandings of eternality lead also to differing understandings of omnipresence. For, from the view that space and time are simply two different aspects of one continuous space-time manifold, it follows that one is located in space if and only if one is located in time. So, if *both* God is located in time (as open theists claim) *and* space and time are different aspects of one space-time manifold (as most contemporary physicists claim), God turns out to be located in space. Since Christians have traditionally held that God, though omnipresent, exists outside space, here lies yet another point of disagreement between orthodox Christianity and open theism. In short, then, the differences between open theists and orthodoxy are deep and extensive.

So even if their understandings of God's nature agree on a few key points—on, say, divine goodness or power—the points of disagreement remain quite significant. And I doubt that, when the views are ultimately fleshed out, much agreement will be found even on these points. For, as I understand them, open theists typically view divine goodness quite differently than Christians have traditionally viewed it.[9] Arguably, moreover, omnipotence properly construed entails omniscience.[10] But, of course, if a particular understanding of omnipotence entails a particular understanding of omniscience, one with a different understanding of omniscience must have *either* a different understanding of omnipotence *or* inconsistent understandings of the two attributes. Thus, on the assumption that all concerned are being consistent, a different understanding of omniscience indicates a different understanding of omnipotence. In the end, then, *perhaps* Christian orthodoxy and open theism can agree at least on this: other than God, who exists necessarily, all beings owe their existence to His creative activity. Beyond this, however, little agreement about the divine nature remains.

From a pastoral point of view, perhaps the most significant disagreement between these rival conceptions of God concerns divine providence and sovereignty. To see this, consider the view of providence entailed by open theism. *If* open theism were true, it would then follow that the God who, according to John 16:13, promised to send His Spirit to lead the church into all truth allowed His children to labor in darkness for almost two thousand years. For, on one hand, the overwhelmingly dominant view within Christendom since the patristic era has been that God enjoys exhaustive foreknowledge. Open theism, on the other hand, is a fairly recent theological development. So if open theism is true, it turns out that most Christians throughout the history of the church have seriously misunderstood the divine nature. And that surely strains one's credulity.

That one lacks exhaustive foreknowledge obviously means that one does not know precisely what will happen. Thus, according to open theists, God is sometimes surprised, sometimes frustrated. Indeed, on Boyd's view, God's uncertainty about the future infects His knowledge of the present. For, he tells us, God lacks knowledge of the *present* character of His creatures; He must test them in order to know whether they are, for instance, faithful.[11] This too strains one's credulity—to the point of breaking.

The divide separating open theists from traditional theists thus turns out to be deep and wide. In affirming exhaustive divine foreknowledge, the *Baptist Faith and Message 2000* places its adherents squarely on the orthodox side of that divide. According to the *London Confession* (1644), "God hath decreed in himselfe from everlasting touching all things, effectually to work and dispose them according to the counsell of his owne will, to the glory of his name. . . ."[12] Such was the God of Baptists in the seventeenth century; and such also is the God of Baptists at the beginning of the twenty-first century.

THAT GOD IS TRIUNE

Like all orthodox Christians, Baptists affirm that God is triune. By this, they mean that, while there exists precisely one God, this God comprises three persons—Father, Son, and Holy Spirit.[13] Now those who deny God's triunity typically do so in one of two ways. Some stress God's "threeness" to the detriment of His "oneness," thus affirming the existence of three distinct gods—a view known as "tritheism." Such a view clearly stands contrary to orthodox Christianity.[14] Others stress God's "oneness" to the detriment of His "threeness." This view—known as "modalism" because it sees the Father, Son, and Holy Spirit not as three distinct persons but rather as different modes of appearance assumed by the one divine person—also stands at odds with orthodox Christianity.

Unfortunately, both the 1925 and 1963 editions of the *Baptist Faith and Message* fail to affirm unequivocally the Baptist commitment to God's triunity. In fact, strictly speaking, one can affirm those editions of the confession but nonetheless deny that the one and only God *is* three persons. For they simply state that God makes Himself known ("is revealed" in 1925; "reveals Himself" in 1963) "as Father, Son, and Holy Spirit." And such language is consistent with the view that one divine person assumes three different personae—appearing at times as Father, at other times as Son, and at still other times as Spirit. Thus, the two earlier editions of the *Baptist Faith and Message* leave room for their adherents to embrace modalism.

Since, however, Christian orthodoxy sees in Scripture neither three gods acting in concert with one another nor one God taking on the roles of three different dramatic personae, but rather one God comprising three distinct but equally divine persons,[15] the 1925 and 1963 editions of the *Baptist Faith and Message* obscure the Baptist commitment to such orthodoxy. The 2000 edition rectifies this problem by inserting 'triune' in the last sentence of Article II's first paragraph—which now states, "The eternal *triune* God reveals Himself to us as Father, Son, and Holy Spirit, with distinct personal attributes, but without division of nature, essence, or being" (emphasis added)—thus making explicit the Baptist rejection of modalism. Since the article's first sentence—which states, "There is *one and only one* living and true God" (emphasis added)—precludes tritheism, the 2000 edition thus places its adherents well within the parameters of historic Trinitarianism. And since Southern Baptists as a people have never intended to be elsewhere, this change in wording—however subtle it might seem—gives clear expression to their intentions.[16]

Now understanding *how* Trinitarianism is true—that is, *how* the one and only God is three distinct persons—proves exceedingly difficult. In fact, the difficulty of understanding the doctrine serves as the impetus for both modalism and tritheism, each of which attempts to make the doctrine intellectually palatable by sacrificing one of its central claims in favor of the other. The difficulty of understanding how both of these claims is true has, moreover, led to charges of inconsistency. But that Trinitarianism is difficult—perhaps even impossible—to understand does *not* make it contradictory.

For, of course, a contradiction asserts that something is at once and in the same way both true and false. So, for instance, to say *both* that

> *Bob Dylan is knockin' on Heaven's door*

and that

> *Bob Dylan is not knockin' on Heaven's door*

is to contradict oneself. One who affirms both of these statements makes an assertion with one breath which he denies with another. Moreover, since both statements cannot possibly be true, one who affirms both of them thus speaks falsely.

Of course, *if* Trinitarianism *were* contradictory, then at least one of its central claims—and therefore the doctrine itself—would be false. So the charge of inconsistency is no small matter. And were Christians to affirm both that

> (1) *there exists one and only one God,*

and that

> (1′) *there does not exist one and only one God,*

they would thus contradict themselves. So also were they to affirm both that

> (2) *there exist three divine persons*

and that

> (2′) *there do not exist three divine persons,*

they would then also contradict themselves. But, while they affirm both (1) and (2), Christians affirm *neither* (1′) *nor* (2′). Indeed, they emphatically deny each of these propositions.

Of course, critics might argue that, in affirming (1) and (2), Christians *implicitly* endorse either (1′) or (2′); for, the argument might go, (1) entails (2′) or (2) entails (1′). Certainly, affirming both (1) and (2) would be contradictory if either of these entailments hold; however, they do not. Or, at least, no one has succeeded in showing that they do; in the absence of a compelling argument to the contrary, then, such an argument fails.

To put the point differently, in affirming that God is both one and three, Christians do *not* affirm that He is one and three *in the same way.* They do not affirm both that

> (1) *there exists precisely one God*

and that

> (1*) *there exist three gods.*

They also do not affirm both that

> (2) *there exist three divine persons*

and that

> (2★) *there exists only one divine person.*

Since (1') follows from (1★), one affirms it if one affirms (1★); and since (2') follows from (2★), one affirms it if one affirms (2★). But Christians deny *both* (1★) *and* (2★). So, while affirming that God is both one and three, they also affirm that He is *not* one *in the same way* that He is three. In so doing they do *not* contradict themselves.

Charges that Trinitarianism is inconsistent thus lack merit. The doctrine may well transcend human understanding. Even so, human inability to understand *how* the doctrine is true does *not* entail its falsehood. Failing to understand how something can be true does not amount to understanding it to be false; to think otherwise is to think much too highly of human reason. Perhaps then the human inability to understand how Trinitarianism is true says more about humankind than about God. Indeed, according to the *London Confession* (1644), "God as He is in Himselfe cannot be comprehended by any but himselfe."[17] Scripture itself portrays God as both one and three; that it does so suffices to show that He is triune, even if we do not understand the "how" of it.

THAT CHRIST IS GOD AND MAN

Setting forth the early church's understanding of the Christ of Scripture, the Symbol of Chalcedon remains the classic statement of orthodox Christology. According to it, Jesus Christ is "truly God and truly man." It goes on to affirm that, with respect to deity, Christ is consubstantial (or coessential) with God the Father; with respect to humanity, He is consubstantial (or coessential) with men. It thus affirms that Christ possesses two natures—one fully divine, one fully human—each of which remains unchanged despite their union in Him, "the property of each nature being preserved."[18]

Article II of the 1925 edition has no section on God the Son; its treatment of Christ is therefore minimal. The 1963 edition's §2 does, however, concern God the Son, stating that Christ took "upon Himself the demands and necessities of human nature." It also describes Him as "partaking of the nature of God and of man." Of course, in becoming human, Christ did indeed take "upon Himself the demands and necessities of human nature"; so also he partook of the nature of man. The 1963 edition is thus consistent with a Chalcedonian understanding of Christ; it does not, however, require such an understanding. For taking on "the demands and necessities" of a nature does not require taking on that nature itself; strictly speaking, one may voluntarily take on the demands and necessities of, say, a parental nature (by graciously raising an orphan) without taking on a parental nature (that is, without becoming a parent).[19] And partaking of the nature of man does not require taking on a human nature. So, for instance, if God the Son had merely taken on a human body, without also taking on a human mind, He would have partaken of the nature of man without having become a man. In such case, one might rightly describe Him as having become *partly* human. Even so, one could not then rightly describe Him as having become *fully* human. For, while man is naturally embodied, one must possess a human mind as well as a human body in order to be fully human.

In the end, then, one can affirm the 1963 edition of the *Baptist Faith and Message* without affirming an orthodox Christology. This sad fact explains the changes in Article II §B of the 2000 edition concerning the nature of Christ. As Baptists have long affirmed, Jesus of Nazareth is not *merely* a partaker of human nature. He is not merely *partly* human; He is rather *fully* human. He did not merely take on the demands and necessities of human nature; rather, He took on that very nature itself. Yet in doing so, He nonetheless remained *fully* divine. So says the *Baptist Faith and Message 2000*; and so say Southern Baptists as a people.

CONCLUSION

Unlike the confession's articles on, say, Baptism and the Lord's Supper or Religious Liberty,[20] its article on God does not set Southern Baptists apart from other Christians. For when it comes to their doctrine of God, Southern Baptists do *not* wish to stand outside the mainstream of historic, orthodox Christianity. On the contrary, they seek to dwell within the midst of that stream. So while the *Baptist Faith and Message 2000*—like its predecessors—distinguishes Baptist faith and practice from that of other communities of Christians, Article II functions primarily to situate its adherents within the midst of the broader community of historic, orthodox Christianity. Although Baptists are not *merely* Christian, neither are they less than Christian.

NOTES

1. Why does the confession's article about God's written Word precede the article about God Himself? Such an arrangement has not always been the norm. In the *London Confession* (1644), for instance, the first two articles concern God's being and nature. Cf. "The London Confession, 1644" in *Baptist Confessions of Faith*, ed. William L. Lumpkin (Valley Forge: Judson, 1959), art. 1, 2, pp. 156–57. Perhaps the impetus for placing the article on the Scriptures at the very beginning of all three editions of the *Baptist Faith and Message* can be found in the modern obsession with epistemological concerns. René Descartes's attempt to achieve certainty apart from prior metaphysical commitments plunged Western intellectuals into an epistemological morass out of which they have not yet emerged. Since the mid-seventeenth century, most intellectuals in the West—including most philosophers and theologians—have sought to pursue their interests without such commitments, working (so to speak) without a metaphysical net. In so doing, they have sought to establish an epistemological foundation for their work—a foundation which will provide a basis for either building a new metaphysics or doing away with metaphysics altogether.

Modern and postmodern thinkers differ not on whether epistemology is more fundamental than metaphysics; they agree that it is. Rather, they differ on whether a satisfactory epistemology—one able to adjudicate disputes across communities of belief and thus serve as an objective arbiter of truth—can be found. On this point, modernists are optimistic, postmodernists pessimistic. Seen in this light, the elevation of the doctrine of Scripture above the doctrine of God turns out to be simply one more attempt—à la modernity—to establish a satisfactory epistemological foundation for one's metaphysical commitments.

2. The following section includes material from Douglas K. Blount, "Togas, Tulips and the Philosophy of Openness," *Southwestern Journal of Theology* 47 (2005), 177–89; used with permission.

3. Among the paradigm's more prominent advocates are Gregory A. Boyd, Clark H. Pinnock, and John Sanders. See, for instance, Boyd's *God of the Possible: A Biblical Introduction to the Open View of God* (Grand Rapids: Baker, 2000); Pinnock's *Most Moved Mover: A Theology of God's Openness* (Grand Rapids: Baker, 2001); and Sanders's *The God Who Risks: A Theology of Providence* (Downers Grove: InterVarsity, 1998). Although these thinkers have popularized open theism among evangelicals, the view is not original with them. Indeed, one finds the view—though not the name—in, e.g., Richard Swinburne, *The Coherence of Theism* (New York: Oxford University Press, 1977; revised, 1993), especially pp. 167–78. For responses to open theism from traditional theists, see Blount, "Togas, Tulips and the Philosophy of Openness"; Millard J. Erickson, *What Does God Know and When Does He Know It? The Current Controversy over Divine Foreknowledge*, revised (Grand Rapids: Zondervan, 2006); John Piper, Justin Taylor, Paul Kjoss Helseth, eds., *Beyond the Bounds: Open Theism and the Undermining of Biblical Christianity* (Wheaton: Crossway, 2003); Bruce A. Ware, *God's Lesser Glory: The Diminished God of Open Theism* (Wheaton: Crossway, 2000); idem, *Their God Is Too Small: Open Theism and the Undermining of Confidence in God* (Wheaton: Crossway, 2003).

4. Boyd, *God of the Possible*, 11, emphasis in original.

5. While I cannot deal satisfactorily with the issue here, it seems worth noting that the alleged inconsistency of creaturely freedom and exhaustive divine foreknowledge is by no means obvious. Indeed, the fact that Christians have historically affirmed their consistency shows that such inconsistency is far from evident. Moreover, Scripture certainly does *not* rule out the consistency of creaturely freedom and exhaustive divine foreknowledge. On the contrary, throughout the history of the church, Christians have seen Scripture as *affirming* their consistency, but I will not press the point here.

Those who reject their consistency do so not for exegetical or theological reasons but rather on philosophical grounds. Such grounds, however, prove dubious. For at least three different philosophical perspectives have been put forward which affirm *both* the understanding of freedom which open theists themselves affirm *and* exhaustive divine foreknowledge. These perspectives—Atemporalism (à la Boethius), Molinism (à la Luis de Molina), and Ockhamism (à la William Ockham)—have each received significant attention in the recent philosophical literature. On these options, see Boethius, *The Consolation of Philosophy* V.vi; Linda Trinkaus Zagzebski, *The Dilemma of Freedom and Foreknowledge* (New York: Oxford University Press, 1991), 36–65; William Ockham, *Predestination, God's Foreknowledge, and Future Contingents*, 2d ed., trans. Marilyn McCord Adams and Norman Kretzmann (Indianapolis: Hackett, 1983); Alvin Plantinga, "On Ockham's Way Out," in *The Analytic Theist: An Alvin Plantinga Reader*, ed. James F. Sennett (Grand Rapids: Eerdmans, 1998), 258–92; Luis de Molina, *On Divine Foreknowledge: Part IV of the* Concordia, trans. Alfred J. Freddoso (Ithaca: Cornell University Press, 1988); Thomas P. Flint, *Divine Providence: The Molinist Account*, Cornell Studies in the Philosophy of Religion, ed. William P. Alston (Ithaca: Cornell University Press, 1998). On the philosophical commitments which undergird open theism, see Blount, "Togas, Tulips and the Philosophy of Openness."

6. Clark H. Pinnock et al., *The Openness of God: A Biblical Challenge to the Traditional Understanding of God* (Downers Grove: InterVarsity, 1994), 7, ellipsis points in original.

7. Pinnock et al., *Openness of God*, 7.

8. Richard Rice, "Biblical Support for a New Perspective" in Pinnock et al., *Openness of God*, 16.

9. Open theists seem to construe love as *the* central divine attribute rather than as one of several equally fundamental ones. Cf. Sanders, *God Who Risks*, 88; Rice, "Biblical Support," 15; and Clark H. Pinnock and Robert C. Brow, *Unbounded Love: A Good News Theology for the 21st Century* (Downers Grove: InterVarsity, 1994).

10. So, for instance, one who understands omnipotence as the possession of maximal power and omniscience as the possession of maximal cognitive power will have obvious reason to affirm that being omnipotent entails being omniscient.

11. Boyd, *God of the Possible*, 63–66.

12. "The London Confession, 1644," art. 3, p. 157.

13. Notice that an orthodox Christology requires an orthodox Trinitarianism. Cf. "The Nicæno-Constantinopolitan Creed" and "The Symbol of Chalcedon" in *The Creeds of Christendom*, vol. 2: *The Greek and Latin Creeds*, ed. Philip Schaff (New York: Harper and Row, 1931; reprint, Grand Rapids: Baker, 1990), 57–61 and 62–65, respectively.

14. It goes without saying that, in standing contrary to historic, orthodox Christianity, such a view also stands contrary to the Bible. For a proper understanding of the claims of

Scripture cannot be contradistinguished from an orthodox understanding of God Himself. In rejecting the latter, then, one *ipso facto* rejects the former.

15. So, for instance, with respect to divine "oneness," Deut. 6:4 affirms the existence of one and only one God; with respect to divine "threeness," Matt. 3:16–17, Mark 1:9–11, and Luke 3:21–22 affirm the existence of three divine persons.

16. The 2000 edition's commitment to orthodox Trinitarianism also manifests itself in changes to §B which affirm the full divinity of Jesus Christ and to §C which affirm the full divinity of the Holy Spirit.

17. "The London Confession, 1644," art. 1, p. 156.

18. "The Symbol of Chalcedon," 62–65.

19. Whatever may be *legally* possible (that is, possible given civil and criminal law), it is *logically* possible (that is, possible given the laws of logic) to raise an orphan without adopting the child.

20. Article VII concerns Baptism and the Lord's Supper; Article XVII concerns Religious Liberty.

· *Article III* ·

Man

Robert B. Stewart

$\mathcal{M}$an is a mystery even to himself. The French philosopher Blaise Pascal, at once aware both of man's greatness and disgrace, asked: "What sort of freak then is man? How novel, how monstrous, how chaotic, how paradoxical, how prodigious! Judge of all things, feeble earthworm, repository of truth, sink of doubt and error, glory and refuse of the universe!"[1] Human beings will never resolve the mystery of man in this life. Nevertheless, Article III of the *Baptist Faith and Message 2000* highlights some critical points about man and his relationship to God. This chapter examines the changes in Article III and proposes what seem to me the best readings of the claims it makes regarding the image of God, human freedom, and original sin.

INITIAL OBSERVATIONS
CONCERNING THE STATEMENT

In the 1925 edition of the *Baptist Faith and Message,* Article III was entitled "The Fall of Man." Subsequent revisions of the confession, being longer and more detailed than that first edition, have entitled this article "Man." As its title suggests, the 1925 edition's third article focuses primarily on the creation of humanity in "God's image" and its subsequent fall. The final section of this essay will address an apparent difference between the 1925 edition and the two later editions.

Changes from the 1963 edition to the 2000 edition are minimal. The 2000 edition of Article III replaces a single sentence in the 1963 edition, "Man was created by the special act of God, in His own image, and is the crowning work of His creation," with two sentences: "Man is the special creation of

25

God, made in His own image. He created them male and female as the crowning work of His creation." It also adds the sentence: "The gift of gender is thus part of the goodness of God's creation." It then replaces yet another sentence, "Through the temptation of Satan man transgressed the command of God, and fell from his original innocence; whereby his posterity inherit a nature and an environment inclined toward sin, and as soon as they are capable of moral action become transgressors and are under condemnation," with two sentences: "Through the temptation of Satan man transgressed the command of God, and fell from his original innocence whereby his posterity inherit a nature and an environment inclined toward sin. Therefore, as soon as they are capable of moral action, they become transgressors and are under condemnation." Furthermore, it replaces "every man possesses dignity" with "every person of every race possesses full dignity." These changes have generated little controversy as they are either merely formal—i.e., rearrangements of statements in the 1963 edition—or intended to make explicit what many believe was implicit in the earlier edition.[2] For example, the substitution of "every person of every race possesses full dignity" for "every man possesses dignity" simply spells out more precisely what was intended in the earlier edition.

Each edition of the *Baptist Faith and Message* has responded to the shifting waves of culture. The statement on gender added to the 2000 edition reflects this. In 1963, few if any American universities had a gender studies department and such fields as feminist biblical studies, feminist philosophy, and feminist theology were in their infancy. No Southern Baptist church then had a woman serving as senior pastor. The inherent goodness of the male/female distinction would not have been questioned; indeed, the issue would not have arisen. But significant changes in the broader culture since 1963 warrant the addition of a statement concerning gender differences.

The *Baptist Faith and Message* is obviously not intended to be a fully developed theological statement on any point that it addresses. In fact, Article III raises as many questions as it answers. Man is a special creation, but special in what way? Man is made in the image of God, but what does this mean? Man is given free choice, but what sort of free choice? Man inherits a nature and an environment inclined toward sin, but what does that mean? How inclined toward sin is man? Does this inclination alone condemn man? Or does it merely make possible his condemnation?

That the confession leaves such questions unanswered should be no surprise. As a general statement, the *Baptist Faith and Message* allows for differences of opinion among Baptists on the fine points of certain doctrines. The remainder of this chapter endeavors to show how I think some of the questions raised by Article III are best answered. In so doing, I recognize that not all Baptists will agree, and I respect their right to differ; for in all its editions, the *Baptist Faith and Message* allows for such differences.

THE IMAGE OF GOD

The Psalmist declares, "What is man that You take thought of him, and the son of man that You care for him? Yet You have made him a little lower than God, and You crown him with glory and majesty!" (Psalm 8:4a) Man differs qualitatively from the rest of God's creation because man alone is made in God's image. But of what does the image of God consist? Throughout Christian history, the dominant position has been that the image of God consists of some ontological property or characteristic possessed by man. This is sometimes referred to as the substantive view.[3] Nevertheless, there has been no universal agreement about what substantive property or characteristic the image of God comprises.

Some, such as the Church of Jesus Christ of Latter-day Saints (Mormons), have supposed that man is an exact duplicate of God the Father—or, at least, that man possesses the potential to become such a duplicate. Man's physical body even mirrors the body that Latter-day Saints believe God has.[4] Latter-day Saints insist that Genesis 5:1–3, which states that Adam begot Seth "in his own likeness, after his own image," parallels Genesis 1:26–27, which states that God creates man in His own image. There is, however, a significant difference between *creating* and *begetting*. One simply cannot get from image to an exact duplicate of the thing imaged. Several biblical passages state explicitly that God is not a man, glorified or otherwise (Num. 23:19; 1 Sam. 15:29; Hos. 11:9). In general, Latter-day Saints reason backwards from man to God, an unfruitful practice that makes God in the image of man.

The substantive property or characteristic most often identified with the image of God throughout Christian history has been the property of reason.[5] James Leo Garrett Jr. notes that most Patristic theologians identified the image of God as residing in man's soul (or spirit or mind) rather than in his body. Usually they held that the image of God was to be identified with reason (*logos*) or mind (*nous*).[6] Some also identified the image of God with the freedom of will to choose either good or evil.[7] Freedom of choice obviously presupposes reason.

Most Baptist theologians have affirmed a substantive view but are hesitant to identify the image of God with any single property, preferring instead to speak of several properties or characteristics that together constitute the image of God. Some prefer to remain silent on what constitutes the image of God, affirming nonetheless that that image is within man rather than simply a function of man.[8]

The second major position taken concerning the image of God is the *relational* view, which understands the image of God not ontologically but relationally. Emil Brunner, a major proponent of this view, distinguished between the *formal* and *material* aspects of the image of God. The formal aspect is that which separates men from animals and makes them responsible before God as free creatures. Brunner insists that, despite the fall of man, all persons retain the image of God in this formal sense.[9] The material aspect, however, consists of the human relating properly and responsibly in love to God by giving "the answer which the Creator intends."[10] Accordingly, the material image of God was lost in the fall and is restored to those who, in keeping with their formal responsibility, trust Christ. Therefore, in one sense the image of God within man is permanent and irrevocable; in another sense it is lost, though subject to restoration.[11] Brunner appears to have subsumed both the doctrine of creation and the doctrine of man under the doctrine of salvation. Furthermore, he seems to have mistaken what the image of God allows man *to do*, i.e., relate to God, for what the image of God *is*. While relating to God is something that man cannot avoid—everyone relates to God in some way, whether correctly or incorrectly—and this is a vital part of what it means to be human, Brunner's position fails to explain what the image of God *is*. Among Southern Baptists, the relational view has been a distinctly minority position, even among those who agree with Brunner on other theological issues.

The third position understands the image of God in a *functional* manner. According to this view, the image of God consists in the Creator giving man dominion over creation. Commenting on this view, Norman Snaith states that the image of God "refers only to man's domination of the world and everything that is in it. It says nothing about the nature of God, but everything concerning the function of man."[12] Although understanding the image of God as man's personal, spiritual capacity, Southern Baptist theologian Frank Stagg concludes that dominion is the central idea expressed in the image.[13] Similarly Daniel Block concludes that, in its original Ancient Near Eastern context, "'imageness' had more to do with the role played by man than with an ontological quality about man."[14] This view correctly emphasizes the connection between the image of God and man's God-given charge to care for creation. Indeed, man is God's steward over the created order.

Walter Eichrodt notes, however, that one reads in Genesis that man was created male and female in the image of God (1:26–27), prior to being given the blessing and direction to rule over the creation (v. 28).[15] Millard Erickson notes that "the use of two hortative expressions—'Let us make man in our image, in our likeness' and 'let them rule'—seems to distinguish the two concepts."[16] He concludes that dominion is *merely a consequence* of the image but not the image itself.[17] But elsewhere in Scripture dominion is mentioned in connection with man's being created in a uniquely high position with respect to the Creator, such as Ps. 8:4–8. Perhaps it is best to say that one reason that man is created in God's image is for the *purpose* of serving as God's steward over creation. This would, however, still distinguish the image itself from a purpose of the image.

It seems best to think of the image as involving something man *is* rather than something he *does* or some *relation in which he stands*. Nevertheless, the relational and functional views highlight a significant dimension of what it means to be human. Man stands in a unique relation to God and serves as God's representative within creation because he is made in God's image, although precisely what this consists of remains something of a mystery. In the end, the Bible itself never states precisely what it means to be made in the image of God. Noting this, Garrett asks, "Could it be that the biblical writers never intended to offer such an interpretation of the image?"[18]

There are, however, some significant consequences of being made in the image of God. First, human life is valuable—indeed, its value requires the highest response when it is wrongly taken (Gen. 9:6). Second, slandering another human is condemned *because man is made in God's image*. According to James 3:9–10, any act directed at another human is in some sense directed at God.[19] Third, men and women are equal before God. Man is made in the image of God *as male and female* (Gen. 1:27). Nevertheless, the *equality* of men and women no more implies a functional identity between them than the equality of God the Father, God the Son, and God the Holy Spirit implies a functional identity between the three divine persons. Both extremes—denying equality on the one hand and ignoring the difference in function on the other—are to be avoided. Fourth, the image of God is *universal*. Here Block states, "Whereas in Babylon the status of 'image of God' was reserved for kings and priests, the Bible democratizes the notion—the children of Adam as a race in general and individual members of the race in particular, are all invested with this status."[20] No other part of creation, no matter how beautiful or intricate, can claim to be made in the image of its Creator. Still, as God Himself is something of a mystery, so also what it means to be made in His image is something of a mystery.

HUMAN FREEDOM

The *Baptist Faith and Message 2000* asserts that man sinned by "his free choice." But what sort of freedom does man possess? Typically, philosophers and theologians distinguish between compatibilist and libertarian freedom. While there are several varieties of compatibilist freedom, each asserts that an action can be both determined and free in a meaningful sense. An action is free, on a compatibilist understanding, so long as the person performing it does what he or she wants to do, i.e., so long as the person performing the action is subject to neither external nor internal compulsion. Libertarian freedom, on the other hand, is a type of incompatibilism; it holds that freedom and determinism are incompatible.[21] Libertarians typically insist that an action is free only if the person performing it could actually choose or reject a given action in a particular circumstance. Which sort of freedom did man have when he chose to disobey his Creator?

Admittedly, the Bible does not address this question directly. Any answer will therefore be conjectural. As such, this is a secondary issue so long as one affirms that, when he fell from innocence, man did so freely. In other words, on the issue of what constitutes genuine biblical freedom, fair-minded Christians—indeed fair-minded Baptists—disagree. And I have no illusions about settling this matter once and for all.

Space does not permit a complete—or even nearly complete—philosophical treatment of this topic. I propose instead to consider what sort of freedom man possessed by posing the question, "Which understanding of freedom fits best with the rest of the *Baptist Faith and Message 2000?*" If the confession includes other sections which imply a particular understanding of human freedom, it then seems preferable to apply that conception of freedom to open-ended statements such as one finds in Article III.

Two articles in the *Baptist Faith and Message 2000* bear on the issue of freedom. The first is Article I on the Scriptures. Christians have traditionally affirmed that the Bible is the inspired word of God. Indeed, the *Baptist Faith and Message* in all its versions affirms that Scripture both is "written by men divinely inspired" and "has God for its author." The latter statement makes it clear that divine inspiration went beyond moving the human authors to write down their thoughts or feelings in light of His revelation, or simply to record God's revelation in history.[22] Since none of the authors of the various versions of the *Baptist Faith and Message* believed the human authors of Scripture were mere typewriters through whom the Holy Spirit pounded out God's message, or the Bible to have been cowritten in the way that a novel, play, or song might be—with one author writing some parts and another writing others, or with one writing lyrics and another music—I can only assume that most believe the human authors to have been genuinely free, though the Holy Spirit somehow superintended the final product. Indeed, most Baptists have affirmed that the Bible results from concursive inspiration, involving both the human and divine authors. According to Millard Erickson,

As authors of Scripture wrote, God placed within their minds the thoughts he wished communicated. This was not a case of the message's already having been revealed, and the Holy Spirit's merely bringing these matters to remembrance, or directing the writer to thoughts with which the writer was already familiar. God created thoughts in the mind of the writer as he wrote. The writer could have been either conscious or unconscious of what was happening. In the latter case, he may have felt that the ideas were simply dawning on him.[23]

But if this is so, in what sense are the human authors free? The answer is that they were free in a compatibilist sense.[24]

Although one may contend that the Bible could nevertheless be exactly what God wanted it to be within a libertarian framework, one must ask, "How then can God be assured of being an *author* of Scripture, if the human author is free to choose to disregard Him?" How can Scripture be the word of God as well as the words of Moses, Matthew, Paul, or Peter? At best, it seems that God merely contributes to writing the text—i.e., making suggestions as to what to write, suggestions which the human author may either follow or disregard.

The other relevant article is Article V, "God's Purpose of Grace," which states, "All true believers endure to the end. Those whom God has accepted in Christ, and sanctified by His Spirit, will never fall away from the state of grace, but shall persevere to the end." All three versions of the *Baptist Faith and Message* affirm the perseverance of the saints, also known as the eternal security of the believer.

How exactly does this come to pass, given human freedom? How is one assured of persevering? Scripture is replete with passages stressing that one's actions are intimately related to one's relationship to God.[25] Yet Baptists affirm that the believer's not falling away results from God's grace rather than human merit or effort. How can both be true? Again, compatibilist freedom seems to work best. God works to ensure that believers *will not* fall away—because they will freely choose to trust Him for their salvation.

Notice the significant difference between "will not" and "cannot." The end result remains the same in either case; the means, however, differ significantly.[26] The former ("will not happen") works *with* the human will, thus ensuring freedom; the latter ("cannot happen") works against the human will, thus denying freedom. The view sketched out above thus allows one to affirm both the sovereignty of God and the freedom of man. The means by which God ensures that believers will persevere is regeneration; in mercy, He washes and renews them by His Holy Spirit (Titus 3:5) and makes them new creatures (2 Cor. 5:17) with new desires so that they freely choose to believe and obey. This sort of perseverance arises out of a dynamic relationship which neither

God nor man wishes to end, rather than a formal contract which neither party can rescind. And it is more in line with compatibilism than with libertarianism.

If I am correct here, and many will think that I am not,[27] it is more consistent to affirm that man has compatibilist freedom than to affirm that he has libertarian freedom. This significantly affects how one understands the entrance of sin into this world as well as the presence of evil more generally. In response to the problem of evil, one may still appeal to a freewill defense, but not as a means of defending God against all objections. Instead, a freewill defense will serve simply as part of a cumulative case for the compatibility of the Christian God with evil existing in creation.[28]

Space does not permit more to be said here.[29] So suffice it to say that, if Baptists are committed to compatibilist freedom when it comes to the inspiration of Scripture and the eternal security of the believer, they should for the sake of consistency be committed when it comes to the freedom mentioned in Article III—unless, of course, they can show that some relevant difference obtains.[30]

EFFECTS OF MAN'S SIN

Concerning original, or inherited, sin, the 1925 edition of the *Baptist Faith and Message* declares that man "transgressed the command of God and fell from his original holiness and righteousness; whereby his posterity inherit a nature corrupt and in bondage to sin, are under condemnation, and as soon as they are capable of moral action, become actual transgressors." The *Baptist Faith and Message 2000* closely follows the 1963 edition, stating about man's fall that he "fell from his original innocence whereby his posterity inherit a nature and an environment inclined toward sin. Therefore, as soon as they are capable of moral action, they become transgressors and are under condemnation."

By including the phrase, "as soon as they are capable of moral action," all three editions seem to affirm an "age of accountability." At first glance, the 1925 edition appears to affirm that man is condemned *prior* to reaching a point at which he is capable of moral action. In the later statements, however, it is clear that man is condemned only after reaching that point.

A growing minority of Southern Baptists hold to a Calvinistic soteriology,[31] affirming at least four of the five points of Calvinism as presented in the acronym TULIP.[32] Generally, these Reformed Baptists insist not only that man inherits "a nature and an environment inclined toward sin" but also that he is in some sense guilty of sin prior to having engaged in morally significant activity. How can those holding this view affirm the *Baptist Faith and Message 2000* in good conscience? Perhaps some will determine that they cannot and no Baptist is required to do so. But many Reformed Baptists do.

The key biblical passage that bears on this issue is Rom. 5:12–19, especially v. 12. In the fifth chapter of Romans, Paul presents the reader with a parallelism—through one man sin and death entered the world because in that one man all sinned. As Adam's sinful act leads to death, so Christ's righteous act leads to life (v. 17). But in order for Christ's atoning death to become effective in one's life, one must confess one's sins and trust God for salvation through Jesus Christ. In other words, there must be an act of moral assent on the individual's part for Christ's righteous act to become salvific for that person. But it is not the human act of turning to Christ that saves; rather, it is the imputation of Christ's righteousness that saves. Turning to Christ in faith is merely the means by which the imputation of Christ's righteousness becomes salvific in one's life.

Similarly, Reformed Baptists may affirm with the *Baptist Faith and Message 2000* that, as a result of the fall, all men "inherit a nature and an environment inclined toward sin." They may also insist that, in some sense, Adam's guilt is inherited as well. For, as Christ's righteousness is imputed, so also is Adam's guilt.[33] Nevertheless, the condemnation for these imputed sins does not become actual (and make one morally accountable before God) until one gives moral assent to Adam's disobedience to God. I do not know if this is the reasoning that Reformed Baptists apply to Article III of the *Baptist Faith and Message 2000*. This interpretation, however, seems right.[34] It also has the added benefit of smoothing out some of the apparent differences between the 1925 edition and later ones. In any case, room exists for both Reformed and other Baptists to affirm the *Baptist Faith and Message 2000*.

In conclusion, since man is made in the image of God, he is a creature of great dignity. Since man is free, he is also responsible for his actions, especially as they impact not only other men but also the whole of Creation. The good news is that, despite human flaws, hope abounds in the person and work of Jesus Christ, God's Son and man's Savior. Because of who man is, he can accept or reject God's invitation of grace; because of who God is, there is a gracious invitation to accept. Praise be to God the Father Almighty, who is mighty in grace and love!

NOTES

1. Blaise Pascal, *Pensees* 131.

2. That Article III has been relatively uncontroversial may be seen by accessing the online essay, "1963 and 2000 Baptist Faith and Message Statements: Comparison and Commentary," found on the website of the Baptist General Convention of Texas (BGCT). The

BGCT essay contends that, with the 2000 edition, the *Baptist Faith and Message* went from being a statement of faith to being a creed. The essay has four columns, the first two displaying the text of the 1963 and 2000 editions side by side. The third column lists the changes found in the 2000 edition, while the fourth column provides commentary on those changes. Significantly, there is no commentary on the changes made to Article III. See www.bgct .org/TexasBaptists/Document.Doc?&id = 610; accessed 30 August 2006.

3. Millard J. Erickson, *Christian Theology*, 2d ed. (Grand Rapids: Baker, 1998), 520.

4. *Doctrine and Covenants* 130:22. Cf. Stephen E. Robinson, "God the Father: Overview," *Encyclopedia of Mormonism*, ed. Daniel H. Ludlow (New York: Macmillan, 1992), 2:548.

5. Thomas Aquinas, *Summa Theologica* I, Q. 93; John Calvin, *Commentary on the Gospel according to John* (Grand Rapids: Eerdmans, 1956), 1:32.

6. James Leo Garrett Jr., "Image of God," *The Encyclopedia of Early Christianity*, 2d ed., ed. Everett Ferguson (New York: Garland, 1997), 1:560–61. See also James Leo Garrett Jr., *Systematic Theology: Biblical, Historical, and Evangelical* (Grand Rapids: Eerdmans, 1990), 1:396–97. Garrett cites Clement of Alexandria, Tatian, Athanasius, Cyril of Jerusalem, John Chrysostom, Ambrose, Cyril of Alexandria, and Augustine of Hippo as holding that the image resided in man's soul. He cites Clement of Alexandria, Origen, Methodius, Eusebius of Caesarea, Gregory of Nyssa, Augustine of Hippo, Athanasius, and Cyril of Alexandria as affirming that the image of God is to be identified with reason.

7. Among these Garrett lists Irenaeus, Tertullian, Basil the Great, Gregory of Nyssa, and Cyril of Alexandria. Garrett, "Image of God," 560–61.

8. John L. Dagg, *A Manual of Theology* (Charleston: Southern Baptist Publication Society, 1857; reprint, Harrisonburg: Gano, 1982), 141–44; Edgar Young Mullins, *The Christian Religion in Its Doctrinal Expression* (Philadelphia: Judson, 1917), 257–60; Erickson, 523.

9. Emil Brunner, *Man in Revolt: A Christian Anthropology*, trans. Olive Wyon (Philadelphia: Westminster, 1947), 64–65.

10. Emil Brunner, *The Christian Doctrine of Creation and Redemption*, trans. Olive Wyon (London: Lutterworth, 1952), 57.

11. Brunner, *Christian Doctrine of Creation and Redemption*, 55–57. One should note that Brunner sees the formal image of God as representing the Old Testament perspective and the material image of God as representing the New Testament and Apostolic perspective.

12. Norman H. Snaith, "The Image of God," *Expository Times* 86 (1974), 24.

13. Frank Stagg, *Polarities of Man's Existence in Biblical Perspective* (Philadelphia: Westminster, 1973), 25–27.

14. Daniel Block, "Man," in *An Exposition from the Faculty of The Southern Baptist Theological Seminary on the Baptist Faith and Message 2000* (Louisville: The Southern Baptist Theological Seminary, 2001), 8.

15. Walter Eichrodt, *Theology of the Old Testament*, trans. J. A. Baker (Philadelphia: Westminster, 1967), 2:127.

16. Erickson, *Christian Theology*, 531.

17. Erickson, *Christian Theology*, 531.

18. Garrett, *Systematic Theology*, 1:400, note 53.

19. See also Matt. 25:40,45; 1 John 4:20.

20. Block, "Man," 9.

21. Many sources discuss this issue in elementary terms. For example, see Charles Taliaferro, *Contemporary Philosophy of Religion* (Malden: Blackwell, 1998), 106–42; J. P. Moreland and William Lane Craig, *Philosophical Foundations for a Christian Worldview* (Downers Grove: InterVarsity, 2003), 267–84.

22. On this point, see Erickson, *Christian Theology*, 214–15; James Barr, "The Interpretation of Scripture. II. Revelation through History in the Old Testament and in Modern Theology," *Interpretation* 17 (1963): 196–97.

23. Erickson, *Christian Theology*, 213.

24. This seems particularly clear if one affirms a verbal, plenary view of inspiration, according to which God insures that the author writes exactly what He intends.

25. See Matt. 24:12–13; 1 Cor. 6:9–10; 1 John 1:6, 2:4–6. Scriptures such as 1 John 1:8–10 also teach that all believers sin.

26. The type of compatibilism for which I am arguing asserts that individuals *want to do* what they do *because of who they are* and they thus choose according to their personalities and psychological characteristics. This is not the opposite of self-determinism, it is the essence of it! I hold to self-determination; an individual *would* choose the same course of action whenever he faces the same situation because of who he is—i.e., he is free to be himself. This is, in my estimation, what ensures that counterfactuals have a truth value.

27. I am not arguing that all Baptists *do* or *must* reason in this way, but rather that they *should*.

28. In my estimation, an appeal to some greater good must be part of *any* Christian response to the problem of evil. Furthermore, a Christian response must be "Christian"— that is, biblical—if it is to address evil fully. Denying Christians the right to appeal to Scripture in responding to the problem of evil unfairly forces them to argue for the Christian God from a position of unbelief.

29. Some may wonder why I do not address the question of Christ's impeccability, i.e., of whether He could have sinned during His earthly sojourn. Doing so would require a longer discussion than this essay permits; moreover, the issue of whether Christ could have sinned is not addressed as explicitly in the *Baptist Faith and Message* as the doctrines with which I have chosen to deal.

30. Perhaps some relevant difference obtains between the freedom man enjoyed prior to the fall and that which he enjoys now. But one must argue for such a difference rather than simply assert it. If there is no such difference, and yet one treats these articles differently regarding human freedom, is one not guilty of special pleading?

31. See, e.g., Collin Hansen, "Young, Restless, Reformed," *Christianity Today*, September 2006, 32–38. Cf. the Founders Ministries website at www.founders.org; the subheading of the site states, "Committed to historic Baptist principles."

32. The five tenets for which TULIP stands are: Total Depravity, Unconditional Election, Limited Atonement, Irresistible Grace, and Perseverance of the Saints (known also as "preservation of the Saints" or "the eternal security of the believer").

33. Whether one conceives of sin as being inherited in an Augustinian or a Federal sense makes no difference on this point.

34. For a position similar to the one I have laid out, see Erickson, *Christian Theology*, 637–56, esp. 652–56. For a Calvinistic perspective, see Wayne Grudem, *Systematic Theology* (Grand Rapids: Zondervan, 1994), 490–501.

· Article IV ·

The Doctrine of Salvation

R. Albert Mohler Jr.

𝒯he doctrine of salvation stands at the very center of the Christian faith. Indeed, God's salvation of His people is the great theme of the Bible. Thus, it is not surprising that the *Baptist Faith and Message* turns to the doctrine of salvation so quickly. In a logical sequence, everything that follows flows from this great doctrine.

The *Baptist Faith and Message 2000* did not emerge from a theological vacuum. As the late John Leith observed, "Generally speaking, creeds have not been written in the quiet periods of history but in those moments of historical intensity when the Church has been engaged by foes from without, or when its mission or life has been endangered from within."[1]

The 1963 revision of the confession, itself occasioned by theological controversy, represented an attempt to revise the historic 1925 edition and to create a new theological consensus for Southern Baptists—a theological consensus that largely reflected the beliefs and views of a denominational elite. The most important aspect of the 1963 revision related to the doctrine of Scripture, and a vaguely neo-orthodox statement was adopted. Controversy over biblical authority had prompted the original adoption of the *Baptist Faith and Message* in 1925, when Southern Baptists swerved to avoid the Fundamentalist-Modernist controversy that was rending the mainline Protestant denominations. At that time, the issue was the straightforward question of supernaturalism. As the 1925 committee reported, "The present occasion for a reaffirmation of Christian fundamentals is the prevalence of naturalism in the modern teaching and preaching of religion. Christianity is supernatural in its origin and history. We repudiate every theory of religion which denies the supernatural elements in our faith."[2]

Controversy over biblical authority also led to the revision of the confession in 1963. Questions related to the historicity of biblical accounts, the veracity of certain passages, and the larger issue of biblical inerrancy (then most often described as infallibility) framed the debate. Interestingly, no major controversy over the doctrine of salvation emerged in the 1925 and 1963 contexts. The same was basically true in 2000, with the exception of one very important question—the exclusivity of the Gospel.

The decision of the 1925 committee to base the *Baptist Faith and Message* on the *New Hampshire Confession* was immediately significant for the doctrine of salvation. In one sense, the doctrine of salvation *was* the catalyst for the adoption of that confession by the Baptist Convention of New Hampshire in 1833. Influenced by the popularity of Free Will Baptist preaching in the area, the New Hampshire convention sought, in the words of William L. Lumpkin, "to restate its Calvinism in very moderate tones."[3] Those moderate tones spread with the popularity of the *New Hampshire Confession*—and that popularity was greatly enhanced by the fact that J. Newton Brown chose that confession for inclusion in his 1853 work, *The Baptist Church Manual*. And, in a move that is highly significant with respect to the doctrine of salvation, Brown personally added two articles. Brown's additions were articles on "Repentance and Faith" and "Sanctification," and both of these added articles became standard in successive editions of the confession.

The decision of the 1925 committee to base a confession for Southern Baptists on the New Hampshire tradition was almost surely made on the basis of the confession's familiarity and stature among Baptists in America—including even Landmarkist groups. As such, the decision was judicious and understandable.

Beyond the issue of familiarity and trust, the New Hampshire tradition also represented the modified Calvinism of Southern Baptists in the early twentieth century. The *New Hampshire Confession* is undeniably Calvinistic in shape and substance—but its Calvinism is also undeniably a modified one. Significantly, the New Hampshire tradition represents a congenial meeting place for Baptists who are traditional Calvinists and those whose Calvinism is more modified. No tenet of traditional Calvinism is denied, but the New Hampshire statement avoids the more rigorously Calvinistic formulations of the *Second London Confession* (1689) and the *Philadelphia Confession* (1742).

In the main, the 1925 committee reproduced the New Hampshire articles (with the addition of Brown's two articles) with only minor editorial changes. "Sanctification" was moved ahead of "God's Purpose of Grace" and language already somewhat outdated was clarified.

In one interesting and unexpected revision, the 1925 committee changed the wording concerning sanctification. Brown's edition defined sanctification as "the process by which, according to the will of God, we are made partakers of his holiness."[4] The 1925 statement defines sanctification as "the process by which the regenerate gradually attain to moral and spiritual perfection through the presence of the Holy Spirit dwelling in their hearts." The revision is at once both more inclined to perfectionistic interpretations and more sentimental than the original. The perfectionism issue would not have been a major concern of Southern Baptists at that time, since the denomination was familiar with the biblical language and would likely have understood "perfection" to mean maturity. Similarly, the 1963 committee retained the 1925 language. In a very different day, the 2000 committee would change "perfection" to "maturity" in order to remove any contemporary confusion.

SALVATION ACCORDING TO THE
BAPTIST FAITH AND MESSAGE

The 1925 statement's article on salvation begins with an eloquent sentence relating to both the person and work of Christ: "The salvation of sinners is wholly of grace, through the mediatorial office of the Son of God, who by the Holy Spirit was born of the Virgin Mary and took upon him our nature, yet without sin; honored the divine law by his personal obedience and made atonement for our sins by his death." The 1963 statement reduced the expression to: "Salvation involves the redemption of the whole man, and is offered freely to all who accept Jesus Christ as Lord and Savior, who by his own blood obtained eternal redemption for the believer."

The 2000 committee, taking the 1963 revision as a foundational text, retained the 1963 language. Thus, explicit references to Christ's mediatorial office and His perfect fulfillment of the divine law do not appear. Sadly, these two vital New Testament doctrines became less familiar (if not altogether unknown) to millions of Southern Baptists as the century drew to a close. Interestingly, the 1963 language regarding "the redemption of the whole man" may reflect the growing influence of psychology and therapeutic concerns. In any event, it was retained by the 2000 committee.

The 1963 committee subsumed the 1925 statement's article on "The Freeness of Salvation" within the new article's first paragraph. Nevertheless, the article clearly states that salvation "is offered freely to all who accept Jesus Christ as Lord and Saviour." The major change made by the 2000 committee had to do with a question that would certainly have been recognized by the committees of 1925 and 1963, but with nothing near the urgency recognized by the 2000 committee. That question is this: Can salvation be found apart from conscious faith in Jesus Christ?

Various strains of universalism can be traced back to the Patristic era. Nevertheless, widespread questioning of the exclusivity of the Gospel did not emerge in mainstream Christianity until the mid-twentieth century. Within some denominations, questioning of exclusive claims began to gain traction shortly after World War II. As far back as 1893, the first World Parliament of Religions (organized in Chicago by Unitarians) revealed a willingness on the part of some theologians to question exclusivity. Growing awareness of religious pluralism and diversity led to new questions. By mid-century, some of the historic denominations of the Protestant "mainline" were ready to announce a "moratorium" on conversionist missions.

Added to this, the Roman Catholic Church was engaged in the process of *aggiornamento* so evident in the massive doctrinal transformations of Vatican II. Cyprian's famous formula, *"salus extra ecclesiam non est,"* was being redefined in inclusivist terms. Inclusivism, as opposed to classic universalism, does not hold that there may be salvation apart from Christ. Instead, inclusivists argue that there may be many ways to salvation *in Christ.* Specifically, they argue that conscious faith in Jesus Christ as Savior and Lord is not necessary. Instead, they argue that the "light" of other religions may be used to draw persons (unknowingly and unconsciously) to Christ.

Other variants of non-exclusivistic thought include the late Karl Rahner's concept of the "anonymous Christian"—a person who follows Christ without ever hearing of Him or responding to His Gospel by faith. Others have argued for a postmortem opportunity to respond to Christ in faith.

Southern Baptists were generally only remote observers of these trends until the 1980s, when some Southern Baptist seminary professors and other leaders began openly to raise the issue. Some went so far as to advocate or propose various inclusivistic or universalistic arguments. Others merely posed the issue as an open question. By the late 1980s, sociologist James Davison Hunter would warn that younger evangelicals were generally open to such proposals.[5]

The 2000 committee took this challenge very seriously, and a clear, concise, and unambiguous sentence was added to the opening paragraph on salvation: "There is no salvation apart from personal faith in Jesus Christ as Lord." This sentence clearly precludes any form of inclusivism or universalism—any suggestion that a sinner can be saved apart from a conscious response of faith in the Lord Jesus Christ prior to the sinner's death.

The modified Calvinism of the New Hampshire tradition is reflected in the *New Hampshire Confession's* placement of the article on regeneration after the articles on justification and the freeness of salvation. This pattern is retained in the 1925 statement, in which regeneration is defined as "a change of heart wrought by the Holy Spirit, whereby we become partakers of the divine nature and a holy disposition is given, leading to the love and practice of righteousness." The statement goes on to add that regeneration is "a work of God's free grace conditioned upon faith in Christ."

Interestingly, the 1963 committee made significant changes in the statement—changes that effectively shifted the confession in a more explicitly Reformed direction. In the first place, the committee moved the article so that it precedes repentance and faith in the presentation. That said, this decision (like the decision of the New Hampshire Baptists) may not reflect any specific intention to imply an *ordo salutis*. But the 1963 committee made another very significant change. Regeneration, described in the 1925 statement as "conditioned upon faith in Christ" is now described as "a change of heart wrought by the Holy Spirit through the conviction of sin, *to which the sinner responds in repentance toward God and faith in our Lord Jesus Christ*" [emphasis added].

What exactly did the committee mean by this change? Herschel H. Hobbs, chairman of the 1963 committee, clearly did not teach that regeneration precedes faith. Even after the committee he chaired made the change noted above, Hobbs argued: "Regeneration is the result of conviction of sin, repentance from sin, faith in Jesus Christ, and the confession of that faith."[6] Thus, the confession itself, as revised in 1963, defines regeneration as the event "to which the sinner responds" in faith even as Dr. Hobbs defined regeneration as "the result" of faith. Does the *Baptist Faith and Message* require a specific order of salvation? Taken as a whole, the paragraphs on salvation attempt to define the doctrine of salvation by looking both backward and forward. A specific *ordo salutis* cannot be argued too strongly from within the text or the context of the *Baptist Faith and Message*. As if to make that point, the 2000 committee moved one very strategic sentence ("Regeneration and faith are inseparable experiences of grace.") to end the paragraph on regeneration, rather than to begin the next.

In the 1925 statement, repentance and faith are described as "wrought in our souls by the regenerating spirit of God." E. Y. Mullins, chairman of the 1925 committee, may have expressed this best: "In strict logic regeneration precedes both faith and repentance if we begin with the true Gospel teaching that all is due to the grace of God. Yet here again fact and apparent logic do not necessarily coincide. The correct view is that regeneration and repentance and faith are simultaneous events in the soul's life. No impenitent or unbelieving soul can be a regenerate soul, just as no penitent believer can be unregenerate."[7]

In the 1925 statement, the article on repentance became the occasion for yet another explication of the offices of Christ and an elaborate definition of repentance in terms of its progress within the believer's conscience. In the 1963 statement repentance is simply defined as "a genuine turning from sin toward God." That statement, retained without alteration by the 2000 committee, explicitly requires repentance as a part of the salvation experience. There is no notion here of any salvation apart from repentance toward God and faith in Jesus Christ. Thus, repentance from sin is not necessary only for some, the more mature and faithful Christians, but for all authentic believers.

The 1963 committee reduced the total number of articles within the confession from twenty-four to seventeen. In order to do this, the committee formatted the statement so that three enumerated paragraphs complete the article. The 2000 committee saw this format as awkward, given the fact that Arabic numerals subdivided an article designated by a Roman numeral. In order to avoid any confusion, the 2000 committee replaced the Arabic numerals with letter designations.

More importantly, the 2000 committee also added a specific paragraph on justification. The 1963 statement simply added a section on justification to the section on repentance and faith. The 2000 statement, while retaining the exact language of the 1963 statement, made justification a stand-alone paragraph. The current language improves upon the 1925 statement by specifying that it is Christ's own righteousness that is the sole ground for the acquittal of sinners: "Justification is God's gracious and full acquittal upon principles of His righteousness of all sinners who repent and believe in Christ. Justification brings the believer into a relationship of peace and favor with God." Given current confusions concerning the doctrine of justification prevalent in the larger evangelical world, it is helpful that the *Baptist Faith and Message* makes clear that sinners are justified by faith alone—on the basis of Christ's righteousness alone.

Sanctification is included under the doctrine of salvation, thus grounding the beginnings of the believer's sanctification in the salvation experience itself. The statement specifies that sanctification begins "in regeneration." Two dimensions of sanctification are explained. In the first place, sanctification is the experience "by which the believer is set apart to God's purposes." Thus, sanctification represents a fundamental reorientation of the believer's life. The lordship of Christ places the believer under a new and conscious sovereignty, and the believer is to be deployed for Kingdom purposes, to live by Kingdom principles, and to live only for the glory of the King.

In the second place, sanctification is the experience by which the believer is "enabled to progress toward moral and spiritual maturity through the presence and power of the Holy Spirit dwelling in him." As mentioned above, the word "perfection" in the 1925 and 1963 statements was replaced in 2000 with "maturity." This change does not reflect a shift in meaning, but is intended only to clarify the meaning of the statement in light of contemporary confusions.

Neglect of the biblical doctrine of sanctification leads to disaster—both individual and congregational. Believers are to pray for, look for, and aim for signs of spiritual maturity and conformity to the image of Christ. All this is, like salvation, all of grace from beginning to end. The indwelling Christ and the presence of the Holy Spirit will gift the believer with growth in grace throughout the believer's life. Just as the confession makes clear, this is a confirmation of regeneration—the fruit of being born again.

Salvation reaches its conclusion in the glorification of all believers. The confession defines glorification as "the culmination of salvation and . . . the final blessed and abiding state of the redeemed." No explicit statement concerning glorification appears in the *New Hampshire Confession* or the 1925 edition of the *Baptist Faith and Message*. This is a strange omission, and the 1963 committee was wise to include a paragraph, though concise, on the glorification of believers. This is a vital New Testament teaching that makes clear and understandable the "already but not yet" nature of our salvation. The salvation of believers culminates in glorification—whereby the believer is transformed so that the Creator is perfectly glorified in the redeemed creature. Like all other aspects of our salvation, this is accomplished only by the unmerited grace of God.

Jaroslav Pelikan once commented that confessions of faith "have their origin in a two-fold Christian imperative, to believe and to confess what one believes."[8] This "Christian imperative" is as old as the faith itself, rooted in the teaching of the apostles and in the warnings of Jesus. After all, it was the Lord who taught His disciples: "So everyone who acknowledges me before men, I also will acknowledge before my Father who is in heaven, but whoever denies me before men, I also will deny before my Father who is in heaven" (Matt. 10:32–33). Southern Baptists, as a convention of churches, did not adopt a confession of faith until 1925. The *Baptist Faith and Message* is an attempt by Southern Baptists to confess the faith "once for all delivered to the saints" (Jude 3), and to do so as an act of theological and biblical integrity.

The doctrine of salvation is central to this confession of our faith. Nothing could be more important than to understand the biblical teaching about the salvation that comes through faith in Jesus Christ. In the *Baptist Faith and Message* the doctrine of salvation serves as a bridge that leads from the problem of human sin to the reality of the church and the framework of the Christian life.

The writing, editing, and revising of a confession of faith is a weighty matter. The tragedy of misstating or misconstruing a doctrine can have eternal consequences. A review of Baptist confessional history demonstrates that the *Baptist Faith and Message 2000* stands squarely in the faithful mainstream of Baptist belief. The 2000 committee found nothing fundamentally wrong with the 1963 statement as it dealt with salvation. For the most part, the 2000 statement is a straightforward representation of the 1963 edition's sections on salvation. The changes to format and vocabulary were intended to clarify and extend the useful life of the confession into the twenty-first century.

The most significant change, of course, was an addition. The statement on the exclusivity of salvation through conscious personal faith in Christ is urgently important. Without this clear and unambiguous statement, some door to inclusivism or universalism would remain open. With the addition of that one sentence, the confession now leaves no room for doubt.

A confession of faith is like a mirror held up to an age. Like a mirror it reveals a great deal about ourselves and the age in which we live. Our epoch is resistant to particularity and distrustful of claims to universal truth. Nevertheless, the church's responsibility is to maintain the apostolic witness in the face of contemporary challenges to truth-telling. In the end, the sum and substance of the article on salvation in the *Baptist Faith and Message 2000* is something every authentic believer—and surely every authentic Baptist—can instantly understand and gladly affirm—*Jesus saves.*

NOTES

1. John H. Leith, ed., *Creeds of Christendom*, 3rd ed. (Atlanta: John Knox, 1982), 2.

2. The quotation is from the preface to the *Baptist Faith and Message 1925*.

3. William L. Lumpkin, ed., *Baptist Confessions of Faith*, rev. ed. (Valley Forge: Judson, 1969), 360.

4. Lumpkin, *Baptist Confessions*, 365.

5. James Davison Hunter, *Evangelicalism: The Coming Generation* (Chicago: University of Chicago Press, 1987).

6. Herschel H. Hobbs, *The Baptist Faith and Message* (Nashville: Convention, 1971), 60.

7. E. Y. Mullins, *Baptist Beliefs* (Valley Forge: Judson, 1912), 43–44.

8. Jaroslav Pelikan, *Credo* (New Haven: Yale University Press, 2003), 35.

· *Article V* ·

God's Purpose of Grace

Daniel L. Akin

*E*phesians 2:8–9 is an important Scripture concerning salvation. It states, "For by grace you are saved through faith, and this is not from yourselves; it is God's gift—not from works, so that no one can boast."[1] These verses address both God's grace and man's faith in the drama of salvation. It affirms that no one is saved apart from the grace of God. It equally affirms that no one is saved apart from faith, a faith that is itself the gift of God.

Few issues ignite a more lively debate than a discussion of the relationship between God's electing purpose of grace and the free agency of man and his responsibility to exercise repentance and faith. The issue is biblically and theologically complex. There is a mystery and a tension in what we discover when we examine Scripture. Maintaining a healthy balance is a challenge, and yet it is clear that is exactly what Article V attempts to achieve.

The article comprises two paragraphs. The first addresses God's gracious electing purpose. The second discusses the doctrine of eternal security and the related concept of the perseverance of the saints. The entire article is firmly rooted in reformed theology, though it is a moderate form of this theological tradition.

ELECTION AND HUMAN RESPONSIBILITY

Article V appropriately begins with God as the author and initiator of our salvation, and what is contained here is a natural corollary to what is found in Article IV on Salvation. Election is said to be the gracious purpose of God. It is instructive to note what *is* and what is *not* stated. Election is an act of grace rooted in the purpose of God. Election unto salvation starts with God, not man. Election to salvation is rooted in grace, not works. It is unmerited and undeserved. And yet the nature and basis of election is not defined. This is somewhat different from "The Abstract of Principles" written by Basil Manly Jr. as the doctrinal confession for the Southern Baptist Theological Seminary in 1859. Its article on Election states, "Election is God's eternal choice of some persons unto everlasting life—not because of foreseen merit in them, but of His mercy in Christ. . . ." The *Baptist Faith and Message 2000*'s article is a milder, less theologically specific statement. It is compatible with "The Abstract of Principles," but it allows also for an understanding of Election that is broader than classical Reformed theology would affirm. It is not Arminian in any historical or theological sense, though those who ground election in God's foreknowledge of man's faith could affirm this statement, since the issue of foreknowledge is not addressed. However, as the last sentence of the first paragraph makes clear, God's purpose in election "excludes boasting and promotes humility." One's faith in Christ and repentance of sin is never an occasion for pride or self-congratulation. God saves persons; they do not save themselves.

In electing persons to salvation, God accomplishes a number of significant and wonderful blessings for unworthy sinners. These blessings include regeneration, justification, sanctification, and glorification. Each of these salvation gifts is noted and expounded in Article IV.

The electing purpose of God is affirmed as being "consistent with the free agency of man, and comprehends all the means in connection with the end." Here the tension in this doctrine becomes evident, often resulting in rigorous debate, which almost always revolves around the subject of Calvinism. For some, this is a theological landmine to be avoided at any cost, even if they are not sure what it means. For others, it signals a recovery of biblical truth growing out of the Reformation of the sixteenth century and its emphasis on the great *solas*—Scripture alone, Christ alone, grace alone, faith alone, for the glory of God alone.

John Calvin (1509–1564) was one of the great theologians of the Reformation. An outstanding biblical scholar, he heralded the theology of both Paul and Augustine (354–430). Like Martin Luther (1483–1546), he emphasized the sovereignty of God, the sinfulness of man, and the necessity of grace for salvation. Later in the seventeenth century, followers of Calvin would systematize his theology and go beyond what Calvin himself taught. This system would be codified with the now famous acronym TULIP. A brief description and comment on each of the five points of Calvinism is helpful at this point.

THE FIVE POINTS OF CALVINISM

Total Depravity—Since the Fall, man is born with a natural bent toward sin. Every aspect of man's being is infected with the disease of sin so that he cannot save himself, neither can he move toward God without the initiating and enabling grace of God. Man is not as bad as he could possibly be, but he is radically depraved. Most Baptists would agree on this point, and the issue is addressed previously in Article III. It is especially difficult to deny some form of human depravity in light of Rom. 3:9–20 and Eph. 2:1–3.

Unconditional Election—God in grace and mercy has chosen certain persons for salvation. This decision is not based on human merit or foreseen faith, but in the goodness and providence of God's own will and purposes. The French theologian Moise Amyraut (1596–1664) referred to this as God's secret or hidden decree. No one is saved apart from God's plan, and yet anyone who repents and trusts Christ will be saved. The tension is obvious, but such tension should be accepted and maintained. John 6:37–47 is helpful at this point.

Limited Atonement—This is an unfortunate phrase, with most five-point Calvinists preferring the term "particular redemption." This teaching affirms that it was the purpose and intention of the atoning work of Christ to provide and purchase salvation for the elect. Thus the work of Christ is *limited* to the elect, and His atonement was made for and purchased a *particular* people (e.g. His sheep, the Church, His Bride). This is a real point of contention for many, and most Baptists today would not embrace this teaching in its classic form. However, we should make a crucial observation that may foster some rapprochement: All Bible-believers limit the atonement in some way. Not to do so is to advocate Universalism, the view that eventually everyone will be saved. My understanding of the Bible is that the limitation of the atonement is in its application, not its provision. In other words I believe that in His death on the cross Jesus Christ died for the sins of the world (John 3:16; 1 Tim. 2:4–6, 4:10; 2 Pet. 2:1; 1 John 2:1–2, 4:9–10), making a universal provision. However, the application is limited to those who receive, by their personal faith in Christ, the free gift of salvation offered to them. One can see, then, that all evangelicals limit the atonement in some sense, but do so in different ways and at different places. Perhaps, then, *sufficient* for all and *efficient* for the elect is an affirmation most Baptists can embrace.

Irresistible Grace—Another unfortunate choice of words, the phrase "effectual calling" is much better. This doctrine asserts that those who are predestined and elected to be saved are called to salvation (Rom. 8:30) effectually or effectively. They are not forced to come but are set free to come and they do so willingly. Timothy George balances this teaching with human responsibility when he writes, "God created human beings with free moral agency, and He does not violate this even in the supernatural work of regeneration. Christ does not rudely bludgeon His way into the human heart. He does not abrogate our creaturely freedom. No, He beckons and woos, He pleads and pursues, He waits and wins."[2]

Perseverance of the Saints—Those God saves He protects and preserves in their salvation. Baptists have historically referred to this as the doctrine of "eternal security," or in popular terminology as "once saved, always saved." This is one point of Calvinism that almost all Baptists affirm, and it is expounded in the second paragraph of Article V. Sometimes misunderstood and falsely caricatured by those rejecting it, perseverance of the saints does not teach that one can live however one chooses, taking advantage of God's grace. Rather, because of the greatness of the gift of our salvation, true believers will be grieved when they sin and will pursue a life pleasing to the God whom they love and who keeps them safely in His hand (John 10:27–29).

This is a summary of the five points of Calvinism, what its advocates call "the Doctrines of Grace." Although it is not as popular among Southern Baptists as it was in the past, there has been a resurgence of its teachings. And one should honestly acknowledge that many wonderful and significant Baptists in the past followed these doctrines, including men like William Carey, Luther Rice, Adoniram Judson, Charles Spurgeon, John L. Dagg, Basil Manly Jr., and James Boyce. Andrew Fuller, John Broadus, and B. H. Carroll also would have considered themselves Calvinists, though they affirmed only four of the five points. They did not advocate particular redemption.

ACCEPTING THE TENSION IN DIVINE SOVEREIGNTY AND HUMAN RESPONSIBILITY

Having taken this brief historical excursion, how might we understand God's electing purpose of grace and at the same time affirm the Scriptural principle of "the free agency of man"?

First, we should affirm the truth both of God's sovereignty and human free will. "The Abstract of Principles," referred to above, reveals a healthy theological balance in its Article IV on Providence. Manly writes,

> God from eternity decrees or permits all things that come to pass, and perpetu-
> ally upholds, directs and governs all creatures and all events; yet so as not in any
> wise to be author or approver of sin nor to destroy *the free will and responsibility*
> of intelligent creatures (emphasis added).

The Bible teaches that God predestines and elects persons to salvation but that He does so in such a way as to do no violence to their free will and responsibility to repent from sin and believe the gospel. Is there a tension here? Yes. Is there divine mystery? Absolutely! I am convinced this is what Paul felt when, at the end of his magnificent treatment of this subject in Rom. 9–11, he concludes with a doxology of praise, writing, "Oh the depth of the riches both of the wisdom and the knowledge of God! How unsearchable His judgments and untraceable His ways" (Rom. 11:33)! If one finds it a challenge to fathom the depths of this doctrine, then one is in good company!

Second, recognize that extreme positions on either side of the issue are biblically unbalanced, theologically unhealthy, and practically undesirable. It is biblical to affirm the truth of all of God's Word. Words like called, chosen, election, foreknowledge, and predestination are in Holy Scripture. We should embrace them, examine them, and seek to understand them. Words like believe, evangelist, go, preach, receive, and repent are also in the Bible. Biblical balance requires that we embrace and affirm these as well.

Theologically we cannot be seduced into living in a theological ghetto that may espouse a nice clean doctrinal system, but that does so at the expense of a wholesome and comprehensive theology. Statements such as, "Election works like this: God voted for you. The devil voted against you. And you cast the deciding vote," must be set aside as an inaccurate reflection of the biblical revelation. On the other hand, attempting to construct a doctrine of double predestination wherein God elects some to damnation, hates the lost, and consigns non-elect infants to the fires of hell is equally irresponsible and lacking in biblical support.

Practically we must not become manipulative using gimmicks in our presentation of the Gospel as if the conversion of the lost depends on us. Neither should we be lulled into an antipathy toward personal evangelism and global missions. Any theology that does not result in a "hot heart" for lost souls is a theology not worth having. Some extreme forms of Calvinism have so warped the minds and frozen the hearts of its advocates that if they saw a person screaming to the top of their lungs—"What must I do to be saved?"—they would hesitate or even neglect sharing the gospel for fear of somehow interfering with the work of the Holy Spirit. If the initials J. C. bring first to one's mind the name John Calvin rather than Jesus Christ, and one fancies oneself more of an evangelist for Calvinism than for Christ, then this latter word of concern applies particularly to that one. We must never forget that the greatest theologian who ever lived was also the greatest missionary/evangelist who ever lived. His name is Paul.

ETERNAL SECURITY/PERSEVERANCE OF THE SAINTS

The second paragraph of Article V is dedicated to the issue of "eternal security," referred to by some as "perseverance of the saints." Contrary to Pelagian and Arminian theologies, this article states, "All true believers endure to the end." Those who depart the faith through theological or moral apostasy walk away because they are not truly in the company of the redeemed, for if they were, "they would have continued with us" (1 John 2:19).

Eternal security is grounded in our union with Christ, God's acceptance of us "in Christ." We are united with Him in death and resurrection. The sanctifying work of the Holy Spirit is also noted as a means by which we are "kept by the power of God" (1 Pet. 1:5). Through the ongoing work of Christ (Heb. 7:25) and the Spirit (Eph. 1:13–14), we "will never fall away from the state of grace, but shall persevere to the end."

The truth of our perseverance should not lead to the false doctrine of perfectionism. Such is the goal for which we strive in this life (Matt. 5:48; 1 John 2:1–2), but its realization is an eschatological reality (1 John 3:1–2). Until then we recognize, "Believers may fall into sin through neglect and temptation." That is why the Bible challenges us to abide in Christ and His Word (John 15:1–11), and warns us to avoid places of temptation (1 Cor. 6:18, 10:12–14; 1 Tim. 6:3–11).

Several motivations are brought forth to encourage our perseverance. The security of our salvation that we enjoy in Christ is never to be the occasion for sinful living. Such a wonderful and secure salvation should prompt holiness and purity, godliness and righteousness. Failure to pursue the "Christ life" will grieve the Holy Spirit (Eph. 4:30). It will impair and hamper the graces and comforts that should accompany our salvation. It will bring shame to the name of Jesus, and it will invite the discipline of the heavenly Father through "temporal" (though not eternal) judgments (Heb. 2:5–13). Yet in spite of the sin believers may commit, "they shall be kept by the power of God through faith unto salvation."

There are few doctrines of Scripture more precious and comforting than the doctrine of eternal security. Spurgeon said, "If there is one doctrine I have preached more than another, it is the doctrine of the Perseverance of the Saints even to the end."[3]

The doctrine of eternal security is necessary to a correct understanding of the Gospel and the truth of the Bible's concept of eternal or everlasting life. If I can lose it, it is not eternal; if I can lose it, it is not everlasting; if I can lose it, I can work my way out of salvation; if I can lose it, my salvation is ultimately dependent on me and not God. And if I can lose it, my confidence, comfort, and hope is pulled out from beneath me and I am suspended in the midair of uncertainty as to my final destiny.

Fortunately, the Bible addresses the doctrine of security clearly and repeatedly. In John 10:27–30, Jesus says, "My sheep hear My voice, and I know them, and they follow Me. And I give them eternal life, and they shall never perish; neither shall anyone snatch them out of My hand. My Father, who has given them to Me, is greater than all; and no one is able to snatch them out of My Father's hand. I and My Father are one." In Rom. 8:38–39, Paul writes, "For I am persuaded that neither death nor life, nor angels nor principalities nor powers, nor things present nor things to come, nor height nor depth, nor any other created thing, shall be able to separate us from the love of God which is in Christ Jesus our Lord." In Eph. 1:13–14, Paul states, "In Him you also trusted, after you heard the word of truth, the gospel of your salvation; in whom also, having believed, you were sealed with the Holy Spirit of promise, who is the guarantee of our inheritance until the redemption of the purchased possession, to the praise of His glory." In Heb. 7:25, the author writes, "Therefore He is also able to save to the uttermost those who come to God through Him, since He always lives to make intercession for them." And in Heb. 13:5, he states further, "Let your conduct be without covetousness; be content with such things as you have. For He Himself has said, 'I will never leave you nor forsake you.'" In 1 John 2:19 the beloved apostle writes, "They went out from us, but they were not of us; for if they had been of us, they would have continued with us; but they went out that they might be made manifest, that none of them were of us." And in 1 John 5:13, he affirms, "These things I have written to you who believe in the name of the Son of God, that you may know that you have eternal life." To all this, Jude adds in a glorious doxology of worship, praise, and adoration, that our God "is able to keep us from falling," and that He will "present us faultless before the presence of His glory with exceeding joy" (Jude 24–25). Thus, the praise of God and the perseverance of the believer are joined in a tightly woven piece of spiritual cloth never to be rent, never to be torn, never to be separated.

An important question of practical theology thus naturally arises: Why do people lack assurance? Why do people doubt their eternal security? At least five reasons present themselves: (1) A faulty understanding of the fact that it is God who does the saving; (2) a faulty method of assurance at the time of salvation (e.g., works, tongues, baptism); (3) doubt of God's faithfulness to keep His word; (4) a lack of proper teaching on the Christian life; and (5) the presence of sin in one's life!

There are at least two ways to help people settle the issue and gain the security they should experience in Christ. First, look to the cross and use God's Word, remembering two crucial truths: By His work on the cross Jesus *obtained* my salvation; and, by His work in heaven Jesus *maintains* my salvation. Second, ask questions regarding one's experience of the Christian life, including: Do you believe the gospel and trust Christ? Do you experience remorse over sin and have a desire to please God? Do you see any evidence of fruit in your life? Does the Holy Spirit witness to your spirit that you are a child of God? When you sin, do you experience the discipline of the Father? Augustus Montague

Toplady said it beautifully: "My name from the palms of His hands eternity will not erase; / Impressed on His heart it remains, in marks of indelible grace. / Yes, I to the end shall endure, as sure as the earnest is giv'n; / More happy, but not more secure, the glorified spirits in heav'n."[4]

CONCLUSION

The *Baptist Faith and Message 2000* is a well-constructed canopy under which varying perspectives on the issue of election can peacefully and helpfully coexist. Pelagians, classic Arminians, and Open Theists will not be comfortable as Southern Baptists. We should love them while also disagreeing with them. There is a place for differing positions on the issues of election, the extent of the atonement and calling, as well as how we do missions, evangelism, and give the invitation. Moreover, we shall be better theologically and practically if we engage each other in respectful, humble, gracious, and serious conversation. As one who considers himself a compatibilist, affirming the majestic mystery of both divine sovereignty and human responsibility, I have been challenged and strengthened in my own theological understanding by those on either side of the issue (i.e., more or less reformed). Because of our passionate commitment to the glory of God, the lordship of Christ, biblical authority, salvation by grace through faith, and the Great Commission, we should work in wonderful harmony with each other, and I am hopeful we always shall.

The great Baptist preacher Charles Spurgeon was a five point Calvinist. He was also a passionate evangelist and soul winner. On August 1, 1858, he preached a sermon entitled, "Sovereign Grace and Man's Responsibility." The words of wisdom that flowed from his mouth on that day could only come from a capable pastor-theologian with a shepherd's heart and a love for the lost. We would do well to heed the counsel of this Baptist hero upon whose shoulders we stand today.

> I see in one place, God presiding over all in providence; and yet I see and I cannot help seeing, that man acts as he pleases, and that God has left his actions to his own will, in a great measure. Now, if I were to declare that man was so free to act, that there was no precedence of God over his actions, I should be driven very near to Atheism; and if, on the other hand, I declare that God so overrules all things, as that man is not free enough to be responsible, I am driven at once into Antinomianism or fatalism. That God predestines, and that man is responsible, are two things that few can see. They are believed to be inconsistent and contradictory; but they are not. It is just the fault of our weak judgment. Two truths cannot be contradictory to each other. If, then, I find taught in one place that everything is fore-ordained, that is true; and if I find in another place

that man is responsible for all his actions, that is true; and it is my folly that leads me to imagine that two truths can ever contradict each other. These two truths, I do not believe, can ever be welded into one upon any human anvil, but one they shall be in eternity: they are two lines that are so nearly parallel, that the mind that shall pursue them farthest, will never discover that they converge; but they do converge, and they will meet somewhere in eternity, close to the throne of God, whence all truth doth spring. . . . You ask me to reconcile the two. I answer, they do not want any reconcilement; I never tried to reconcile them to myself, because I could never see a discrepancy. . . . Both are true; no two truths can be inconsistent with each other; and what you have to do is to believe them both.[5]

Here is a good place to stand. Here is a theology of "God's purpose of grace" we can all affirm in service to our Savior.

NOTES

1. All references to Scripture are taken from the Holman Christian Standard Bible (HCSB) unless otherwise noted.

2. Timothy George, *Amazing Grace: God's Initiative—Our Response* (Nashville: LifeWay, 2000), 74.

3. Charles Spurgeon, *The Metropolitan Tabernacle Pulpit,* vol. 18 (Pasadena, Texas: Pilgrim, 1984), 337.

4. Augustus Montague Toplady, "A Debtor to Mercy Alone," *Psalms & Hymns of Reformed Worship* (London: Wakeman Trust, 1994), Hymn no. 574.

5. Charles Spurgeon, *The New Park Street Pulpit,* vol. 4 (Pasadena, Texas: Pilgrim, 1991), 337–43.

Article VI

The Church

Malcolm B. Yarnell III

$\mathcal{A}$rticle VI of the *Baptist Faith and Message 2000* concerns the New Testament church.[1] Although our churches are often called "Baptist," Baptist Christians have sought to develop the doctrine of the church according to the Bible. The principle of *sola scriptura*, Scripture as the final authority, is applied with thoroughness to the Baptist doctrine of the church. Baptists privilege neither the authority of tradition nor experience nor reason, but Scripture, for only Scripture is inspired and inerrant. To be a Baptist is to be a biblical Christian; to be a Baptist church is to be a biblical church.[2] In the following six sections, the biblical doctrines of the church's identity, activity, polity, ministry, and glory will be discussed. First, however, the name of the church is considered.

THE CHURCH'S NAME:
WHAT DOES 'CHURCH' MEAN?

The Greek word for church is *ekklesia*, a compound of the terms *kalein*, "to call," and *ek*, "out." The common Greek *ekklesia* was an assembly composed of duly called members. The Septuagint utilized *ekklesia* to translate the Hebrew Old Testament *qahal*, denoting various gathered assemblies in Israel. When the New Testament writers spoke of the Christian congregation, they preferred *ekklesia* to *synagoge*, because the latter indicated a contemporary Jewish assembly. Of 114 occurrences in the New Testament, *ekklesia* refers thrice to non-Christian gatherings (Acts 19:32,39,41) and twice to the assembly of Israel (Acts 7:38; Heb. 2:12), while the remainder refer to congregations of Christians. Of the remaining Christian references, over 90 percent indicate a particular local congregation or the local congregation in a generic sense, while a few indicate an eschatological, spiritual gathering of Christians.[3] The New Testament also teaches about the church with various metaphors or images, such as "the temple of God," "the household of God," "the bride of Christ," "the body of Christ," "the fellowship of the Holy Spirit," and "a royal priesthood."[4]

The English term 'church' derives ultimately from the Greek *kuriakon*, "belonging to the Lord." *Kuriakon* indicated Christian houses of worship in the Constantinian era. Germanic soldiers in the Roman army thus called a church building, *kirika*. Returning to their homes, they took with them the term, which became the Anglo-Saxon *circe*, German *Kirche*, Scottish *kirk*, and English 'church.'[5] To distinguish the New Testament doctrine of the church from the Roman hierarchy, the Protestant martyr William Tyndale translated *ekklesia* as "congregacion" or "congregacyon."[6] 'Congregation,' derived from the Latin *congregatio*, thus became synonymous with 'church,' emphasizing the church as a democratically gathered people rather than a building.[7]

Many scholars discern a twofold sense of church in the New Testament: the particular local church, and the whole gathering of the faithful. But the attachment of various other adjectives to the church lacks explicit biblical precedent—for instance, the "catholic" (i.e., universal) church versus the "local" church; the "invisible" church versus the "visible" church; the church "militant" versus the church "triumphant"; or the "mixed" church versus the "pure" church. Also lacking biblical precedent is the ascription of the term to a building rather than a people, the constriction of the term to a hierarchy of Christian clergy, or the description of national, linguistic, or denominational groups as churches. Structural, clerical, and supra-local organizational understandings of "church" are historical corruptions of the biblical doctrine.[8]

THE CHURCH'S IDENTITY:
WHAT IS THE CHURCH?

Our confession identifies a Baptist church as "a New Testament church." According to John A. Broadus, the first Baptist distinctive is that "the Bible alone is a religious authority; and in regard to Christian institutions the direct authority is of course the New Testament."[9] B. H. Carroll distinguished Baptists from Protestants by noting that the Baptist principle is, "The New Testament, the only law of Christianity," versus the Protestant confusion of Old and New Testaments. Only in the New Testament may be found "the true idea of the Christian church, or its members, or its ordinances, or its government, or its officers, or its sacrifices, or its worship, or its mission, or its ritual, or its priesthood."[10] The New Testament principle is forsaken by Roman Catholics and Protestants when they privilege Old Testament law to the detriment of New Testament revelation. Unlike Roman Catholics, Baptists do not appoint sacerdotal priests who offer propitiatory sacrifices, because the New Testament teaches that the royal priesthood belongs to all Christians who offer spiritual sacrifices (1 Pet. 2:5–9; Rom. 12:1). Unlike the Reformed, Baptists do not justify baptizing infants with the analogy of Old Testament circumcision, because the New Testament teaches that baptism is to be given to those who profess Christ as personal Lord (Matt. 28:18–20; Mark 16:14–16).[11]

The church's one foundation is the Lord Jesus Christ, the Word of God (1 Cor. 3:11; John 1:1). Upon Christ, the cornerstone, the apostles and prophets built the church "for a dwelling place of God in the Spirit," indicating the Trinitarian basis of the church (Eph. 2:19–22; 1 Pet. 2:6–8). Christ Himself builds the church through the apostles' confession of Him (Matt. 16:13–19). Biblical preachers recognize they are merely instruments of God who must proclaim the unique headship and unequaled primacy of Jesus Christ over the church, which is His body (Col. 1:18; Eph. 1:22). The New Testament presents the church as intimately dependent upon Jesus Christ, and as organically developing in Him by the Spirit (Eph. 1:23, 2:19–22). It is through the church's proclamation of God's Word that others come to know the hidden wisdom of God, "the unfathomable riches of Christ" (Eph. 3:8–11). He who builds on any foundation other than Christ or through any means other than the proclamation of His Word invites judgment (1 Cor. 3:10–15). The church is the dearly beloved bride of Jesus Christ, for whom He cares. Honoring the Lord Who has sacrificed everything for her, Christians treat His church with the utmost respect (Eph. 5:22–32).

Currently, the spiritual body of Christ takes form through the establishment of local congregations. In the Tabernacle and then the Temple, the omnipresent God was specifically present to Old Testament Israel (2 Sam. 7:5–7; Isa. 6:1). In the New Testament, the omnipresent God is particularly manifested in the powerful presence of Jesus Christ in the local church.[12] The Gospels record only two occasions when Jesus spoke of the *ekklesia*, and in the second occurrence, Matt. 18:15–20, he used the term twice. The modern English Baptist movement arose after intense examination of this seminal text.[13] Matt. 18 offered Baptists theological support for establishing churches without governmental permission. Baptists rejected authorization by England's king, for King Jesus gave His authority to the disciplined, covenanted, gathered, separated congregation of His people. In vv. 15–17, Christ's form of church discipline demands a careful redemptive process which leaves the final temporal decision to the entire congregation. In v. 18, the church's decision on earth is given heavenly sanction, indicating a concurrence between God and His people.

In v. 19, Christ binds Christian access to divine authority with covenantal agreement among God's people. The Greek word, *symphonesosin*, translated here as "agree," indicates both harmonious fellowship and formal acquiescence to a legal contract or covenant between persons.[14] A church covenant establishes fellowship between Christians horizontally on the basis of joining themselves to God vertically. It summarizes the people's promise to watch after one another according to the "gospel rule or order" of Matt. 18. Church covenants and confessions of faith are the "basic church documents."[15] In v. 20, Christ says that, where two or three gathered in covenant, He would be present to them. Since Jesus Christ is Prophet, Priest, and King to His people, His congregation participates derivatively in His offices. The New Testament thus speaks of the church as a "royal priesthood" (1 Pet. 2:9), indicating the church's authorization to proclaim God's Word as a prophethood, to worship the Triune God freely as a priesthood, and to govern itself under Jesus Christ as a kingship. Because Christ offers His authority only through local covenants, each congregation is necessarily independent and autonomous. Since Christ gave His authority to the local congregation, the local congregation may not presumptuously surrender it to anybody.

The church is composed only of the born again who witness to their conversion in believers' baptism. This New Testament practice ensures separation from the wicked world; in other words, regenerate church membership is a New Testament distinctive of the church. People gathered by the Spirit of Holiness necessarily separate from the wicked. Churches which fail to distinguish believers from unbelievers disobey God's direct command (2 Cor. 6:14–18). The visible indication of membership is believers-only baptism by immersion. In Scripture, baptism always follows the hearing of the Word and personal conversion (Matt. 28:19–20; Mark 16:15–16; Acts 8:35–38, 10:44–48, 16:30–33, 19:1–5). As the Anabaptist martyr Balthasar Hubmaier declared, "the one who wants to be baptized with water must *beforehand* have the certain knowledge of a good conscience toward God through the Word of God."[16]

Baptism always entails entrance into a church. During Pentecost, those who received Peter's preaching of the Gospel "were baptized, and that day were added about three thousand souls" to the Jerusalem church (Acts 2:41,47). Therefore, a New Testament church is correctly defined as a "congregation of baptized believers," while baptism is defined in Article VII of the *Baptist Faith and Message 2000* as a "church ordinance."[17] Baptism follows conversion; baptism and church membership go hand-in-hand.

THE CHURCH'S ACTIVITY:
WHAT DOES THE CHURCH DO?

An ordinance is a command given by Christ for the church's continual observance. The ordinances recall Christ's blood atonement on the cross and resurrection from the dead, as well as the doctrine of the Trinity.[18] The two ordinances of Christ are baptism, intended for believers only, and the Lord's Supper, intended for members in good standing with the local church. Christ commanded that baptism be continually practiced by the church until the end of the age (Matt. 28:18–20) and that the Lord's Supper be continually observed by the church until His triumphal return (Matt. 26:30; Mark 14:25; Luke 22:16; 1 Cor. 11:26). Baptism by the church is a responsibility and a testimony that brings a new believer into local church membership through visible identification with the Triune God. The Lord's Supper is a memorial celebration that manifests the believer's continuing communion with Christ and His church.

The local church is ruled by the laws of Christ. The church may not give itself or its members any new laws, but must faithfully execute Christ's laws. The church may not legislate, but must execute the laws given by Christ. These laws are conveniently summarized in the two ordinances, the two great commandments to love God and one another, and the disciple's bearing of the cross (Matt. 22:34–40, 25:31–46; Mark 8:34). The burden given by Moses cannot be borne, but the yoke given by Christ is light. Therefore, the early church was wary of enforcing the old law or creating new laws. The apostles required only what the Lord required, proclaiming that salvation comes "through the grace of the Lord Jesus" (Acts 15:10–11,28; Matt. 11:28–30).

Spiritual gifts are intended to edify the church. The primary purpose for the gifts is building the congregation, not oneself (1 Cor. 12:7, 14:1–5; Eph. 4:12). Among God's gifts to the church are the apostles, whose teaching is recorded in Scripture, and pastors and teachers, who proclaim the Bible (Eph. 4:11). Chief among the rights and privileges of the churches is the ability to approach the throne of God in Christ (Heb. 4:16). The gifts of the Spirit and the presence of Christ empower the church to act; the ordinances and laws of Christ define the limits of the church's actions; and the Great Commission defines the direction of the church's actions (Mark 16:15; Luke 22:47–48; John 20:21).

The church remains on earth "to extend the gospel to the ends of the earth" by bearing witness to Christ in all places and at all times (Acts 1:8). Our Lord's Great Commission includes four necessarily progressive, continuing, and interrelated actions: "going" to the lost throughout the world; "making disciples" by evangelism; "baptizing" new disciples into a local church; and "teaching" all that Jesus Christ commanded (Matt. 28:18–20). Those who neglect any aspect of the Great Commission, including believers-only baptism and the teachings of our Lord, may not be considered Great Commission Christians. Chief among the ecclesial teachings of our Lord are the preaching of the Gospel, the meaningful celebration of the ordinances, and redemptive church discipline.

Thus, following the Reformers of the sixteenth century, some Baptists consider preaching, the ordinances instituted for worship, and church discipline to be "marks of the church."[19] The marks of the church have been of some controversy between Baptists and non-Baptists, especially with regard to the necessity of scriptural precedent in ecclesial practices.[20] These marks indicate the four temporal means by which Christ builds, begins, preserves, and manifests His church. First, the free preaching of the Gospel is the means by which the lost repent and believe, thus building the church (Mark 1:14–15). Second, believers-only baptism is the symbolic act of obedience which begins the new disciple's membership in a local church through his personal confession and public identification with the death and resurrection of Jesus (Matt. 28:18–20; Rom. 6:3–6). Third, redemptive church discipline preserves the integrity of the regenerate church (Matt. 18:15–17). Fourth, the Lord's Supper through its meaningful symbolism manifests believers' continuing communion with the local church (Matt. 26:26–30; 1 Cor. 10:16–17).

THE CHURCH'S POLITY:
HOW IS THE CHURCH GOVERNED?

The New Testament church is *ruled* by Jesus Christ, *governed* by the congregation, *led* by pastors, and *served* by deacons.[21] In Article VI, the rule of the church is introduced in the section on the church's identity. Jesus Christ is the unique Head of His church, meaning the church is ruled only by Him. Any person or group claiming part of Christ's unique rule denies His Lordship. The full life of the body of Christ, the church, comes through its Head, Christ Himself, who died for her. He is preeminent, brooking no rival in allegiance or law (Col. 1:18; Eph. 1:22). As one English Baptist concluded, "the Church is called a Christian Church because it is redeemed by the blood of Christ, governed by the law of Christ, and formed for his praise."[22]

There are five general forms of church government advocated among Christians—Romanism, Episcopalianism, Presbyterianism, Congregationalism, and Quakerism. Romanism believes Christ granted all authority to one person, the Pope, the Bishop of Rome, who is considered the successor of Peter and the vicar of God on earth, who has been granted all doctrinal and juridical authority, and in whose fellowship the church subsists.[23] Episcopalianism, characteristic of both Eastern Orthodoxy and Anglicanism, looks to bishops as the successors of the apostles and locates ecclesial authority in their unity. In Episcopalianism, the bishop is elevated above the elder and the local churches.[24] Third, in Presbyterianism, the distinction between bishops and elders is deemed an extra-biblical innovation. However, elders are divided between ruling and teaching elders, the board of elders governs the local church, and synods above the local churches govern the elders.[25]

In Congregationalism, the granting of authority is by Christ to the apostles rather than to one apostle; indeed, the gift of authority is from Christ to the entire congregation (cf. John 20:19–23; Matt. 18:15–20). Baptists embrace democratic congregationalism as the only biblical form of church government. Congregationalism is "that form of church governance in which final human authority rests with the local or particular congregation when it gathers for decision-making. This means that decisions about membership, leadership, doctrine, worship, conduct, missions, finances, property, relationships, and the like are to be made by the gathered congregation except when such decisions have been delegated by the congregation to individual members or groups of members."[26] The first English Baptists agreed that decisions were to be made under the public leadership of the minister, but decisions with regard to communion of members and election of leaders may never be delegated.[27]

Baptist congregationalism is deeply grounded in the New Testament witness. In Matt. 18:15–20, final temporal authority for excommunication resides with the congregation. Jesus was clear that findings by the "brother" followed by the "one or two more" were preliminary steps before the ultimate decision by the entire church. In Acts 6:3, the Jerusalem congregation itself was charged with choosing seven men who were obviously Spirit-filled and widely respected to be put in charge of mundane church matters. In Acts 13:2–3, the Holy Spirit led the Antioch congregation to set apart Barnabas and Saul for missionary work by laying hands upon them. In Acts 15:22, the apostles and elders along "with the whole church" of Jerusalem chose messengers to deliver their message to the associated Antioch church. In 1 Cor. 5:2–5, Paul informs the church it was responsible for disciplining an immoral man by assembling together to excommunicate him. In 2 Cor. 2:6, Paul asks the same church to restore a man who had been sufficiently disciplined by "the majority."[28] In v. 10, Paul considers himself bound by the congregation's decision in this matter. In 1 Tim. 5:19–20, Paul instructs the churches through Timothy to judge an elder only upon the witness of two or three, and to rebuke a sinning elder in the presence of all. Numerous other texts reinforce congregationalism as the only biblical polity.[29]

In the fifth form of governance, Quakerism, the locus of human authority is within the individual Christian, so that the "inner light" of the Spirit is elevated above the written Word. Quakers, mystics, rationalists, and other individualistic Christians may gather temporarily in loose assemblies, but these groups are denied any binding authority. Although Baptists voluntarily associate in local congregations, we also recognize that the congregation is divinely instituted and given authority to discipline. On the other hand, individualists see the congregation as a human institution without governance over the Christian. As Congregationalists, some Baptists tend toward Presbyterianism while others tend toward Quakerism. There are dangers in both extremes.[30]

THE CHURCH'S MINISTRY:
WHO SERVES AND LEADS THE CHURCH?

There are two New Testament church offices, that of the pastor and that of the deacon. The three major Greek New Testament terms describing a pastor are: *episcopos*, "overseer" or "bishop"; *presbyteros*, "elder"; and *poiman*, "shepherd" or "pastor." In the Pauline ministerial manual of Acts 20, *episcopos* and *presbyteros* are interchangeable (vv. 17, 28), while the task of this church officer is *poimainein*, "to shepherd," the church of God. Peter also utilized the three terms interchangeably (1 Pet. 5:1–2). Paul's list of qualifications for the office of an *episcopos* in 1 Tim. 3:1–7 parallels that of the *presbyteros* in Titus 1:5–9, who is also identified as an *episcopos* (v. 7). The New Testament does not make an official distinction between the bishop who oversees and the elder who pastors a local church. Reflecting the New Testament, Baptists thus reject the historical elevation of bishops over elders.

The pastor is charged by God to lead the people of God. Pastoral leadership is exercised entirely through the proclamation of the doctrine and Word of God. The pastor's authority is nothing more, nor less, than the fervent, faithful, watchful, exemplary labor of preaching God's Word, for which he is accountable. Simply put, the Word of God is the pastor's entire authority. Since the Word of God is all-powerful, what more could he possibly need? However, the pastor may not deviate from God's Word (1 Tim. 5:17; Heb. 13:7,17; Titus 1:10–14). Because God uses the pastor instrumentally to proclaim His powerful, effective, and returning Word, both honor and responsibility fall upon ministers. Ministers are described by Paul as "servants," "God's fellow workers," "a wise master builder," "attendants of Christ," "stewards of the mysteries of God," "tutors in Christ," and "fathers." These seven metaphors indicate both the high honor and the heavy responsibility of Christian ministry (1 Cor. 3:5,9,10; 4:1,15). The list of qualifications for a pastor is stringent, because the office is distinguished and entails a severe accountability (1 Tim. 3:1–7; Titus 1:5–9).

The pastor is God's gift to the local church and should be honored. Such honor includes appropriate financial support for his official and familial needs, and protection from spurious accusations (Eph. 4:11; 1 Tim. 5:17–19). Typically, Southern Baptists employ one pastor in the local church, but in recent years there has been a trend toward multiple elders. The biblical and contextual arguments in favor of single eldership include the existence of multiple house-churches in a city, the transitional state of the early church, single presidency in the period's synagogue, the assignment of one "angel" to each of the seven Asian churches (Rev. 1–3), and the common biblical paradigm of multiple leaders overseen by a single leader.[31] The biblical argument in favor of multiple elders relies upon the plural form of reference to elders in various cities in the New Testament. However, this argument assumes the corporate plural without due consideration for the distributive plural.[32] Those advocating multiple elders often recall seventeenth-century Reformed theology as mimicked by some nineteenth-century Southern Baptists.[33] Although latitude with regard to the number of elders may be exercised, the division of "teaching elders" from "ruling elders" or the co-option of congregational governance by a "board of elders" is without biblical support.[34]

Diakonos originally indicated a table-waiter, but the broader meaning became that of a "servant" or "minister." In some sense, all New Testament Christians were servants and ministers, but there is an office of deacon as well (Phil. 1:1). The seven chosen to minister to the mundane needs of the early Jerusalem Church in Acts 6 have sometimes been identified as deacons. The qualifications and honor of a deacon are outlined in 1 Tim. 3:8–13. *Gunaikas* in v. 11 has been variously translated as "wives" and "women," the latter translation recently understood as indicating deaconesses. However, the translation of "wives" is preferable in light of Paul's avoidance of the term "deaconess" here, the separate and shorter list of qualifications for these women, the three-fold household structure of the passage, and the later extended discussion of an office for women in the same book.[35] Paul's reference to Phoebe as a *diakonon* probably indicates general Christian service rather than ecclesial office (Rom. 16:1). In the late twentieth century, some Southern Baptists also considered the novel idea of ordaining female pastors. Although the concept was culturally vogue, it contradicts biblical precedent regarding order in creation and the church, and is thus firmly denied in our confession (1 Tim. 2:11–15; 1 Cor. 14:34–35). Unequivocally, both men and women should offer themselves for general Christian service in the church.[36]

THE GLORIOUS CHURCH:
WHEN IS THE CHURCH UNIVERSAL?

The Baptist Faith and Message 2000 focuses upon the local church, in line with the New Testament emphasis. But, as previously noted, the New Testament has two senses of church—as *both* a particular local congregation *and* the gathering of all the faithful. Many refer to the second sense with the terms "spiritual church," "general church," or "universal church." Some even speak of the "invisible church." Our confession uses none of these terms, but prefers the biblical language "of all the ages, believers from every tribe, and tongue, and people, and nation" (cf. Rev. 5:9).[37]

Historically, Baptists disagree as to whether the church is "universal." Landmark Southern Baptists, such as J. R. Graves and J. M. Pendleton, disliked the term 'universal church,' although the latter affirmed the second sense of the church as "the redeemed in the aggregate."[38] J. L. Dagg, the first Southern Baptist systematic theologian, affirmed "the church universal," by which he meant "the whole company of those who are saved by Christ."[39] Whether they use the term, all Baptists firmly reject the Roman idea that the church is "Catholic" or "universal in any sense of embracing all churches in some objective form of organization."[40] H. E. Dana preferred to speak of "the spiritual church," although he did not reject the term "universal."[41] W. A. Criswell indiscriminately used the adjectives "figurative," "spiritual," and "universal," while Herschel Hobbs called it "the church general." Both Criswell and Hobbs distinguished the church from "the kingdom of God." The church is related to the kingdom, having been given the responsibility for extending His kingdom.[42]

Recognizing that the kingdom of God is related to but distinct from the church, *The Baptist Faith and Message 2000* treats each entity with its own articles (cf. Article IX). The kingdom concerns God's sovereign rule over all creation, and His particular rule over His acknowledged subjects. Unlike the Landmarkism of J. R. Graves, which effectively questioned the participation of non-Baptists in the kingdom, most Southern Baptists do not equate the kingdom with the sum total of local Baptist churches. Although Southern Baptists disagree with their doctrines or practices, we do not deny the existence of other Christians and their churches. On one hand, Southern Baptists treasure our personal relationships with Christians of other traditions, even as we maintain our biblically derived convictions concerning the church. On the other hand, Southern Baptists have been notably wary of interdenominational cooperation. Christian unity is found in the common spiritual harmony of Christ's people, not in a supra-local bureaucracy (cf. Article XIV).[43]

The phrase "invisible church" is especially unfortunate, for it implicitly denies the gathering of the church. An *ekklesia* is a visible gathering of identifiable people at a particular place and time. Can something that is not visibly identifiable really be a congregation? The downgrading of the church's visibility and locality has encouraged the development of ecclesiologies with little basis in Scripture. For instance, some carelessly refer to amorphous gatherings of like-minded Christians as "the ecumenical church" or "the evangelical church." However, such a "church" has no covenant, confession, meeting place, or shared ordinances.[44] Again, some postmodern Christians advocate the "emerging" or "emergent church." But again there is apparently no way to determine membership in this "church."[45] Ecumenism, evangelicalism, and emergentism are better described as "movements" or "conversations." To lend the title "church" to formless entities grants them biblical status without biblical warrant. These may be movements, but they are not churches.

A general church may be discerned in a few New Testament passages. In Matt. 16:18, the gates of hell will not ultimately prevail against the church. In Eph. 1:22, Christ is the head of the entire church. While the image of "body of Christ" refers to a local church in 1 Cor. 12:12–27, it may denote all of the redeemed in Eph. 5:23–32. In vv. 23 and 25, the particular instance of a husband-wife relationship is compared to the relationship between Christ and His church: "Christ is head of the church; and He is Savior of the body." However, there is no exegetical clue militating against the application of each of these generic references to a particular church.

In Hebrews, however, it is difficult to limit *ekklesia* to the common local sense. After rehearsing the hall of faith in chapter 11, Heb. 12 eschatologically considers the Old Testament faithful as "a cloud of witnesses" whom the letter's recipients will approach, along with "an innumerable company of angels," to form "the general assembly and church of the firstborn who are registered in heaven" (vv. 1,22,23). In Eph. 5:27, Paul refers to "a glorious church" that Christ will present to Himself made entirely holy. Eph. 3:21 also concerns this eschatological congregation, for Christ is the agent by which the church glorifies God "throughout all ages, world without end." These biblical passages indicate that in one sense, the church will one day include all Christians. We may speak of that church as existing proleptically or potentially but not as yet in actuality.

With regard to this "glorious church," B. H. Carroll noted its composition from three parts—some of its members are now in heaven, some are now on earth, and some are not yet even born. "It follows that . . . *there is as yet no assembly*, except in prospect" (emphasis in original).[46] In other words, the glorious church, which many call "universal," currently exists only in concept, not in actuality. "When the calling out is ended, and all the called are glorified, then the present concept of a general assembly will be a fact." Carroll warned against speculating regarding the invisible church. "All teaching in the direction that there now exists a general assembly which is invisible, without ordinances, and which is entered by faith alone, will likely tend to discredit the particular assembly, which does now really exist and which is the pillar and ground of truth."[47] The glorious church will exist only at the consummation, and efforts to currently identify it detract from God's ordained instrument in our time, the local church. The church which contains all the redeemed will exist only in glory.

CONCLUSION

Although Baptists may and should agree with other Christians concerning many doctrines, we must part ways with regard to the doctrine of the church. Baptists may agree with Eastern Orthodox and Roman Catholics concerning the doctrines of the Trinity and the Person of Christ, but only because these doctrines are biblically established. Baptists may agree with Lutherans and the Reformed concerning the doctrines of the atonement and justification, but only because these doctrines are biblically established. Baptists graciously but firmly disagree with many other Christian groups regarding our doctrine of the regenerate church, which is begun in the post-conversion symbolic practice of believers-only baptism by immersion, and which is congregationally governed and locally autonomous, but only because our doctrines of the church are biblically established. The biblical doctrine of the church affects numerous other articles in *The Baptist Faith and Message*, including those dealing with Salvation, Baptism and the Lord's Supper, and the Kingdom of God, as well as Cooperation and Religious Liberty.

NOTES

1. Appreciation is expressed to Jason Duesing, Madison Grace, Jason K. Lee, Paige Patterson, and the participants of *Oxford 2006* for their insightful comments upon earlier drafts of this essay.

2. Some Hispanic Baptist churches are self-identified as *biblica bautiste*, "Biblical Baptist." The phrase is redundant but instructive. Baptists received their name as a result of their commitment to scriptural precedent, visibly practiced in the recovery of believers-only baptism by immersion.

3. Dana finds 96 local or generically local uses and 13 spiritual or eschatological uses. H. E. Dana and L. M. Sipes, *A Manual of Ecclesiology*, 2nd ed. (Kansas City: Central Seminary Press, 1944), 33–69. Cf. Edwin C. Dargan, *Ecclesiology: A Study of the Churches* (Louisville: Dearing, 1897), 25–35; K. L. Schmidt, s.v. "*ekklesia*" in *Theological Dictionary of the New Testament*, ed. Gerhard Kittel, trans. Geoffrey W. Bromiley (Grand Rapids: Eerdmans, 1965), 3:501–36; James Leo Garrett Jr., *Systematic Theology: Biblical, Historical, and Evangelical*, 2nd ed. (North Richland Hills: BIBAL, 2000–2001), 2:504–6; John S. Hammett, *Biblical Foundations for Baptist Churches: A Contemporary Ecclesiology* (Grand Rapids: Kregel, 2005), 26–29. These sources indicate a long history of concern with the biblical doctrine of the church. For earlier treatments, see B. H. Carroll, *Ecclesia: The Church* (Louisville, 1908; reprint, Paris, Arkansas: Baptist Standard Bearer, forthcoming), and historic Baptist sources available at www.BaptistTheology.org.

4. Paul S. Minear, *Images of the Church in the New Testament* (Philadelphia: Westminster, 1960); Malcolm Yarnell, "*Oikos Theou*: A Theologically Neglected but Important Ecclesiological Metaphor," *Midwestern Journal of Theology* 2 (2003), 53–65.

5. S.v. "Church" in *Oxford English Dictionary* (New York: Oxford University Press, 2006).

6. *The New Testament Translated by William Tyndale: The Text of the Worms Edition of 1526 in Original Spelling*, ed. W. R. Cooper (London: British Library, 2000), passim. Thomas More, the Roman Catholic polemicist, objected to Tyndale's use of "congregation" for undermining the clerical priesthood. *The Complete Works of St. Thomas More* (New Haven: Yale University Press, 1968ff), 6:286–88.

7. The medieval university of Oxford, which Tyndale attended, was governed by "Congregations," the directly democratic gatherings of scholars. G. R. Evans, *John Wyclif: Myth and Reality* (Oxford: Lion Hudson, 2005), 73–74.

8. Cf. "Not the Walls but the Faithful are the Church," in Yves Congar, *Christians Active in the World*, trans. P. J. Heburne-Scott (New York: Herder and Herder, 1968), 29–37. The reference to "the church throughout all Judea and Galilee and Samaria" in Acts 9:31 was "geographical, not organizational in meaning." James Leo Garrett Jr., "The Congregation-Led Church: Congregational Polity," in *Perspectives on Church Government: Five Views of Church Polity*, ed. Chad Owen Brand and R. Stanton Norman (Nashville: Broadman & Holman, 2004), 171.

9. John Andrew Broadus, *The Duty of Baptists to Teach Their Distinctive Principles* (Philadelphia: American Baptist Publication Society, 1881), 6.

10. Carroll believed the Old Testament was the inspired Word of God, but that its law and typology was fulfilled by Christ. Therefore, Christians "should not go to the Old Testament to find Christian law or Christian institutions." Benajah Harvey Carroll, *Baptists and their Doctrines: Distinctive Baptist Principles* (New York: Revell, 1913), 7–11.

11. Classic Reformed theology argues that Calvinist soteriology negates both personal decisions for Christ and believers-only baptism. Richard A. Muller, "How Many Points?" *Calvin Theological Journal* 28 (1993), 425–33.

12. The relationship between Old Testament Israel and the New Testament church has fostered some debate between evangelical theologians. Reformed theologians advocate the Replacement theory, that Israel has been replaced by the church or that Israel is the Old Testament church; classic Dispensationalism considers the church a parenthetical interruption in the divine plan for Israel; other evangelicals, such as the current author, consider both Israel and the church as comprising the one people of God who find reconciliation only through faith in Jesus Christ. Cf. Walter C. Kaiser Jr., "Israel as the People of God," in *The People of God: Essays on the Believers' Church*, ed. Paul Basden and David S. Dockery (Nashville: Broadman, 1991), 99–108.

13. Douglas Shantz, "The Place of the Resurrected Christ in the Writings of John Smyth," *Baptist Quarterly* 30 (1984), 199–203; James R. Coggins, "The Theological Positions of John Smyth," *Baptist Quarterly* 30 (1984), 246–64.

14. Otto Betz, "*symphoneo*," in *Theological Dictionary of the New Testament*, ed. Kittel, trans. Bromiley (1974), 9:304–9.

15. Cf. "Covenant of Grassy Creek Baptist Church" (1757), in John A. Broadus, *Baptist Confessions, Covenants, and Catechisms*, ed. Timothy and Denise George (Nashville: Broadman & Holman, 1996), 201–3; Charles W. Deweese, *Baptist Church Covenants* (Nashville: Broadman, 1990), ix.

16. Balthasar Hubmaier, "On the Christian Baptism of Believers" (1525), in *Balthasar Hubmaier: Theologian of Anabaptism*, trans. H. Wayne Pipkin and John H. Yoder (Scottsdale: Herald, 1989), 117.

17. Evangelical ecumenists often argue against *The Baptist Faith and Message* that baptism is a mere Christian ordinance—rather than a church ordinance administered by the church's appointed leaders—on the basis of an atomistic and presumptive reading of Acts 8:36. Against the ecumenists' atomistic reading of this passage, it should be noted that Philip the Evangelist was an appointed leader of the Jerusalem church (Acts 6:5); the Ethiopian's membership in the Jerusalem church thus continued until a local church was later established in Ethiopia. Against the ecumenists' presumptive reading of this passage, it should be noted that Philip was miraculously led by the Spirit to engage in this activity, evidenced by his physical translation, while modern ecumenists claim no such verification for their irregular activities.

18. Northamptonshire Baptist Association, *The Beauty of Social Religion* (Northamptonshire, England, 1777), 10n; W. A. Criswell, *The Doctrine of the Church* (Nashville: Convention, 1980), 81–82.

19. Early Baptist confessions correlated the threefold office of Christ as Prophet, Priest, and King with the three marks of the church—prophets preach, priests worship, and kings govern. *The Confession of Faith, Of those Churches which are commonly (though falsly) called Anabaptists* (London, 1644), arts. 10–21; *An Orthodox Creed, or a Protestant Confession of Faith, Being an Essay to Unite and Confirm All True Protestants* (London, 1679), art. 17. Both confessions are reprinted in *Baptist Confessions of Faith*, ed. William L. Lumpkin (Valley Forge: Judson, 1959). Cf. Mark Dever, "The Noble Task: The Pastor as Preacher and Practitioner of the Marks of the Church," and R. Albert Mohler Jr., "Discipline: The Missing Mark," in *Polity: Biblical Arguments on How to Conduct Church Life*, ed. Mark Dever (Washington, D.C.: Center for Church Reform, 2001), 3–18, 43–56.

20. Thomas White considers the exact administrator of baptism a matter of the "well-being" (*bene esse*) of the church rather than of its "being" (*esse*). White, *What Makes Baptism Valid?* (Fort Worth: Center for Theological Research, 2006), 6, 10; available at www.BaptistTheology.org. A third useful category, in addition to the common categories of *esse* and *bene esse* would be that of "indifference" (*adiaphora*). Indeed, the exact form of baptism may not be of the *esse* of the church, but neither is it a matter of theological indifference, for the form of baptism is dominically established and scripturally revealed.

21. "Rule," "govern," and "lead" have been used indiscriminately in recent Baptist literature. The distinctions made here may contribute some clarity to the ongoing debates over polity.

22. Charles Stovel, *Hints on the Regulation of Christian Churches* (1835), 17, cited in J. H. Y. Briggs, *The English Baptists of the Nineteenth Century* (Didcot: Baptist Historical Society, 1994), 22.

23. Romanism seeks biblical support for its position in Christ's granting of the keys to Peter, whom Romanists believe is the "rock" upon which the church is built (Matt. 16:18–19). While Protestants dispute the Roman interpretation, even Romanists agree that the transference of authority from Peter to the first bishop of Rome and thence to subsequent bishops of Rome relies on extrabiblical tradition.

24. Episcopalianism recognizes that the distinction and elevation of a bishop from elders is of post-apostolic origin. Ignatius of Antioch is the first church father to distinguish clearly bishops from elders and to elevate the bishop above the congregation, although he does see the bishop as a "first among equals" in regards to the elders. Hans von Campenhausen, *Ecclesiastical Authority and Spiritual Power in the Church of the First Three Centuries* (Peabody: Hendrickson, 1997), 97.

25. The historical development of Reformed polity in the sixteenth and seventeenth centuries is exhaustively documented in James L. Ainslie, *The Doctrines of Ministerial Order in the Reformed Churches of the 16th and 17th Centuries* (Edinburgh: T. & T. Clark, 1940).

26. Garrett, "The Congregation-Led Church," 157.

27. John Smyth, *The Differences of the Churches of the Seperation* (1608), cited in Malcolm Yarnell, "Changing Baptist Concepts of Royal Priesthood: John Smyth and Edgar Young Mullins," in *The Rise of the Laity in Evangelical Protestantism*, ed. Deryck Lovegrove (New York: Routledge, 2002), 239.

28. "Democracy" is popularly understood in a more secular sense as a mere plurality; however, Baptist democracy is best characterized by a filial consensus void of crass politics.

29. Acts 1:21–26, 9:26–28, 11:22, 14:27,15; Gal. 6:1; 1 Cor. 6, 16:3–4; 2 Cor. 8:22–24; Phil. 2:25; 2 Thess. 3:6; Rev. 2:14–16,20–25. Cf. Daniel L. Akin, "The Single-Elder-Led Church: The Bible's Witness to a Congregational/Single-Elder-Led Polity," in *Perspectives on Church Government*, 28–33; Garrett, "The Congregation-Led Church," 158–72.

30. The Baptist historian W. W. Barnes considered the Presbyterian tendency a significant danger in his day. William Wright Barnes, *The Southern Baptist Convention: A Study in the Development of Ecclesiology* (Fort Worth: Seminary Hill, 1934), 78–79.

31. Akin, "The Single-Elder-Led Church," 64–67; Paige Patterson, "Single-Elder Congregationalism," in *Who Runs the Church? 4 Views on Church Government*, ed. Steven B. Cowan (Grand Rapids: Zondervan, 2004), 147–52.

32. The corporate plural assumes multiple elders in one congregation in each city, while the distributive plural allows for the development of single elders in multiple congregations in each city. Expositional neglect of the distributive plural would have the absurd result of exhorting all the deacons in a church to marry the same woman. Cf. 1 Tim. 3:11.

33. Samuel E. Waldron, "Plural-Elder Congregationalism," in *Who Runs the Church?* 187–221; James R. White, "The Plural-Elder-Led Church: Sufficient as Established—The Plurality of Elders as Christ's Ordained Means of Church Governance," in *Perspectives on Church Government*, 269–79; Mark Dever, *By Whose Authority? Elders in Baptist Life* (Washington, D.C.: 9 Marks, 2006). Although the founding president of the SBC, William Bullein Johnson, favored multiple elders, his own church disciplined him over his adamantly held peculiar positions. Gregory A. Wills, *The First Baptist Church of Columbia, South Carolina, 1809 to 2002* (Nashville: Fields, 2003), 1–21, 26–37. Cf. idem, "The Church: Baptists and Their Churches in the Eighteenth and Nineteenth Centuries," in *Polity: Biblical Arguments on How to Conduct Church Life*, ed. Mark Dever (Washington, D.C.: Center for Church Reform, 2001), 31–32.

34. Daniel Akin and Paige Patterson promote single-elder leadership but believe the number of elders in a church is a matter of some indifference. Samuel Waldron, an advocate of multiple elders, concludes in a somewhat contradictory manner that single-elder

churches, although "not necessarily sinful," yet suffer a "deficiency." Akin, "The Single-Elder-Led Church," 64; Patterson, "Single-Elder Congregationalism," 134; Waldron, "Plural-Elder Congregationalism," 213–14.

35. 1 Tim. 3 progressively considers the deacon's personal qualities first (vv. 8–10), followed by his wife's qualities (v. 11), then his conduct of the household (v. 12).

36. Dorothy Kelley Patterson, "Why I Believe Southern Baptist Churches Should Not Ordain Women," *Baptist History and Heritage* 23 (July 1988), 56–62. Cf. *Biblical Manhood and Womanhood*, ed. John Piper and Wayne Grudem (Wheaton: Crossway), 1991.

37. Affirmation of the church as the aggregate of the redeemed did not appear in the *New Hampshire Confession* of 1833 nor in its immediate successor, the 1925 version of the *Baptist Faith and Message*. A shorter form of this affirmation appeared first in the 1963 revision of the *Baptist Faith and Message*. Cf. Lumpkin, *Baptist Confessions of Faith*, 365–66, 396.

38. James Madison Pendleton, *Baptist Church Manual* (1867; reprint, Nashville: Broadman & Holman, 1966), 5; idem, *Christian Doctrines: A Compendium of Theology* (1878; reprint, Valley Forge: Judson, 1985), 329.

39. John Leadley Dagg, *Manual of Theology. Second Part. A Treatise on Church Order* (1858; reprint, Harrisonburg: Gano, 1982), 100.

40. Dana, *Manual of Ecclesiology,* 56–57.

41. Dana, *Manual of Ecclesiology*, 67–68.

42. Criswell, *The Doctrine of the Church*, 27–29, 40–41; Herschel H. Hobbs, *Fundamentals of Our Faith* (Nashville: Broadman, 1960), 127–28.

43. If Landmark Baptists conflate the church with the kingdom, the Social Gospel falsely opposes the kingdom to the church, while evangelical ecumenists downplay the church in favor of the kingdom. Leon McBeth, *The Baptist Heritage: Four Centuries of Baptist Witness* (Nashville: Broadman, 1987), 451; Briggs, *English Baptists of the Nineteenth Century*, 22–27; Jason G. Duesing, "J. L. Dagg's Understanding of the New Testament Church as Local and Universal in light of Nineteenth Century Landmark Ecclesiology," unpublished paper delivered at the 9th Annual Ph.D. Conference, Southeastern Baptist Theological Seminary, Wake Forest, NC, May 2003.

44. Contrary to the biblical emphasis and Southern Baptist concerns, when letting "the evangelical church speak for itself," J. I. Packer and Thomas C. Oden stress the universal church, downplay the local church and its ordinances, and do not consider any Southern Baptist confessions. Packer and Oden, *One Faith: The Evangelical Consensus* (Downers Grove: InterVarsity, 2004), 117–29. D. G. Hart believes that evangelicalism is little more than a marketing construct. See his *Deconstructing Evangelicalism: Conservative Protestantism in the Age of Billy Graham* (Grand Rapids: Baker, 2004).

45. D. A. Carson and John Hammett retain the designation, "emerging church" or "emerging church movement," but neither indicates how the group might be biblically identified as a "church." D. A. Carson, *Becoming Conversant with the Emerging Church: Understanding a Movement and Its Implications* (Grand Rapids: Zondervan, 2005), 11–44; Hammett, *Biblical Foundations for Baptist Churches*, 321–31.

46. B. H. Carroll, *Baptists and Their Doctrines: Sermons on Distinctive Baptist Principles* (New York: Fleming H. Revell, 1913), 42–43.

47. Carroll, *Baptists and Their Doctrines*, 44, 48.

· *Article VII* ·

Baptism and the Lord's Supper

John S. Hammett

*A*rticle VII of the *Baptist Faith and Message 2000* presents a traditional state-ment of Baptist beliefs concerning baptism and the Lord's Supper. It follows the *Baptist Faith and Message 1963* verbatim and is similar in substance to Baptist confessions of faith throughout history. Yet among moderate Baptists, there have been calls for substantive changes in both of these ordinances,[1] and even among traditional Baptists, there is often poor understanding of the rationale behind Baptist practice and considerable room for improvement in the practi-cal celebration of these ordinances. Clearly, then, there is a need for a renewed consideration of Baptist thinking on baptism and the Lord's Supper. This article deals with some general issues common to both of these acts, and then addresses the specific affirmations made for each.

GENERAL ISSUES

The Proper Terminology

The word most often used in Christian history for these acts has been 'sacra-ment,' and there is nothing inherently problematic about the word itself. It derives from the Latin *sacramentum*, originally used for an oath of loyalty made by a Roman soldier to his commanding officer. Baptist theologian A. H. Strong refers to baptism and the Lord's Supper as sacraments "in the sense of vows of allegiance to Christ, our Master."[2] In that sense, the word is perfectly acceptable. However, Catholic theology has defined a sacrament as an act that conveys saving grace, and thus Baptists, in their theology and confessions of faith, have tended to avoid the term sacrament and have used the term 'ordi-nance,' signifying that these acts are ordained by Christ for the church.

The Proper Number

Baptism and the Lord's Supper have been almost universally recognized by Protestants as the only two ordinances, with foot washing claimed as a third by a small number of Baptists. Since the twelfth century, Catholics have practiced seven sacraments—baptism, confirmation, the Eucharist (or the Lord's Supper), penance, matrimony, holy orders, and extreme unction (also called last rites or anointing of the sick). Among Baptists, ordinances have been defined by two criteria: (1) ordinances must have been directly instituted by Christ, and (2) they must be directly related to the gospel.[3] On these grounds, Baptists (and others) have maintained that only baptism and the Lord's Supper qualify as valid ordinances.

The Proper Administrator

The *Baptist Faith and Message 2000* does not speak to the issue of who may properly baptize or lead the church in the observance of the Lord's Supper. Typically, pastors have been charged with leading the church in these acts. But given the Baptist belief in the priesthood of all believers, there is no theological reason why one must be ordained to administer the ordinances. Furthermore, since Baptist theology sees the ordinances as entrusted to the church, the church may designate whomever it chooses to lead them in these acts. However, pastors are normally the appropriate persons to do so.

The Proper Setting

There is widespread agreement that the ordinances belong in a special way to churches. The *Baptist Faith and Message 2000* calls baptism "a church ordinance" and limits the Lord's Supper to "members of the church." This seems justified, in view of the New Testament descriptions of baptism and the Lord's Supper as well as the meaning of both of these practices, as argued below. Therefore, they are not appropriate exercises for an individual family, a home Bible study, or a youth group. They may certainly be celebrated outside of church buildings, but their meaning can be fully expressed only when they are celebrated by the body of believers of a church.

The Proper Perspective

One helpful way to approach the ordinances is to consider the human action and the divine action involved in these practices. In other words, what do we do and what does God do? The *Baptist Faith and Message,* like most Baptist confessions of faith, focuses on human actions: we obey, testify, proclaim, and remember. Our emphasis on the symbolic nature of the ordinances has led us to be cautious about saying that God acts in them. Yet God is surely present to bless His people when they gather to worship and honor Him, and at least two major Baptist confessions of faith describe God as acting in the Supper to confirm the faith of believers and nourish them spiritually.[4] It seems that Baptist celebration of the ordinances could benefit from approaching them with the expectation that God will be present to bless His people when they gather to obey and honor Him.

BAPTISM: THE ORDINANCE OF COMMITMENT

It was their practice of baptism that most visibly distinguished the earliest Baptists from others and earned them their name. They differed both in whom they regarded as the proper subjects of baptism (namely, believers only, not infants) and in what they regarded as the proper mode of baptism (namely, immersion rather than pouring or sprinkling). But underlying these visible differences was their view of the meaning of baptism. That topic demands first attention.

The Meaning of Baptism

New Testament teaching on baptism centers around the idea of identification with Christ. The *Baptist Faith and Message 2000* cites Rom. 6:3–5 and Col. 2:12, texts which speak of our identification with Christ in His death, burial, and resurrection. This language is echoed in the text of the article, which speaks of "the believer's death to sin, the burial of the old life, and the resurrection to walk in newness of life in Christ Jesus."

But to identify with Christ is also to identify with the church, Christ's body. Acts 2:41 connects baptism with being added to the church. In fact, except for the Ethiopian eunuch (Acts 8:36–39), all the accounts of baptism in the book of Acts seem to be connected to a church—whether established or just beginning. This is why the *Baptist Faith and Message* describes baptism as a "church ordinance," and makes it prerequisite to church membership.

Baptists have historically insisted that baptism is not salvific, that it is not essential to salvation. It does not accomplish identification with Christ, but symbolizes the identification that happens when one places faith in Christ. It symbolizes the believer's faith and testifies to that faith, but it does not create faith. Yet it should not be devalued. A beautiful if imperfect analogy is provided by a wedding. A wedding ceremony does not create love between two people; they have already said "yes" to each other well before the wedding.

Yet at the wedding the couple's love is publicly confessed, celebrated, and confirmed. In the same way, baptism does not create faith or unite one with Christ, but it is the event by which faith is confessed, celebrated, and confirmed. It is the ordinance of commitment.

Who May Be Baptized?

The early Baptists' understanding of the meaning of baptism brought them into conflict with the established churches of their day. Those churches practiced infant baptism, while Baptists insisted on baptism for believers alone. Despite the argument from the so-called household baptisms in the book of Acts, the analogy proposed between circumcision and baptism, and the longstanding practice of infant baptism in history, Baptists saw the plain teaching of the New Testament as limiting baptism to believers alone and thus excluding infants.[5] Article VII of the *Baptist Faith and Message 2000* is clear on this point, referring to faith or belief five times in ten lines.

An important, related question not addressed by this confession is the age at which one can be baptized. Historically, believer's baptism was closely associated with adult baptism, and to this day, the baptism of preteen children is rare in Baptist churches outside North America. But the average age of baptismal candidates in North America has been dropping for decades. Some say that baptism should immediately follow faith, even in cases of young children. Others offer two objections. First, some think genuine conversion, involving a real experience of repentance, requires more cognitive ability than young children possess. Second, some argue that even if children can believe at an early age, baptism should occur only when the church is able to see evidence of the reality of faith in a child's life, which in the case of a young child may require a number of years. For reasons like these, there have been a number of suggestions for a minimum age for baptism, ranging from as low as seven to as high as after a child leaves his parents' household, with around twelve gathering the support of others.[6] While setting an exact age may be difficult, the language describing baptism as symbolizing "death to sin, the burial of the old life, and the resurrection to walk in newness of life in Christ Jesus" surely raises questions about the appropriateness of the baptism of younger children.

The Mode of Baptism

The earliest English Baptists practiced baptism by pouring in the first decades of their existence, but by 1639 Particular Baptists embraced immersion as the proper mode. It was enshrined in the First London Confession of 1644 and soon became universal among Baptists. Baptists saw three important supports for immersion. The first was the simple meaning of the word *baptizo*. Even John Calvin acknowledged that the word means to immerse, though he himself believed that the mode was of no importance.[7] Baptists, with their zealous biblicism, took the meaning of the biblical word to its baptismal conclusion. Second, immersion seemed a particularly apt way of symbolizing death, burial, and resurrection (as per Rom. 6:3–5). Third, immersion matches the biblical descriptions (such as the one given in Mark 1:10) of people being baptized and then coming out of the water. While there may be some room for pouring or sprinkling in exceptional circumstances (e.g., the baptism of a paraplegic or someone pathologically afraid of water), immersion is biblically, theologically, and symbolically preferable.

Contemporary Controversy Over Baptism

Despite the longstanding support for believer's baptism among Baptists, some have recently questioned the necessity of baptism as a prerequisite for church membership and participation in the Lord's Supper. G. Todd Wilson questions requiring a long-time believer who was baptized as an infant to receive believer's baptism prior to joining a Baptist church. He states that "baptizing a believer who has already been walking with God is a contradiction of the New Testament meaning of baptism."[8] But if believer's baptism is a matter of obedience, Wilson's approach would seem to prefer no obedience to delayed obedience. Some no doubt see baptism as a minor issue, having little practical importance, and the issue of infant baptism versus believer's baptism as simply an unimportant difference of interpretation, especially in a post-denominational era when denominational distinctives are seen as more a matter for embarrassment than emphasis. The *Baptist Faith and Message 2000* takes a contrary position. It describes believer's baptism as "an act of obedience." It is included in the Great Commission's command to "make disciples . . . baptizing them" (Matt. 28:19) and in the command concluding Peter's sermon on the day of Pentecost, "Repent and be baptized" (Acts 2:38). Baptists have not believed that differences among Christians concerning what constitutes proper baptism should diminish the importance of obedience to Christ's command. Thus, we ask those who identify with our churches to walk in obedience to this command. The connection between baptism and participation in the Lord's Supper leads us to consideration of the second ordinance.

THE LORD'S SUPPER:
THE ORDINANCE OF RENEWAL

While baptism is a one-time initiatory rite, the Lord's Supper is a continuing rite that churches observe repeatedly. For most of Christian history, it has been the central act of worship, and is the only act for which we have explicit biblical instruction (1 Cor. 11:23–34). This ordinance goes by a number of names, most of which have some biblical support. It is called "communion" in 1 Cor. 10:16 and "the Lord's Table" in 1 Cor. 10:21. The phrase "the breaking of bread" in Acts 2:42 and 20:7 probably refers to this ordinance, though it might refer simply to a meal. The term "eucharist," taken from the Greek *eucharistia* which means "thanksgiving," is used by some denominations and is found in 1 Cor. 11:24 and in each of the gospel accounts of the institution of the Supper (Matt. 26:26–27; Mark 14:22–23; Luke 22:17–19). The word "Mass," derived from the Latin *missa*, has been the traditional Catholic term for centuries, though the trend since Vatican II has been to return to the biblical term "eucharist." The most common term among Baptists has been "the Lord's Supper," reminding us that the rite originally involved a meal and implying renewal or nourishment. As a physical meal renews our bodies, so the Supper is an occasion of spiritual renewal.

THE DEBATE OVER "THIS IS MY BODY"

The word "memorialize" in Article VII positions the *Baptist Faith and Message 2000* within a longstanding debate. That debate has to do with the meaning of the phrase spoken by Jesus at the institution of the Supper, "This is my body." While there was some diversity even into the ninth century, the view eventually affirmed by the Catholic Church in the Fourth Lateran Council of 1215 sees Christ as referring to His own physical body. This interpretation led to a view called transubstantiation, which affirms that when a properly ordained priest lifts the elements and says, "This is my body," God performs a miracle. While the outward appearance and chemical composition of the bread and wine remain the same, the inner reality or metaphysical substance is changed (transubstantiated) into the actual, physical body and blood of Christ. This is sometimes called the doctrine of real presence. At the time of the Reformation, Luther objected to several aspects of Catholic doctrine respecting the Supper, such as the idea that it involves a re-crucifixion of Christ, that a priest has the power to bring about the miracle of transubstantiation, and that it provides grace apart from faith. But Luther did not object to the doctrine of real presence. However, he saw Christ's real presence coming not from a metaphysical change in the elements, but as guaranteed by the words of Christ, which he took strictly literally. Christ's presence was there "in, with and under" the elements, a view that came to be called consubstantiation. Ulrich Zwingli participated in a famous debate with Luther in which he pointed to numerous passages in Scripture where "this is" clearly means "this signifies." Zwingli's name is thus associated with the view called memorial, according to which the bread is not Christ's physical body, but a memorial meant to signify and commemorate that body. Shortly after Luther and Zwingli, Calvin offered a mediating view according to which the presence of Christ in the Supper is not physical, but spiritual. That view came into many Reformed confessions, and was adopted by one major Baptist confession,[9] but the more widely held view among Baptists is the memorial view, reflected in the use of the word "memorialize" in the *Baptist Faith and Message*.

The Significance of the Supper

As stated above, the Lord's Supper originally involved a meal, and even today involves physically "partaking of the bread and the fruit of the vine." As noted in the *Baptist Faith and Message 2000*, this is a "symbolic act." As physical food renews the body physically, the Lord's Supper renews the body of Christ, the church, spiritually. Returning to the analogy suggested above, if baptism may be compared to a wedding ceremony, the Lord's Supper may be compared to an anniversary celebration in which the vows taken at the wedding are renewed.

Renewal takes place in the Supper on a number of levels. First, the remembrance of our Lord's death should lead to a renewal of our repentance, because we remember that His body was broken to free us from sin. How can we live in sin when His body was broken to liberate us? Second, the Supper should be an occasion to renew our faith. In partaking of it, we "proclaim the Lord's death" (1 Cor. 11:26). We remember that this death is our only hope, and we renew our commitment to trust in Christ alone. That faith focuses on His death, the body broken and the blood shed, but it also emphasizes His resurrection, victory over death, and promised return. As this document puts it, in the Supper we "anticipate His second coming." Finally, the Lord's Supper is also an occasion for renewing our commitment to the church. 1 Cor. 11:18 sees the Lord's Supper as a time when the church "comes together." 1 Cor. 10:16–17 associates the Lord's Supper with the unity of the body; and some see the judgment spoken of in 1 Cor. 11:29–30 for failure to properly discern "the body" as a reference not to Christ's physical body, or the bread broken in the Supper, but to the church as Christ's body.[10] The Lord's Supper is supremely the time when the church renews its love for and commitment to one another. This relates especially to the question of open versus closed communion, which is perhaps the most controversial aspect of the statement on the Lord's Supper in the confession.

Open versus Closed Communion

One question over which there has been disagreement among Baptists, and between some Baptists and most other Protestants, concerns who may properly partake of the Lord's Supper. There is widespread agreement that the Lord's Supper is for the Lord's people; it should thus be restricted to believers. There is also widespread agreement that of the two ordinances, baptism should come first and then the Lord's Supper. The disagreement comes with the question of participation by believers who, according to Baptist thought, have not been properly baptized. Such believers may have been baptized as infants; or they may have been baptized by sprinkling or pouring. Baptists, however, do not regard such practices as proper and valid baptisms. The *Baptist Faith and Message 2000*, in common with most Baptist confessions of faith, sees proper baptism as "prerequisite to the privileges of church membership and to the Lord's Supper."[11] This position is variously called strict communion, restricted communion, close communion, and perhaps most commonly closed communion. The opposing view, which sees the Lord's Supper as open to all believers, is called open communion.

Advocates of open communion have objected to closed communion on a number of grounds.[12] Most important seem to be objections that the Supper is the Lord's, not the church's, and that it is harsh, unloving, offensive, and wrong to exclude from the Lord's Table any who belong to Him. Moreover, the lack of proper baptism, which is doctrinally secondary, admittedly not necessary for salvation and widely disputed among evangelical Christians, seems to them an insufficient ground for exclusion from the Lord's Supper.

Those who support closed communion offer four reasons for their position. First, they note that virtually all denominations agree that baptism should precede participation in the Lord's Supper. The disagreement is then over what is proper baptism and Baptists believe the evidence supporting believer's baptism is quite strong. Second, it is a logical outgrowth of the Baptist view of the church and the Lord's Supper as an ordinance for the church. If the Lord's Supper is for the church, and the church is composed of properly baptized believers, then the Lord's Supper is for properly baptized believers. Third, closed communion is supported by the relational aspect of the Lord's Supper. It is not just about renewing our commitment to the Lord, but also to the body of believers. One who is not baptized and thus not a member of the local body celebrating the Lord's Supper cannot realistically renew unity with or commitment to that body. Some advocates of closed communion believe participation should be limited to the members of the local church in question. Most Baptists, however, allow what is called "transient communion," which permits participation by those who—though not members of that local church—are members of a church "of like faith and order," meaning one which practices believer's baptism. Fourth, those who support closed communion see open communion as denigrating the importance of obedience to Christ's command to be baptized. In fact, according to Mark Dever, the command to be baptized is so serious that, if someone was admitted to church membership but refused to obey such a clear command of Christ, the church would be obligated to discipline him immediately.[13]

Until fairly recently, most Baptists have supported closed communion, with some notable exceptions, such as John Bunyan, Robert Hall, and C. H. Spurgeon.[14] However, the twentieth century has seen significant movement away from closed communion. In the last decade, four authors from the moderate wing of Baptist life have voiced strong opposition to closed communion,[15] and anecdotal evidence seems to indicate that a growing number of Baptist churches are practicing open communion. Perhaps this movement toward open communion is due to increased interaction of Baptists with other Christians in parachurch gatherings where differences over baptism have not hampered fellowship. Perhaps it is part of the overall post-denominational attitude characteristic of evangelical Christianity. Or perhaps open communion is attractive simply because it seems more hospitable, inclusive, and loving. But an equally possible reason for the movement toward open communion is a lack of awareness of the case for closed communion, which remains strong. The design and purpose of the Lord's Supper cannot be fully experienced apart from a commitment to those with whom one shares the Supper. Thus, it is primarily for the members of a local body of believers. A recognition of the fact that the body of Christ extends beyond the local body of believers gives some grounds for the practice of transient communion, but to extend communion to unbaptized Christians seems to denigrate Christ's command to be baptized. Certainly, we can and should experience fellowship with other believers across denominational lines, but there are other contexts for such fellowship. The Lord's Supper, as the ordinance in which we renew our commitment to both Christ and each other, is not such a context. The *Baptist Faith and Message 2000* clearly affirms closed communion.

NOTES

Much of the material in this chapter is drawn from my chapter on "More than Simple Symbols: Baptism and the Lord's Supper" in *Biblical Foundations for Baptist Churches: A Contemporary Ecclesiology* (Grand Rapids: Kregel, 2005), 257–98. Used by permission.

1. John Tyler, *Baptism: We've Got It Right . . . and Wrong* (Macon: Smyth & Helwys, 2003) and several of the contributors to *Baptism and the Lord's Supper*, ed. Walter B. Shurden,

Proclaiming the Baptist Vision, vol. 5 (Macon: Smyth & Helwys, 1999) call for changes in the requirement of believer's baptism by immersion for church membership and participation in the Lord's Supper.

2. A. H. Strong, *Systematic Theology* (Philadelphia: Judson, 1907), 930.

3. Stanley Grenz, *Theology for the Community of God* (Nashville: Broadman & Holman, 1994), 676.

4. The idea of spiritual nourishment in the Lord's Supper is present in Article 32 of the Second London Confession and in Article 33 of the Orthodox Creed.

5. Defenses of believer's baptism have been standard among Baptists, ranging from the early Anabaptist Balthasar Hubmaier, "On the Christian Baptism of Believers," to the nineteenth century J. L. Dagg, *Manual of Theology; Second Part: A Treatise on Church Order* (Philadelphia: American Baptist Publication Society, 1858; reprint, Harrisonburg: Gano, 1982), to A. H. Strong's classic *Systematic Theology,* to more recent works by Paul K. Jewett, *Infant Baptism and the Covenant of Grace* (Grand Rapids: Eerdmans, 1978) and Fred Malone, *The Baptism of Disciples Alone: A Covenantal Argument for Credobaptism Versus Paedobaptism* (Cape Coral: Founders, 2003).

6. See the discussion of this question in John S. Hammett, *Biblical Foundations for Baptist Churches: A Contemporary Ecclesiology* (Grand Rapids: Kregel, 2005), 122–24, 271–73.

7. John Calvin, *The Institutes of the Christian Religion,* ed. John T. McNeill, trans. Ford Lewis Battles, The Library of Christian Classics, vol. 21 (Philadelphia: Westminster, 1960), 1320 (4.15.19).

8. G. Todd Wilson, "Why Baptists Should Not Rebaptize Christians from Other Denominations," in *Baptism and the Lord's Supper,* ed. Walter B. Shurden, Proclaiming the Baptist Vision, vol. 5 (Macon: Smyth & Helwys, 1999), 43.

9. The Second London Confession, in Article 32, adopted verbatim a paragraph from the Westminster Confession affirming Christ's spiritual presence in the elements. The Philadelphia Confession of Faith reproduces the same paragraph unchanged. However, nowhere else in Baptist confessions is this idea clearly affirmed.

10. Gordon Fee, *The First Epistle to the Corinthians,* The New International Commentary on the New Testament, ed. F. F. Bruce (Grand Rapids, Eerdmans, 1987), 563–64.

11. Limitation of the Lord's Supper to baptized church members is stated in the Orthodox Creed of 1679, the New Hampshire Confession of Faith, the Articles of Faith of the Sandy Creek Association, the Abstract of Principles, and all three editions of the *Baptist Faith and Message.* It is implied in the First London Confession and not addressed in the Second London/Philadelphia Confession. However, Free Will Baptists have historically held that the Lord's Supper should be given to all who are disciples of Christ, baptized or not, though their view is the minority one. See the discussion in Hammett, *Biblical Foundations for Baptist Churches,* 283–88.

12. In the mid-nineteenth century, Baptist theologian J. L. Dagg enumerated and responded to ten objections to closed communion. See Dagg, *Manual of Theology,* 214–25.

13. Mark Dever, *A Display of God's Glory,* 2nd ed. (Washington, D.C.: Center for Church Reform/9 Marks Ministries, 2001), 52–53.

14. The controversies in Baptist life over open versus closed communion are traced in Timothy George, "Controversy and Communion: The Limits of Baptist Fellowship from

Bunyan to Spurgeon," in *The Gospel in the World: International Baptist Studies*, ed. David Bebbington, Studies in Baptist History and Thought, vol. 1 (Waynesboro: Paternoster, 2002), 38–58.

15. The opposition is found in a book by John Tyler, *Baptism: We've Got It Right . . . and Wrong*, and in three articles from *Baptism and the Lord's Supper*, ed. Walter B. Shurden. The articles are G. Todd Wilson, "Why Christians Should Not Rebaptize Christians from Other Denominations," Thomas Clifton, "Fencing the Table," and Fisher Humphreys, "A Baptist Theology of the Lord's Supper."

The Lord's Day

John S. Hammett

This article is one of the most surprising in the *Baptist Faith and Message 2000* because, in spite of a rather significant change, it has sparked little discussion. The change comes in the last sentence. The 1925 and 1963 editions have after the words, "both public and private," the following phrase: "and by refraining from worldly amusements, and resting from secular employments, works of necessity and mercy only being excepted."[1] The 2000 edition replaces that specific phrase with one which leaves how an individual observes Sunday to his conscience. This less stringent attitude can also be seen in another, much smaller change. Whereas the earlier editions say that the Lord's Day "should be employed in exercises of worship and spiritual devotion," the 2000 edition says the Lord's Day "should include exercises of worship and spiritual devotion." What could be the rationale for such changes, and what do they mean for Baptist faith and life?

Some might suggest that the authors of the *Baptist Faith and Message 2000* have simply caved in to the changes within American society, in which Sunday has become for some just another day of work and for most just another weekend day for pleasure and recreation. However, in view of the strongly counter-cultural stance of other articles in the confession, this explanation seems unlikely. A more likely explanation is that the changes developed from biblical and theological reflection on the relationship between the Old Testament Sabbath and the New Testament Lord's Day, reflection sparked perhaps by a number of studies on the topic that have appeared since the publication of the 1963 edition of the *Baptist Faith and Message*.[2]

THE SABBATH AND THE LORD'S DAY

The key issue is the application of the Fourth Commandment, the command to "Remember the Sabbath day by keeping it holy" (Exod. 20:8), to Christians. That command seems to be the basis for the prohibition of "worldly amusements" and "secular employments" on Sunday, for the prohibition of work and the setting apart of the day as holy are prominent in Old Testament teaching on the Sabbath. The close connection between the Sabbath commandment and the Baptist view of the Lord's Day is seen in earlier Baptist confessions of faith which call the Lord's Day the "Christian Sabbath."[3]

However, the transference of the Old Testament Sabbath to the Christian Lord's Day is not clearly seen in the New Testament itself. In fact, in view of the prominence of the Sabbath in Judaism, and the numerous Sabbath controversies in the gospels, there is surprisingly little about the Sabbath in the New Testament. It is the only one of the Ten Commandments not specifically reaffirmed in New Testament teaching, and Paul treats Sabbath observance as an issue of Christian liberty (Rom. 14:5; Col. 2:16) rather than a matter of Christian obedience.

The worship formerly observed on the Sabbath came to be observed on the first day of the week. This is highlighted in the *Baptist Faith and Message 2000*. For the idea of commemorating Christ's resurrection by worship on the first day of the week does seem to be present in the New Testament itself. Acts 20:7 and 1 Cor. 16:1–2 show Christians gathering on the first day of the week; and by the time of Rev. 1:10, the day had acquired the title of "the Lord's Day," justifying the claim that "the first day of the week was the Christian day of regular corporate worship in the church of Asia at the end of the first century."[4] Beyond that, while the precise origins of Sunday worship cannot be proven to go back to the resurrection itself, the repeated use of the phrase "the first day of the week" in the resurrection narratives is suggestive. Once Christians began to worship on Sunday, the link to the resurrection would have been inevitable. Richard Bauckham concludes that we have no reason to think that Christian observance of Sunday as a day of worship was ever disconnected from the idea of commemoration of Christ's resurrection.[5]

The element of rest came to be interpreted as fulfilled in Christ, for all who believe in Him "enter that rest" (Heb. 4:3), which is a rest from our own work and a rest of faith (Heb. 4:9–10). As A. T. Lincoln puts it, "the true Sabbath, which has come with Christ, is not a literal, physical rest but is seen as consisting in the salvation God has provided."[6] This understanding was shared by some early English Baptists. In 1645, Robert Garner wrote, "by Sabbath here, we are to understand the Lord Jesus only, Who Alone is the Sabbath of Rest of Believers under the Gospel."[7] However, in the late patristic and throughout the medieval period, physical rest came to be re-associated with Sunday.

This development happened in stages. First, by the time of Constantine, rest on Sunday was seen as a convenient way to allow Christians to have plenty of time to worship. But this lacked a theological rationale and was even criticized by some as encouraging sinful idleness.[8] Augustine paved the way for such a justification by his view of the Ten Commandments as the centerpiece of Christian moral teaching. Although he himself interpreted the Sabbath rest spiritually, the result of his elevation of the Decalogue "was to exalt the Sabbath commandment to a place of significance it might not otherwise have attained."[9] After Augustine, physical rest was seen as part of Christian obedience to the Ten Commandments, but was transferred from the Sabbath (or seventh day) to the Lord's Day (or first day). Although Luther and Calvin broke with the almost unanimous medieval understanding of Sunday as the Christian Sabbath, and saw worship on Sunday as a convenience rather than a command and theologically distinct from the Sabbath, the medieval view came back into Protestant thought with their successors, especially the Puritans. In fact, the emphasis on obedience to the Sabbath command was so strong that some Puritans took their obedience to the logical conclusion and became Seventh-Day Baptists.[10] But the overwhelming majority of Baptists have followed the dominant Puritan model and observed Sunday as the Christian Sabbath.

In the twentieth century, many Southern Baptists were troubled by the growing secularization of American society and sought to preserve Sunday as a day of rest and worship. W. O. Carver, longtime professor at the Southern Baptist Theological Seminary, in 1940 called for the state "to recognize and encourage the observance of the Lord's Day as a day of religious worship" but acknowledged that people should not be forced to worship.[11] More recently, many Baptists have been involved in an organization called the Lord's Day Alliance, which argues for the preservation of Sunday as a day of worship and rest, not only on religious grounds, but also on the grounds that all humans need a day of rest. In fact, they see the preservation of the Lord's Day as something "upon which the stability and well-being of our nation depend."[12]

The statement on the Lord's Day in the *Baptist Faith and Message 2000* does not necessarily oppose such efforts. I myself refrain from certain activities on Sunday as a spiritual discipline, and encourage others to do likewise. But the confession's statement does signal a shift in how the relationship of the Sabbath command and the Lord's Day is perceived. Basically, the statement leaves the two unrelated. Aside from the inclusion of Exod. 20:8–11 in the list of Scriptures appended to the article, nothing in the statement relates the Lord's Day to the commands to rest on the Sabbath day and to remember to keep it as a holy day. The Lord's Day is described as a "Christian institution," not as instituted by the Ten Commandments. It is for worship, but there is no mention of rest. Activities on the Lord's Day are left as a matter of Christian freedom, as in Rom. 14:5 and Col. 2:16. While not stated, the implication seems to be that in Christ the Sabbath command to rest is fulfilled when we rest in Him in faith. Our practice of the Lord's Day is based on New Testament teaching and example, not on an Old Testament command.

PRACTICAL IMPLICATIONS

It may still be possible to make a case that resting from work on Sunday is healthy for a variety of reasons. Bodies still need physical rest, and ceasing from work can be one way of expressing the truth that we live by faith, not by our works. It is certainly true that worship should be a priority. Some argue as well that Sabbath rest is grounded in the model of God's rest on the seventh day of creation and that the principle of one day in seven for rest is God's desire for all humanity. Many in the Reformed tradition regard the Sabbath, along with parenthood, marriage, and work, as creation ordinances, given by God for the good of all and to be observed by all.[13] But there is no command regarding the Sabbath in Genesis as there is for parenthood, marriage, and work, and the pagan nations around Israel, while criticized for many ethical violations and idolatry, were never cited for violating the Sabbath command. Harold Dressler concludes from his study of the Sabbath in the Old Testament that "the Sabbath was inaugurated for the people of Israel to be celebrated as a weekly sign of the covenant. The Sabbath is not viewed as a universal ordinance for all mankind but as a specific institution for Israel."[14] This seems to be the view informing the *Baptist Faith and Message 2000*. Sabbath rest may be prudent or beneficial, but it is not commanded.

What are the implications of this view of the Lord's Day for individual Southern Baptists and their churches? Increasingly, believers are facing challenges as they live in a post-Christian world that sees Sunday as just another day, as the second half of the weekend. Increasingly, employers want employees to work on Sunday, community groups choose to schedule meetings on Sunday, college athletes find themselves scheduled to compete on Sunday, and even children's soccer teams play on Sunday. Courts may afford some protection to Christian workers under the claim that such requirements infringe on their freedom to worship, and we may try to persuade organizations that we are involved in to avoid Sunday meetings and games, but they may find our arguments for treating Sunday as a special day unconvincing.

How should Christians respond to such difficult situations? Some may choose to avoid jobs that involve Sunday work, to withdraw from teams and organizations that meet on Sunday. Others may feel called, for a variety of reasons, to maintain their involvement in these activities, but also want to be involved in their churches. The *Baptist Faith and Message 2000* makes these choices a matter of Christian conscience, rather than command. Churches should recognize the importance of offering Sunday evening, Wednesday evening, and other worship and small group times for those who seek to live under the Lordship of Christ, but are also called to be salt and light in areas of society that no longer recognize Sunday as a special day.

NOTES

1. There is one very small difference between the two. The 1925 edition has the word "works of necessity and mercy," while the 1963 edition uses the singular "work."

2. D. A. Carson traces the recent interest in the topic to the work of Willy Rordorf, *Sunday: The History of the Day of Rest and Worship in the Earliest Centuries of the Christian Church* (London: SCM, 1968). Carson states that this book was the catalyst for "hundreds of articles" and "a substantial number of books," including the one in which Carson's statement appears. See D. A. Carson, "Introduction," in *From Sabbath to Lord's Day: A Biblical, Historical and Theological Investigation*, ed. D. A. Carson (Grand Rapids: Zondervan, 1982), 14.

3. This phrase is found in the Second London Confession, the Philadelphia Confession, the Orthodox Creed, and the New Hampshire Confession. Early Baptist thinking on this topic seems to be most influenced by English Puritan teaching, as seen especially in the Westminster Confession of Faith. Phrases like the command to observe "public and private exercises of . . . worship" on the Sabbath, and to refrain from "worldly employments and recreations" with the exception of "duties of necessity and mercy" seem to be echoed in the Baptist confessions mentioned above, all of which appeared after the Westminster Confession. See the discussion in Paul Jewett, *The Lord's Day: A Theological Guide to the Christian Day of Worship* (Grand Rapids: Eerdmans, 1971), 151–55.

4. R. J. Bauckham, "The Lord's Day," in *From Sabbath to Lord's Day*, 232–33.

5. Bauckham, "The Lord's Day," 236.

6. A. T. Lincoln, "Sabbath, Rest, and Eschatology in the New Testament," in *From Sabbath to Lord's Day*, 215.

7. Robert Garner, *A Treatise on Baptism* (1645; reprint, Paris, Arizona: The Old Faith Baptist Church, n.d.), 30, cited in Tom Wells and Fred Zaspel, *New Covenant Theology* (Frederick: New Covenant, 2002), 235.

8. R. J. Bauckham, "Sabbath and Sunday in the Post-Apostolic Church," in *From Sabbath to Lord's Day*, 286.

9. Bauckham, "Sabbath and Sunday in the Medieval Church in the West," in *From Sabbath to Lord's Day*, 300. Jewett, *The Lord's Day*, 90, agrees with Bauckham's evaluation.

10. These historical developments are traced by R. J. Bauckham, "Sabbath and Sunday in the Protestant Tradition," in *From Sabbath to Lord's Day*, 312–34, and Jewett, *The Lord's Day*, 100–108.

11. W. O. Carver, *Sabbath Observance: The Lord's Day in our Day* (Nashville: Broadman, 1940), 82.

12. James P. Wesberry, "Preserving Our Liberty by Observing the Lord's Day," in *The*

Lord's Day, compiled by James P. Wesberry (Nashville: Broadman, 1986), 25. The Lord's Day Alliance is an interdenominational organization, with at least twenty-three denominations represented on its board of directors. It has been in existence since 1888.

13. A typical representative of this position is that given by Roger T. Beckwith and Wilfrid Stott, *This Is The Day: The Biblical Doctrine of the Christian Sunday in its Jewish and Early Church Setting* (Greenwood, South Carolina: The Attic, 1978), 6–7.

14. Harold H. P. Dressler, "The Sabbath in the Old Testament," in *From Sabbath to Lord's Day,* 34.

The Kingdom

Russell D. Moore

$\mathcal{I}$n contemporary America, notes one liberal Old Testament scholar, "we have no king but Elvis."[1] It is certainly hard to see how the concept of "Kingdom" translates into a world where the only king most children see is the Neighborhood of Make Believe puppet monarch on *Mister Rogers' Neighborhood* television reruns, and the only royal family most adults can think of is the idle, scandal-plagued celebrities across the Atlantic. This unfamiliarity with the idea of a "kingdom" has led some to wonder whether the phrase "kingdom of God" really works in this cultural context at all.[2] The Baptist confessional witness insists that it does. Part of the strangeness of the gospel in our time is the central claim of Jesus' message—the universe is not a democracy but a monarchy. The Kingdom of God is not simply a metaphor for the Christian life. It is the defining purpose of God's plan for the cosmos. This being the case, the Baptist confession about the Kingdom has everything to do with every other conviction Baptists hold. The fact that a "king" is so hard to imagine in contemporary America is one more reason that the Baptist faith, like that of the New Testament churches themselves, is meant to be countercultural.

THE KINGDOM AND THE BAPTIST
CONFESSIONAL TRADITION

In one sense, every Baptist church's baptistery is a statement of faith on the Kingdom of God. The Anabaptist and Baptist confessions of faith that preceded the *Baptist Faith and Message* all assume a newness of Kingdom activity in the coming of Jesus. This is why, for instance, they rejected a theocratic model of church/state relations and confessed the new covenant to include only believers, not their unregenerate children. The first London Confession of Faith (1644) identifies the "spiritual kingdom" of God on earth with the church (Article 33), a Kingdom presence that necessitates a holy and regenerate body of believers in covenant with one another. The confession likewise looks to the day when the Kingdom is "fully perfected" with the rule of Christ after His second coming. The Second London Confession (1689) and its derivative statements—the Philadelphia (1742) and New Hampshire (1833) confessions as well as the *Abstract of Principles* of the Southern Baptist Theological Seminary (1859)—all assume the same basic Kingdom framework. The *Baptist Faith and Message* clarifies the Southern Baptist witness on the Kingdom by addressing the issue in its own article of the confession.

From the 1963 statement to the 2000, the only change in the article on the Kingdom was spelling, from "kingdom" with a small "k" to "Kingdom" with a capital "K." The transition from the 1925 to 1963 statements, however, was much more substantive, reflecting the theological contexts of the two ages of twentieth century Baptist kingdom theology and the influence of the two primary theological shapers of the documents, E. Y. Mullins and Herschel Hobbs. All three documents stand in a long Baptist confessional tradition that affirms the primacy of God's kingdom purposes in the mission of the churches.

The 1925 version of the *Baptist Faith and Message* statement on the Kingdom is strikingly individual and non-ecclesial, defining the Kingdom as "the reign of God in the heart and life of the individual in every human relationship, and in every form and institution of organized human society." The statement identifies the "chief means of promoting the Kingdom of God on earth" as "preaching the gospel of Christ, and teaching the principles of righteousness contained therein." Skirting potentially divisive millennial issues, the statement affirms that the Kingdom "will be complete when every thought and will of man shall be brought into captivity to the will of Christ." This article emerges in an early twentieth century Protestant religious context engaged with the Social Gospel of Walter Rauschenbusch and others who argued that the Kingdom of God means the transformation of the social, political, and economic orders. Such transformation begins with individual ethical reformation, as seen in Social Gospel pamphleteer Charles Sheldon's 1896 novel *In His Steps,* in which a town's farmers, businessmen, and religious leaders lead a societal reformation by asking in their personal decisions, "What would Jesus do?"[3] Most Southern Baptists circa 1925 did not embrace a Social Gospel vision of the Kingdom, but the ethos of the Protestant American establishment was heavily influenced by the postmillennial optimism of the movement.

The 1925 statement echoes—at points virtually word-for-word—E. Y. Mullins's writings on the Kingdom of God in his 1912 book *Baptist Beliefs.* Like the proponents of the Social Gospel, Mullins identifies the Kingdom with ethical improvement in the structures of society and like them he grounds this in individual ethical improvement. But, for Mullins, the accent is on the individual, in keeping with his emphases on personal experience and the competency of the individual soul before God. Mullins is careful to note that the Kingdom "is not to be identified with any outward ecclesiastical or civil government."[4] Like the later *Baptist Faith and Message* statement, Mullins affirms the Kingdom as both the general sovereignty of God and the historically manifested rule of Christ, arguing that the latter assumes the former.[5]

On the Kingdom, the 1963 and 2000 versions of the *Baptist Faith and Message* represent a marked theological improvement on the 1925 article. The revised article is more community-focused and Christocentric, identifying the completion of the Kingdom not vaguely in language of a day in which wills are brought into conformity with Christ but concretely at "the return of Jesus Christ and the end of the age." This statement maintains the priority of personal regeneration and the (at least partially) future nature of the Kingdom, *contra* Social Gospel theology, even as it affirms that Christians should work for God's will to be realized in the present age. As with 1925, the article on the Kingdom in the 1963 statement explicitly reflects the Kingdom theology of its primary author, in this case Herschel Hobbs. In a 1964 book on doctrine, Hobbs explains the tension between the realized and future aspects of the Kingdom, and maintains the cosmic extent of God's Kingdom program. Noting the redemption of the creation promised in Scripture, Hobbs contends that Jesus came "to establish God's reign, not only in men's hearts, but over all things in the universe."[6] As in the *Baptist Faith and Message 1963*, Hobbs sees the Kingdom as salvific in purpose and meaning. The universal acknowledgement of Christ's lordship in passages such as Phil. 2:10–11 is, for Hobbs, a crucial aspect of the Kingdom's future realization. "This does not mean universal salvation," Hobbs makes clear. "The saved will have submitted to God by faith prior to Jesus' second coming. The lost will be submitted to an acknowledgement of God's rule by force, the force of God's will, at the final judgment."[7] The *Baptist Faith and Message 1963* summed up these themes in Hobbs's understanding of the Kingdom, a summation that reflects the Baptist consensus so well that in 2000, despite a new generation, a denominational restructuring, and tumultuous decades of doctrinal controversy, the article remained virtually unchanged.

THE KINGDOM AS GENERAL SOVEREIGNTY

The first *Baptist Faith and Message* was written in the context of a Southern intellectual culture grappling with Darwinism—the idea that a blind force was at work in the universe, randomly bringing forth varieties of men and things. By the end of the century, such challenges to Christian theism had only accelerated. In the face of any idea that the cosmos juts about, driven by chance, the *Baptist Faith and Message* affirms that God's Kingdom includes His "general sovereignty over the universe." This aspect of God's Kingdom is more fully explained in Article II.A, which asserts that "God as Father reigns with providential care over His universe, His creatures, and the flow of the stream of human history according to the purposes of His grace."

This affirmation of God's cosmic sovereignty is an essential component of the biblical story, present from the very beginning when He is revealed as Creator of all that exists (Gen. 1–2). The Psalmist exults that God is "a great King above all gods" (Ps. 95:3), and that "the Lord reigns" both in the heavens and throughout the earth (Ps. 99:1).[8] David, himself the king of Israel, confesses, "The Lord has established his throne in the heavens, and his kingdom rules over all" (Ps. 103:9). All divine and human kingships are derivative of and accountable to the sovereignty of this regal Creator God. Thus, the God of Israel brings to nothing the competing sovereigns of Pharaoh of Egypt (Exod. 1–15) and Nebuchadnezzar of Babylon (Dan. 4:28–37). It is this general sovereignty of which the divine voice says to the humiliated Babylonian emperor "the Most High rules the kingdom of men and gives it to whom he will" (Dan. 4:32).

As the *Baptist Faith and Message* article on God notes, this kingship is tied particularly to God's Fatherhood. The king to whom God grants the nations as an inheritance is spoken of as God's son (Ps. 2:6–8; 2 Sam. 7). Of this future messianic king, God announces, "He shall cry to me, 'You are my Father, my God and the Rock of my salvation.' And I will make him the firstborn, the highest of the kings of the earth" (Ps. 89:26–27). This pattern of divine patriarchy, reflected in human father-headship in the creation family structure, the tribes of Israel, and the church community, reflects God's archetypal identity as both Father and King. Thus, the apostle Paul can write, "For this reason I bow my knees before the Father from whom every family [literally, every "fatherhood"] in heaven and on earth is named" (Eph. 3:14).

Neither godly human patriarchy nor the divine patriarchy, however, can be compared to the oppressive, tyrannical Pharaoh-like "kingship" of the dictators of this fallen age. Thus, Samuel warns the people of Israel that exchanging divine kingship for human kingship will mean the opposite of God's providential sovereignty—a king who uses his rule for his own selfish purposes. The divine kingship, however, is mysterious and all-encompassing, but, through the revelation of God in Christ, believers know that "all things work together for good, for those who are called according to his purpose" (Rom. 8:28), and that this sovereignty moves toward God's ultimate goal, that we be "conformed to the image of his Son, in order that he might be the firstborn among many brothers" (Rom. 8:29).

God's general sovereignty over the universe may seem obvious, since it is everywhere assumed in both Old and New Testaments. Southern Baptists do not have consensus on precisely how God's sovereignty relates to the free will of human and angelic beings. On this point, confessional architect Mullins was a modified Calvinist while Hobbs was a modified Arminian.[9] The question of how "general" God's "general sovereignty" may be is a point of often-heated discussion among confessionally orthodox Baptists. But the *Baptist Faith and Message* statement at this point corrects a long-standing Baptist temptation toward a revision—or outright rejection—of God's kingly reign over the universe. Despite the central place of "Kingdom of God" language in his work, for instance, Walter Rauschenbusch was not quite as sure about what it means for God to be King. "Our universe is not a despotic monarchy, with God above the starry canopy and ourselves down here," he wrote. "It is a spiritual commonwealth with God in the midst of us."[10] Contemporary Baptist theologian Gregory Boyd echoes Rauschenbusch when he writes: "The cosmos is, by divine choice, more of a democracy than it is a monarchy."[11] Of traditional models of God's kingship, theologian E. Frank Tupper, formerly of the Southern Baptist Theological Seminary writes:

> God does not control everything, and God does not control anything completely. Could God have prevented the murder of the infants in Bethlehem? If the providence of God happens within the limits of a historically conditioned context, if context is critical for content, the answer would have to be 'Probably not,' indeed, a cautious but necessary 'No.'[12]

Against such views of a democratic—and essentially chaotic—universe, the *Baptist Faith and Message* affirms the reign of God over all things seen and unseen. But, even so, the revisionist complaint may seem valid. If the universe is a monarchy, then why do we see all around us sin, suffering, death, and unspeakable evil? To this, the *Baptist Faith and Message*, drawing from the Scriptures, answers with a particular kingship—the Kingdom of Christ.

THE KINGDOM AS PARTICULAR KINGSHIP

The *Baptist Faith and Message* asserts that the second aspect of the Kingdom of God is "his particular kingship over men who willfully acknowledge him as King." The Kingdom of God is instead the reign of God through His human mediator-king over a world in submission to His righteous rule. This envisions the restoration of the Edenic order when God ruled through a human vice-regent, Adam, and put "all things under his feet" (Ps. 8:5–8). This human rule is now disrupted, as the king and queen of the cosmos listened to a beast (over whom they were to rule) rather than to the Word of God. Thus, in animal predation, decay, natural disturbances, and death, we hear the universe asking, with its Creator, "Adam, where are you?" (Gen. 3:9) This is why Jesus' announcement of the dawning Kingdom is accompanied by the casting out of demons and the overturning of death and sickness. The Kingdom is the assumption of what God always intended—the rule of a human mediator King over the entire cosmos. Now the universe waits expectantly for that unveiling—the revelation of the sons of God—which will mean its liberation from the occupying principalities and powers (Rom. 8:20–23).

For now, the Kingdom is hidden. Citing Psalm 8, the writer of Hebrews notes, "We do not yet see everything in subjection to him" (Heb. 2:8). At the same time, Hebrews affirms that we do see "Jesus, crowned with glory and honor because of the suffering of death, so that by the grace of God he might taste death for everyone" (Heb. 2:9). The *Baptist Faith and Message* reflects the New Testament's "already/not yet" tension of Kingdom fulfillment.[13] In Jesus, the Kingdom promises to Abraham, to David, to the nation of Israel are fulfilled (2 Cor. 1:20). And yet, He now waits in heaven for all enemies to be placed under His feet. Jesus rules, but He rules over those who, as the *Baptist Faith and Message* puts it, "voluntarily acknowledge Him." Just as Jesus compares the Kingdom's advance in the present era to the silent expansion of yeast or the slow growth of a small seed into a mighty tree (Matt. 13:31–33), Southern Baptists affirm that the Kingdom's presence now comes not through shock and awe in the skies above us, but in the quiet invincibility of the Spirit, who works through the preaching of the Gospel.

This "already" aspect of the Kingdom is called in the *Baptist Faith and Message* the "realm of salvation." This emphasizes the biblical teaching that salvation is never simply about the isolated rescue of an individual soul. The saved sinner becomes part of a Kingdom community, an organic body, the assembly of the heavenly places—the church. This is why Baptists do not baptize babies, and why church membership is so important in Baptist churches. The church is a colony of the coming Kingdom, ruled by Christ Himself (Eph. 1:20–23). To admit into membership (or keep in membership) within the church one who has not experienced the new birth is to contradict Jesus' announcement that, "unless one is born again, he cannot see the kingdom of God" (John 3:3). The gifts of the Spirit at work in any given Baptist church are not about the organization of committees. They represent the triumph of Christ over demonic world rulers, a triumph that is manifested in His distribution of the spoils of war to His band of brothers and sisters (Eph. 4:8–16).

The fullness of the Kingdom, however, does not arrive apart from Jesus' own presence as the promised King. While Baptists confess that the Kingdom has come in Christ, a reality we see in our churches, we also confess that the "full consummation of the Kingdom awaits the return of Jesus Christ and the end of the age." This fits with the *Baptist Faith and Message* statement on Last Things, which avoids a particular millennial stance while maintaining a "fundamentalist" (in the best sense of that too-often-maligned word) stance on the necessity of hope in a future, visible, cosmic reign of Jesus as the Second Adam, the Son of David, and the incarnate Word of Yahweh. This future aspect of God's reign is precisely why the apostle Paul tells the churches that we do not yet judge the world (1 Cor. 5:12) but only the membership of the church itself. We are not yet kings ruling over the nations (1 Cor. 4:8). That awaits the return of the Messiah who alone has authority to rule coercively over the nations "with a rod of iron" (Rev. 3:26–27; cf. Ps. 2:8–9).

The futurity of the Kingdom is a critical piece of the Baptist confessional witness to religious liberty and the separation of church and state. The *Baptist Faith and Message's* Article XVII stands or falls on the Baptist concept of the Kingdom. Because, as Jesus announces to the Roman governor, "If my kingdom were of this world, my servants would have been fighting" (John 18:36). We must not compel salvation through the power of Caesar's sword because no legislation can persuade the human heart. We must not support our churches through tax dollars because we are, within the church assembly, citizens of Mount Zion, ruled by Christ Himself. Thus, while Baptists affirm the good and proper role of the state, we understand that the focus of Kingdom activity in the present age is the church—not the civil government.

The Baptist confessional witness to the future consummation informs us of what God defines as justice and peace. The article on the Kingdom calls Christians "to pray and to labor that the Kingdom may come and God's will be done on earth," echoing the prayer modeled by Jesus (Matt. 6:10). Thus, Articles XV on the Christian and the Social Order and XVI on Peace and War look to the "principles of righteousness, truth, and brotherly love," principles revealed in the Kingdom agenda of Jesus, for clarity on the kinds of evils against which the church must struggle in the present age. These articles, however, are informed by Baptist Kingdom theology just as much on the limits to that struggle. Article XV affirms that any social activities are "truly and permanently helpful only when they are rooted in the regeneration of the individual by the saving grace of God in Jesus Christ." Article XVI notes that the Christian is to work for peace and against war, but it points to the Gospel alone as the "true remedy for the war spirit." This focus on both the "already" and "not yet" poles of Kingdom fulfillment do not answer every question about how the

Christian church is to live and move in this era, but it does remind us of the dangers of both ungodly passivity and messianic utopianism.

This holistic Kingdom vision is precisely why the Southern Baptist cooperative effort is so focused on personal evangelism and world missions. While Christians must minister to the whole person—meaning the feeding of the hungry, the clothing of the naked, the rescuing of the threatened—such activity apart from the preaching of the Gospel is not consonant with the Great Commission. The Kingdom of God will one day be cosmic and material—a renovated new earth in a redeemed universe (Rev. 21–22). But the only human beings who will enter this new creation are those who have already experienced its first fruits—through union with the resurrected Christ through the Spirit of holiness.

CONCLUSION

At one level, it may appear that most contemporary Westerners know nothing of kings or kingdoms. Most of us live in democratic republics in a global economy that promises an ever-expanding democratic vision. Personal choice, not the will of some monarch, is the rule of this epoch. And yet none of us— believer or unbeliever—is as unfamiliar with the idea of a kingdom as we may pretend. The Jewish religious leaders of Jesus' day assured Him that they, too, were under the authority of no master. But Jesus reminded them that "everyone who commits sin is a slave to sin" (John 8:34, cf. 2 Pet. 2:19). All around us are those who believe themselves to be free and autonomous, yet they are captive to their own passions and desires, to the god of this age (2 Cor. 4:4). The confession of the Kingdom of God is not then simply a statement about the eschaton—although it is certainly that. With our confession that God's purpose is the formation of a Kingdom for His Christ, we are asserting that we will walk in a new pattern of life, a new creation that has dawned in the empty tomb, witnessed to in our baptisms. Whatever our conviction about the "priesthood of the believer," we know that this cannot mean a rootless individualism. We are, after all, in Christ not a collection of freelance clerics but a "kingdom of priests" (Exod. 19:6; 1 Pet. 2:9–10). This community of the future, seen in churches committed to a regenerate membership and a missionary expansion, is always in every place countercultural. It testifies to the sadness and futility of sons of Abraham saying, "We have no king but Caesar," in the hearing of Jesus and to the heartbreaking deadness of contemporary Americans joking, "We have no king but Elvis" in the presence of the church. The churches' confession of the Kingdom of God reminds us that, whatever the ruling order looks like now, there will come a day when every knee will hit the pavement, and every mouth will shout the words the entire cosmos has longed for millennia to hear: "Jesus is Lord."

NOTES

1. Patrick M. Arnold, *Wildmen, Warriors, and Kings: Masculine Spirituality and the Bible* (New York: Crossroad, 1991), 212.

2. Brian McLaren, *The Secret Message of Jesus: Uncovering the Truth that Could Change Everything* (Dallas: W, 2006), 138–48.

3. For the story of Sheldon and the "What Would Jesus Do?" movement, see Timothy Miller, *Following in His Steps: The Biography of Charles M. Sheldon* (Knoxville: University of Tennessee Press, 1988).

4. E. Y. Mullins, *Baptist Beliefs* (Valley Forge: Judson, 1912), 56.

5. Mullins, *Baptist Beliefs*, 56.

6. Herschel H. Hobbs, *What Baptists Believe* (Nashville: Broadman, 1964), 117.

7. Hobbs, *What Baptists Believe*, 117.

8. Unless otherwise noted, all Scripture references are from the English Standard Version.

9. For a discussion of Herschel Hobbs's Arminianism and its role in Baptist theology, see Mark T. Coppenger, "Herschel Hobbs," in *Baptist Theologians*, ed. Timothy George and David S. Dockery (Nashville: Broadman, 1990), 444–45.

10. Walter Rauschenbusch, *A Theology for the Social Gospel* (New York: Macmillan, 1917; reprint, Louisville: Westminster/John Knox, 1997), 49.

11. Gregory A. Boyd, *God at War: The Bible and Spiritual Conflict* (Downers Grove: Inter-Varsity, 1997), 58.

12. E. Frank Tupper, *A Scandalous Providence: The Jesus Story and the Compassion of God* (Macon: Mercer University Press, 1995), 110.

13. For a fuller discussion of the "already" and "not yet" poles of Kingdom fulfillment, see Russell D. Moore, *The Kingdom of Christ: The New Evangelical Perspective* (Wheaton: Crossway, 2004).

· Article X ·

Last Things

Paige Patterson

*W*hether contemporary Baptists owe their origin to the Anabaptists of the Radical Reformation or the English Separatists of the seventeenth century, one thing is certain. A variety of eschatological opinion has been found among almost all Anabaptist and Baptist groups. Both the committee of fifteen, charged in 1998 with the assignment of revisiting these issues, and the messengers to the Annual Meeting of the Southern Baptist Convention in the year 2000 were keenly aware of these differences. As with each of the articles of the *Baptist Faith and Message*, the committee and the convention were faced with discovering the essential fabric of Baptist belief, while leaving the "frills" of the details to individuals who advocated the varying positions.

Baptists like B. H. Carroll and George W. Truett embraced post-millennialism. W. A. Criswell, R. G. Lee, and most of the evangelists in the denomination, as well as others, preached a vigorous pre-millennialism with a pre-tribulation rapture perspective. Meanwhile, theologians like Ray Summers, Ray Frank Robbins, and Curtis Vaughn espoused amillennialism. When amillennialism temporarily quiesced in Southern Baptist life, numerous professors, and not a few pastors, embraced what was denominated "Historic Pre-millennialism," which was popularized by George Eldon Ladd in *The Blessed Hope* and other books.

While these views were vigorously embraced and often preached by Baptist adherents, on the whole Baptists have been model kingdom citizens when agreeing on the essentials of a doctrine of last things without attempting to press one another unrelentingly on the particular details. Article X of the *Baptist Faith and Message 2000* is a classic case in point.

THE HISTORY OF ARTICLE X

As indicated in their prefaces, the *Baptist Faith and Message* documents of 1925, 1963, and 2000 are all built on the sturdy foundation of the *New Hampshire Confession* of 1833. Although Article XVIII of the 1833 confession, entitled "Of the World to Come," is quite different from Article X in the 2000 confession, the essentials are nevertheless apparent. Article XVIII reads,

> [We believe] that the end of this world is approaching; that at the last day, Christ will descend from heaven, and raise the dead from the grave to final retribution; that a solemn separation will then take place; that the wicked will be adjudged to endless punishment and the righteous to endless joy; and that this judgment will fix forever the final state of men in heaven or hell, on principles of righteousness.

Article XVIII of the *New Hampshire Confession* carries the same general themes found in the *Baptist Faith and Message*, including the fact that the present order is not eternal and will be brought to a conclusion by the return of Christ. The wicked and the righteous will both be judged, and eternal states of heaven and hell will be ushered in. There is no mention in the article of millennial expectation, multiple judgments, or the relationship of the church to the tribulation. In fact, no period of tribulation is addressed at all.

When the committee of E. Y. Mullins, L. R. Scarborough, C. P. Stealey, W. J. McLaughlin, S. M. Brown, E. C. Dargon, and R. H. Pitt began to work toward the final form of the *Baptist Faith and Message* statement of 1925, their draft of what became Article X found its way into the finally accepted version. Interestingly, the state convention presidents, who served as a committee for the revision of the *Baptist Faith and Message* in 1963, made no change in Article X, so that in the 1963 version it remained the same as in 1925.

As the Annual Meeting of the Southern Baptist Convention in 2000 drew near, many people, knowing that the specially appointed committee of fifteen would bring their recommendation, thought that the nature of Article X would surely be altered. There was perhaps good reason to anticipate this. Twelve of the fifteen named to the committee were pre-tribulation, pre-millennialists. These men and women believe that the return of Christ will be initiated by His appearance in the heavens with the rapture as the Lord takes to Himself every genuinely born-again believer on the face of the earth. This event will be followed by seven years of unparalleled tribulation, at the end of which Christ will return to the earth to establish one thousand years of His millennial reign over all the earth. Since twelve of the fifteen members of the committee essentially endorsed such a view, many messengers expected that a change would be recommended in this article. What actually transpired was that the process employed by the committee was first to review every article of the 1963 version of the *Baptist Faith and Message* to ascertain whether a change was merited. This procedure made the overall assignment of the committee much easier, since many of that version's articles were left to stand unaltered. Such was the case concerning the article on last things.[1] Even though the committee members were overwhelmingly of a pre-millennial persuasion, they recognized the vast diversity in Southern Baptist life on this issue and felt, along with the 1925 and 1963 committees, that the article as written focused on those essentials held by almost all Baptists.

ANALYSIS OF ARTICLE X

Those who do not take time to read carefully often secure only a cursory understanding. In the case of the *Baptist Faith and Message*, one then misses much of what the authors of the 1925 confession, reaffirmed by the 1963 and 2000 committees, wished to say. What follows is an analysis of twelve clear affirmations that are bound up in Article X.

First, the document affirms the sovereignty of God over both time and circumstances. The initial sentence reads, "God, in His own time and in His own way will bring the world to its appropriate end." The cosmos is not somehow in control of its own destiny, nor are the forces of evil determining its future. God will bring the world to an appropriate end. He does so on His timetable, and He does so with His own choice of methodology and circumstances. Although these circumstances in some degree, including the time of the eschaton, are clearly discussed in Holy Scripture, the authors of the confession were quite willing to recognize that, while the interpretation of those passages involved differences, God's sovereignty over both the timing and the circumstances was clear in Holy Scripture.

Second, the present order is not eternal. The sentence again focuses on the fact that "God . . . will bring the world to its appropriate end." The present order of things was not intended to be eternal. Rather, God has been guiding the entire process of history to the designed climax, which He prescribed from eternity past and which alone can be the "appropriate end" of all things.

The third declaration in the document specifies that whatever transpires in the end is based securely on the promise of Christ Himself. Jesus cautioned His disciples against allowing their hearts to be troubled by assuring them that He was going away to prepare a place for them; and if He prepared that place, He would surely come again to receive them to Himself, so that where He was, they would be also (John 14:3). The high priest himself was the recipient of the same promise when Jesus answered his question, "Are you the Christ, the Son of the Blessed?" Jesus responded, "I am. And you will see the Son of Man sitting at the right hand of power and coming with the clouds of heaven" (Mark 14:62). Therefore, the developments that take place in the end times are now based solidly in the providence and the sovereignty of God and take place in accord with the promise of Christ.

Fourth, Christ will return personally to the earth. Those who find the possibility of a personal return of Christ unthinkable have often attempted to "spiritualize" the prophecies of Christ's return. But the committees working on the *Baptist Faith and Message* eliminated that possibility by stressing that Jesus would come personally. In so doing, they affirmed the message of the angels who, after the ascension of Christ, said, "Men of Galilee, why do you stand gazing up into heaven? This same Jesus, who was taken up from you into heaven, will so come in like manner as you saw Him go into heaven" (Acts 1:11).

Fifth, not only will Christ return personally, but He will return "visibly in glory." And, that return will be "to the earth." Against the idea that, while He might return personally, His coming would only be known to believers or perhaps even unknown to them, the authors of this article declare that His return will be visible and in glory. When Jesus came in the incarnation, there was a sense in which His deity was veiled in His humanity. But His return at the end of the age is said to be in glory. The visibility of this return neither establishes nor eliminates the possibility of Christ's coming to receive His church to Himself in a way that is not known to all men. However, the structure of the sentence does make clear that at some point Christ's return to the earth will be visible, apparently to all.

The authors of Article X next move to the consequences associated with the return of Christ at the end of the age. The first is that the dead will be raised, a point eliminating the possibility of annihilationism or the prospect that physical death is the terminating point of human existence. From what follows, i.e., that all of the dead, both the righteous and the wicked, will be raised and have continued existence seems clear.

Seventh, at that time "Christ will judge all men in righteousness." Jesus Himself made the point that the Father had given "all judgment to the Son" (John 5:22). The authors of Article X affirm their belief that Christ, the Savior of all men, will also be the Judge of all men. Further, they affirm that His judgment will be righteous, precluding the possibility of injustice and thus going beyond the mere affirmation that Christ's judgment will be carried out in a righteous way, carrying the concept of both justice and rectitude.

The authors next concern themselves with the result of Christ's judgment as it pertains to the unrighteous. "The unrighteous will be consigned to hell, the place of everlasting punishment." Most recent public surveys have indicated that more than half of Americans believe there is a place called hell. Certainly to listen to discussions among even secular postmoderns, hell seems not far from their thoughts, even if its contemplation is much more infrequent than references to it. But, however much the general public believes in the concept, its inclusion by the committee developing the *Baptist Faith and Message 2000* is a fascinating holdover from the 1925 and 1963 confessions. In 1925, or even in 1963, hell was still a doctrine addressed with some regularity in the churches. By 2000, even in evangelical pulpits, hell was seldom discussed or even mentioned with great frequency. Still, it was clearly the conviction of the authors of the *Baptist Faith and Message 2000* that Southern Baptists overwhelmingly believe that a place called hell will be the eternal home of those who reject Christ and are therefore considered "unrighteous." Although no definition for hell is provided in the statement, the references to biblical passages following the article make it clear that the place of punishment mentioned in this document is a literal place anticipated by Jesus as well as the apostles.

Furthermore, the authors follow the 1925 and 1963 confessions in saying that hell is a place of "everlasting punishment." Here the authors intended to deny that the Bible presents hell as a place of confinement where one is purged of his sin and from which one can expect eventual release or as a place where after some suffering the soul is forever annihilated. The retribution of hell is an ongoing and everlasting event from which there is no reprieve.

Once again the authors did not think it necessary to elaborate on how this concept is consistent with a God of love and justice. The initial statement claiming God's sovereignty over time and circumstance, as well as earlier statements in the confession, are deemed quite sufficient to answer the question, even if some mystery remains in the human family.

Ninth, the authors now broach the positive results of Christ's judgment. "The righteous in their resurrected and glorified bodies will receive their reward and will dwell forever in Heaven with the Lord." The first declaration here refers to glorified bodies. Salvation is thus construed as being complete only with the salvation of the body. Whereas some, as in Greek thought, would have imagined that the body was perpetually evil just because of its materiality and that the soul's liberation from the body would be the object of salvation, the biblical writers understood that salvation would affect not only the spirit or soul of a man but also eventually his body. The body is the artistry of God and suffered in the Fall. Therefore, the body also must be eventually affected by the atonement of Christ, and that is observed in its glorification. The writers of the confession do not say anything about the nature of that glorified body. The Scriptures cited with the article, however, speak of it as a real body no longer bound by space and time and, therefore, by the illnesses and sorrows that typify human existence in the present body. The body is seen as one that will not suffer pain, death, or sorrow but rather will be modeled after the glorified body of our Lord in His resurrection (Phil. 3:20–21; 1 John 3:2).

Tenth, the righteous will also "receive their reward." Here the subject of reward is introduced without the necessity of further comment. The greatest reward is without doubt direct access to God eternally. The reward that is a part of salvation also includes heaven itself. Furthermore, the Scriptures speak of rewards, reminding believers that there will be a distinction in heavenly rewards. Because the Scriptures do not dwell at length on the nature of these distinctions or even the nature of the rewards themselves, the writers of the confession are also silent.

Eleventh, the righteous will "dwell . . . in heaven with the Lord." Here both intimate, direct access to the Lord and the existence of a place called heaven are clearly affirmed by the confessors. Heaven is therefore seen not to be just a state but an actual place, notably a place where the Lord dwells. Descriptions of heaven, such as those that occur in Revelation 20 and 21 as well as John 14, are specifically recounted in the passages appended to the end of the discussion but are not elaborated in the text. To note that heaven is a place where the Lord Himself dwells is sufficient.

Finally, that dwelling is said to be "forever." Just as the unrighteous are consigned to hell for "everlasting punishment," so the righteous "dwell forever" in heaven with the Lord. This affirmation once again underscores the ongoing existence of humankind under the very different circumstances of a heavenly abode. This experience is to be uninterrupted and without end.

These twelve declarations make up the essence of the doctrine of last things as propounded first by the *New Hampshire Confession of Faith* and then altered by the authors of the 1925 version of the *Baptist Faith and Message* and confirmed by the committees in 1963 and again in 2000. Conclusions then are the following:

1. While Baptists have wide-ranging beliefs regarding exactly how the end times will progress, the twelve matters specified in Article X are nearly universally affirmed by Southern Baptists. Furthermore, from the *New Hampshire Confession of Faith* of 1833 until the 2000 version of the *Baptist Faith and Message* nearly 170 years later, almost no change has taken place in Baptist teaching regarding the essentials of the doctrine of last things. This circumstance alone is significant.

2. Observation of the appended scriptural support reveals, as in most of the articles, an overwhelming preponderance of New Testament evidence with very few Old Testament citations. Old Testament attesta-

tion comes from Isaiah 2:4 and 11:9. Interestingly, these two passages both focus on conditions that pre-millennialists most often see as having to do with a millennial earth. In any case, the sovereignty of Christ the Judge is thematic in both. Isaiah 2:4 indicates that He will judge the nations and rebuke many people, but the end result will be that "they shall beat their swords into plow shares and their spears into pruning hooks," indicating conditions of total peace brought not by the efforts of men but rather by the sovereign rule of God. Isaiah 11:9, on the other hand, indicates also that under the sovereign reign of Christ "they shall not hurt nor destroy my holy mountain for the earth shall be full of the knowledge of the Lord as the waters cover the sea."

3. New Testament support begins with Matthew 16:27, which anticipates the return of the Son of Man with the glory of His Father and with His holy angels. And, noting that He returns to provide rewards, Matthew 18:8–9 stresses the seriousness of spiritual decisions, mentioning the agonies of those who are cast into "hell fire." Matthew 19:28 sees the coming of a day of regeneration and includes one of only two uses of the word "regeneration" (Gk. *paliggenesia*) in the New Testament. Used once in Titus 3:5 of personal regeneration, here in Matthew 19:28 the subject of cosmic regeneration seems to be the emphasis. Since that is not discussed in the article, the reference may rather be to the latter part of the verse where the disciples are told they will be sitting on twelve thrones judging along with the Master. The remaining references in the book of Matthew are all found in the discourse in which the Lord particularly addressed many of the things that would happen in the end times. The itemized verses address the clear visibility of the Lord's return (Matt. 24:27,30) and the fact that no one knows when Christ is going to return except the Father (Matt. 24:36), giving rise to the necessity of being prepared for His coming (Matt. 24:44). The long section in Matthew 25:31–46 emphasizes the judgments associated with the return of Christ. Jesus as reigning Judge with all power is emphasized in Matthew 26:64.

Mark 8:38 and 9:43–48 emphasize strategic judgments associated with the Lord's return, with verses in the longer passage being among the most vivid expressions of eternal punishment found anywhere in the New Testament. Luke 12:40,48 gives support for the doctrine of rewards for the saints as well as for the severity of punishment for those who are lost. Luke 16:19–26 includes the story that Jesus told concerning the rich man and Lazarus and emphasizes the certainty of separation in the eternal state when the wicked are confined in an intolerable place. In this text, the rich man finds a place denominated "hades," whereas Lazarus finds himself comforted "in the bosom of Abraham." The agonies of the rich man's experience in hell are vividly described. Luke 17:22–37 focuses on the words of Jesus concerning the kingdom and culminates in a separation of people from the earth with the coming of Christ, resulting in one in bed being taken while the other is left; two women grinding together, one being taken and the other left; two men walking in the field, one taken and the other left. The final passage from Luke 21:27–28 focuses again on the coming of Christ in power and great glory and the fact that at this point the saints will know their redemption "draws near."

John 14:1–3, the only passage cited from John's gospel, is an important attestation to the doctrine of last things because it focuses on the promise of Jesus. Jesus promised that if He were to go away, He would come again and receive His disciples to Himself after making special preparation for them in heaven. This promise is further underscored by the angels in Acts 1:11, where the promise is made to the disciples who have observed His ascension that He will come again in the same way. Acts 17:31, on the other hand, seems to underscore the fact that God has chosen His own time and way, having "appointed a day on which He will judge the world in righteousness by the Man whom He has ordained."

Romans is the most intensely theological book in the Bible. Yet, only Romans 14:10 is cited in Article X. In this passage Paul informs the Romans that they will "all stand before the judgment seat of Christ." The passage is apparently used to support the affirmation that "Christ will judge all men in righteousness." First Corinthians is understandably cited three times. First Corinthians 4:5 warns that believers are to be slow about judgments, knowing that ultimately Christ will bring everything to light and reveal even the "counsels of the hearts." First Corinthians 15:24–28,35–58 comprises a portion of the extensive discussion of Paul relating to the resurrection and focuses on the fact that "the dead will be raised." Second Corinthians 5:10 repeats the counsel of Romans 14:10 that all will appear before the judgment seat of Christ.

Philippians 3:20–21 is included in the list of passages to emphasize the nature of the resurrected body or, as Article X suggests, the "glorified bodies of believers." Colossians 1:5 emphasizes the hope laid up for the believer in heaven, while Colossians 3:4 affirms that, when Christ appears in heaven, believers will appear with Him in glory.

First Thessalonians 4:14–18 and 5:1ff constitute a long discussion by Paul with the Christians at Thessalonica about the comfort to be found in Christ's coming and what is to be anticipated in the Day of the Lord. Believers are cautioned in the passage that the coming will be sudden and involve judgment as well as redemption. 2 Thessalonians 1:7ff continues that theme, refuting those who think that the coming of Christ might have already taken place and affirming that, when the Lord comes, there will be no doubt left in anyone's mind. However, 2 Thessalonians 2 anticipates the mystery of lawlessness that will be unleashed in the last days, about which nothing is said in this article on last things. However, the movement of the entire chapter is to stress the importance of standing firm despite the events of the last days.

First Timothy 6:14 speaks of Christ's appearing and the need of the saints to be blameless in the day of His appearing. Second Timothy 4:1,8 stresses both his appearing and the fact that rewards will be given on that final day of judgment. Titus 2:13 calls for believers to be constantly looking for the "blessed hope and glorious appearing of our great God and Savior Jesus Christ." This verse is particularly important because of the clear identification of Jesus as God as well as the indication of the certainty of His coming.

Hebrews 9:27–28 is cited as evidence that, while men are appointed once to die, there is a reckoning, or judgment, to follow. However, the promise given to believers is that for those who love Him, "He will appear a second time apart from sin for salvation." This reference comes the closest of any in the New Testament to speaking of a "second coming." James 5:8, on the other hand, seems to suggest that believers are to be patient, knowing that the coming of the Lord is "at hand."

In 2 Peter 3:7ff, the discussion focuses on the fact that God is very long-suffering, not willing that any should perish but that all should come to repentance. Nevertheless, the day of the Lord is going to come as a thief in the night, and the very elements of the cosmos will be burned up and melted in fervent heat. The believer is to look forward to that day, knowing that God's justice will be done and there will emerge a new heaven and a new earth. Of the Johannine epistles, 1 John 2:28 is cited, indicating a certain lack of knowledge about the future but nevertheless confidence that He will appear. First John 3:2 further observes that, when He comes, "we shall be like Him for we shall see Him as He is." Jude 14, in which the Lord is said to be coming with "ten thousands of His saints," is also cited.

Finally, the authors could easily and simply have cited virtually the entire book of Revelation. However, they chose to be selective, citing 1:8, the vivid promise that Christ is not only alive but that He holds the keys of death and the grave. Revelation 3:11 is cited where the Lord states, "Behold, I am coming quickly," making use of the disputed Greek term, *tachu*, which may also mean "certainly." Finally, Revelation 20:1–22:13 is a long passage describing the new order, the new Jerusalem, and the delights of the heavenly kingdom.

Evaluating the list of Scriptures appended to Article X, the authors of the 1925 confession, as well as those who followed in 1963 and 2000, must have experienced some frustration deciding which passages to cite. Even allowing for the sparse citations from the Old Testament, the New Testament literature alluding to the last days is so vast that space limitations provide for little more than representative passages. However, a careful analysis of these texts shows once again that the passages were chosen to support the twelve main ideas that have been presented in the body of this chapter. God's sovereignty over the end of historical time as well as the prospect of Christ as the Judge are issues most prominently documented by the Scripture references. Furthermore, the results of that judgment as either eternal punishment in hell or eternal bliss in glorified bodies in heaven are further underscored by the references.

CONCLUSION

The major changes in language occurred between the *New Hampshire Confession* of 1833 and the *Baptist Faith and Message* of 1925. However, even these changes are less significant than they may appear upon first reading. The language of the article on last things in the 1925 confession is in fact more specific, but once again notably there is no change in the 1963 or 2000 versions. This unanimity among Baptist people regarding the twelve affirmations that appear to be made in the confessional statement is remarkable.

What may be seen as most remarkable about the 2000 statement is that within a postmodern ethos, which generally desires to skirt issues of judgment, the Southern Baptist Convention has maintained the emphasis from former years on the certainty of the judgment of God, associating that judgment with the return of the Lord, insisting that there are two classes of people—the righteous and the unrighteous—and that all people will spend eternity in either heaven or hell. These themes for the most part appear to be distasteful to a postmodern generation. The certainty of the personal and visible return of Christ, together with God's sovereignty over all of history, are also themes that are less commonly heard in sermons in churches in the present generation. Indeed, God's full knowledge of the future, which is implied throughout the discussion of last things is contrary to the contemporary "openness theology," which raises questions about what God can know with certainty of future events.

On the other hand, Article X has its genesis in Article I on the Scriptures. If the Scriptures are divinely inspired and constitute a "perfect treasure of divine instruction," then one must take seriously the rather clear declarations of Scripture that sustain the thoughts embodied in Article X. Of course, there are concerns about interpretation; but most Baptists, even if inclined to see spiritual lessons rather than physical realities in some of those passages relating to the end times, would apparently endorse the reality of the affirmations in Article X in a decisively literal way. For Southern Baptists, then, one can only conclude that the sovereignty of God over history, culminating in the return of Christ and the end of the age including eternal states of heaven and hell, remains not only the testimony of Scripture as understood by Baptists but also adds significant understanding to the following article on evangelism and missions. Eschatology, or the doctrine of last things, thus remains a vital component in the confessional faith of Southern Baptist people.

NOTES

1. Confirmed by the author in a conversation with committee member Richard Land on March 5, 2006.

· Article XI ·

Evangelism and Missions

Keith E. Eitel

There is no definition of doctrine anywhere in the SBC Constitution or Bylaws. I often referred to this original purpose when I was president of the SBC Foreign Mission Board (now International Mission Board).

Some 'Ultra-Conservative Resurgence' leaders argued with me that doctrine, not missions, was the unifying force. It took me awhile to recognize that they were a different kind of Baptist. Some Baptists do believe doctrine is the most important element in a convention. This explains why many of them gave only minimal support to the SBC before taking control and changing its nature. They have now redefined the Southern Baptist Convention and have made doctrine its controlling force.[1]

$\mathcal{S}$eismic reverberations are still felt from that fateful moment on June 14, 2000, in Orlando, Florida, when the Southern Baptist Convention (SBC) officially adopted a confession of faith known as the *Baptist Faith and Message 2000*.[2] Perhaps the most violent aftershocks stem from the leadership of the International Mission Board (IMB) requiring field missionaries to affirm the newly adopted confession.

R. Keith Parks's statement above reflects the grounds for the divide among Southern Baptists. Elements within the Convention prefer to gather around causes related to missionary activity as the ground of being designed to hold the Convention together. Others see that the purposes of missionary activities presuppose the reliability of the Bible, sound theology, and a faith and practice that will motivate and sustain missionaries as they engage global spiritual lost-ness with the uniquely true claims of Christ regarding salvation. The source of these presuppositions is the Bible itself. If anything, the rephrasing of the *Baptist Faith and Message* in 2000 was designed to address contemporary challenges related to the way humanity may know about God's existence, His Truth, and His desire to connect with us through that redeeming Truth. The necessary question is, How can a Convention unify around missionary causes

111

while simultaneously embracing elements of truth decay that threaten the very foundation of the Gospel itself? Without a reliable Bible, we have no God-given mission. The controversy in the SBC that has ensued since 1979 aims at recovering historic Baptist views of the Bible and thereby preserving the Convention's justification for faith, life, and evangelistic missionary activity.[3]

From the requirement that missionaries sign the new confession, a continental divide emerged which culminated in some missionaries being dismissed.[4] The reason given by some missionaries for not signing the confession is that, to them, the act symbolized a shift from a "confession" to a "creed" and thereby signified a radical redefinition of what it means to be Southern Baptist.[5] This chapter explains and defends the revision of the *Baptist Faith and Message,* specifically the changes made to the eleventh article which sets forth the SBC's understanding of evangelism and missions. It itemizes changes in the article by comparing it in both the 1963 and 2000 versions of the *Baptist Faith and Message.* Additionally, it explains what was left intact. Finally, this chapter provides an argument in support of the IMB's requirement that missionaries sign the newly revised confession of faith.

THE SCOPE AND MEANS OF BIBLICAL EVANGELISM: STATEMENT ADDITIONS

Change is inevitable. Evangelism and missiology are realms of Christian experience where change is keenly sensed because the interface between cultures makes worldview comparisons and contrasts so sharply focused. Hence, those engaged in communicating the Gospel across sets of cultures, whether foreign or a multifaceted culture like that of North America, are constantly challenged by shifting relevance. Explaining timeless truths that have eternal significance while being "cutting edge" in the means and methods used requires a delicate balancing act. What may be the most significant choices made in the near future will not be what is changed in communicating the Gospel but what is left intact.[6] In other words, we can become so relevant that we lose the distinctive quality of the eternal, transcultural Gospel message. The apostle Paul clearly recognized this danger when addressing the Galatians and warned them about even well-meaning messengers that may alter the once delivered, eternal message and pronounced his judgment on their actions that such should be "accursed."[7] This should be warning enough for those of any era, especially Southern Baptists, to take care to avoid defining the content of the message in any way other than in keeping with Paul's understanding of salvation by grace alone through the finished work of Christ upon the cross! It follows, then and only then, that one must identify those who should hear this message and determine how it should be told to them. Each of these issues has eternal significance.

On June 14, 2000, the SBC passed the *Baptist Faith and Message 2000*. In so doing, the Convention spoke specifically and directly about evangelism's scope and communicative means in a fresh way. The breadth of the task is delineated in the statement added to the 1963 statement. The wording of the newer document specifies that our "Lord Jesus Christ has commanded the preaching of the gospel to all nations."[8] Thus, the source of the message to be spoken is Christ Himself and its recipients are all nations.[9] These are not geopolitical entities *per se*. These are rather unique groupings of peoples that share language, culture, and heritage. One nation-state may have thousands of such gatherings or clusters of peoples. The job is not complete until Christ is honored among all the nations as per His determination. By this statement, the framers of the *Baptist Faith and Message 2000* indicate full recognition of this scriptural emphasis that Southern Baptists must affirm in order to demonstrate our obedience to the full implications of Christ's commissioning.

Additionally, the *Baptist Faith and Message 2000* includes a statement addressing a specific way that the Gospel witness is to be communicated. Every believer is to live in such a way as to foster consistent witness to the Gospel message and is to do so "by verbal witness undergirded by a Christian lifestyle." This statement is not meant to restrict Christians to only one means of witness. Quite the contrary, the statement from the 1963 version of the *Baptist Faith and Message* that "other methods in harmony with the gospel of Christ" will be acceptable and encouraged was left in place. Why then did those who drafted the 2000 version believe it necessary to emphasize verbal witness, stating that a "Christian lifestyle" should enhance that witness? Probably it is because of the contemporary inclination to settle for engaging primarily in a "lifestyle evangelistic" approach.[10] This is often a nonverbal witnessing technique that, when used by some, turns out to be less than biblical because it fails to proactively proclaim the Gospel, settling instead for some form of reactive witness. In other words, we find no examples in Scripture of lost people simply surmising the content of the Gospel message on their own and knowing intuitively how to appropriate God's amazing grace by simply watching a Christian. Commands to *go, preach,* and *teach* are abundant in Scripture. Such activities will certainly be enhanced by a godly lifestyle that is congruent with the message being communicated, but lifestyle in isolation is a poor substitute for proclaiming the Gospel.[11]

By advocating personal initiative in direct verbal proclamation of the Gospel, the latest edition of the *Baptist Faith and Message* affirms the essence of the 1963 edition while also addressing a fault embedded in a model of evangelizing so prevalent in these days of increasing universalistic or pluralistic tendencies. The spirit of our times encourages Christians and others to cower in the context of rampant religious chaos; the Bible, however, directs believers to engage the lost-ness of a fallen world and "speak the truth in love."[12]

MOTIVATION AND SPIRITUAL CONDITION
FOR BEARING WITNESS:
STATEMENT PRESERVATIONS

In a time of globalization and heightened religious pluralism, why would one leave one's culture, familiar customs, family, and home to undergo a nearly complete life transformation by living in another culture and facing the challenges of trying to relate to the people of that culture at a deep enough level to communicate truths that will radically alter their worldview and affect their eternal spiritual condition? The motivational base for doing such things has usually been the scriptural commands of Christ to engage a world in need of the Gospel.[13] An emerging ideology whose motivation should parallel or complement an obedience-based one has been allowed by some to eclipse it. The absence of worship among many of the nations or peoples of the world shifts the reason to a faith-based response, expressing our love of Christ as a reason to go. In other words, to honor Christ and demonstrate the genuineness of our love for Him, we go to preach the Gospel so that authentic worship will emerge among all the peoples of the earth.[14]

While this certainly aims at a worthy goal, it should not replace the duty-based motivation also seen in Scripture. Each rationale intertwined will certainly strengthen all Gospel bearers as they go into the world. During times of discouragement, these motivations will anchor witnesses with twin truths. First, believers did not initiate such activities on their own, but rather they are essential to being an obedient Christian, in accordance with the Lord Jesus Christ's expectations for believers of all time. Second, we demonstrate a faith-love response to His grace, which has been poured out on us, when we extend His church into all the nations or peoples of the earth. Genuine praise of the one true God will emerge among those peoples and glorify Him further throughout the ages.

The *Baptist Faith and Message 2000* emphasizes the "duty and privilege of every follower of Christ and of every church of the Lord Jesus Christ to endeavor to make disciples of all nations." This duty should not feel like an act of drudgery akin to what one feels when forced to pay taxes. If the fact of privilege is not forgotten, the duty becomes an honorable assignment that results in the extension of praise to Him among the nations. Being privileged to go to the nations, according to the *Baptist Faith and Message 2000,* depends on being the recipient of saving grace and thus regenerate. "Missionary effort on the part of all," the confession states, "rests thus upon a spiritual necessity of the regenerate life. . . ."

In one sense evangelistic and missionary activities are things about which a believer has no choice because one's total spiritual being is changed. When we are revolutionized and transformed by the saving grace of Christ, such activity becomes part of what we—having been made new in Christ—must do. Hence, regenerate beings simply must speak forth and declare the mercies of the God of their salvation to the ends of the earth.

TO SIGN OR NOT TO SIGN

In January of 2002, Jerry A. Rankin, president of the International Mission Board (IMB) of the Southern Baptist Convention (SBC), issued a letter requiring all those then serving as IMB missionaries to affirm the *Baptist Faith and Message 2000* by signing it. This was an apparent reversal of his often-cited feelings on the matter. Siegfried Enge, now a retired missionary, recalled that in "December 2000, Jerry Rankin pledged . . . that as long as Rankin is president of the International Mission Board, no missionary would be required to sign a doctrinal statement."[15] Some missionaries felt betrayed by their president's reversal as well as his unwillingness to defend them against what they thought was a wrong act on the part of the Board's trustees.[16]

To many Christians outside the SBC, that the requirement to sign an evangelical doctrinal statement caused such tumult might seem odd. But the SBC has been in the process of transition and reform since 1979.[17] The *Baptist Faith and Message 2000* represents but one milestone in the progress of this reform movement, albeit a major one. The statement, as revised, addresses challenges to biblical theology that have emerged in the past fifty years or so. Yet there were at least two streams of reaction to the IMB requiring missionaries already under appointment to sign the document. The first reactionary stream came from many of the missionaries themselves and generally involved a reaction against what they perceived as "creedalism" (i.e., the imposition of some theological standard other than Scripture, no matter how true to Scripture that standard might be). The second stream of reaction arose from among those committed to a "postmodern" view of Baptist theology and closely aligned to "moderates" within the SBC.

In an open letter addressed to "family and friends in the U.S. and colleagues in Japan," Ron Hankins and Lydia Barrow-Hankins explained why they were willing to suffer the consequences of early resignation by refusing to sign the *Baptist Faith and Message 2000*. Their concerns revolved around three core issues. First, they said, those who are "missions-minded" are supposed to be "inclusive," implying that any sort of "creedal" statement like the one under consideration is necessarily exclusive. Second, they saw the requirement by the trustees of the IMB that missionaries sign the statement as reflecting "coercive" political action foreign to their perception of what it means to be Baptist. Third, they claimed that requiring Baptists to sign a "creed" is of paramount importance because doing so means that "Southern Baptists are no longer 'Baptist' in faith and practice."[18] Here arises the concern for what it means to be Baptist. History and precedent, they indicated, were primary considerations motivating their refusal. But within SBC life are multiple traditions. And the model they embraced reflects a relatively recent phenomenon. Baptists have created confessions of faith since the beginning of their history—even before their formal institution, if one sees the beginnings of Baptist distinctives in Anabaptist traditions.[19] These confessional statements have been used primarily to regulate the voluntary association of Baptists throughout their history. When autonomous local churches align to work together, they need reasonable proof of like-mindedness to insure that the work develops toward mutually agreeable outcomes. Missionary activities require similar biblical convictions as prerequisite to working collectively toward the achievement of what Christ's commissioning entails. Articulating those convictions through biblical exegesis and stating them as an interpretative guide are essential for any voluntary association of individuals or churches working collectively.

However, a more recent tradition allows experience to guide interpretation and tends practically to downplay the Bible's role. This tradition emerged with an influential Baptist theologian of another generation. E. Y. Mullins ushered in an Enlightenment tradition that allows experience and individualism to trump the clear teaching of Scripture. As noted at the beginning of this chapter, this tradition is reflected among some of the leaders—at least past ones—within the IMB.[20]

The other stream of opposition comes from those advocating some form of postmodernism. The theory of religious truth upon which this movement is founded militates against collective affirmation of doctrinal beliefs as the basis for doing cooperative work. Taking Scripture to speak clearly makes one guilty of embracing the philosophical perspective of "modernity." These folks view embracing that perspective negatively simply because it fosters a degree of certainty when interpreting the Word of God.[21] One such advocate notes,

> The 2000 revision of [the *Baptist Faith and Message 2000*], however, reflects the current modernist concern for clarity and proposition as the standard of truth. It inserts the view that confessions, such as the 2000 BFM, serve as 'instruments of doctrinal accountability.' In other words, rather than a collective statement of

belief, confessions are to be seen as clear propositional expressions of Scriptural intent.[22]

Without clarity, certainty, or propositional truth that is attainable, understandable, and applicable, how does one conclude that missionary work is even necessary? Postmodern Baptists, expressing opposition to the *Baptist Faith and Message 2000*'s affirmation of Scripture as propositional truth, have difficulty building a Biblical theology of missions.

> Postmodernists, therefore, reject the validity of any grand account (or 'metanarrative') that presumes to fit the situation of *every* person in *all* places at *any* time, not only because such comprehensive narratives are understood as socially constructed local stories but also because their forced application to universal settings is oppressive.[23]

SUMMATION

The net effect of both streams of Baptist missionaries who reject the *Baptist Faith and Message 2000* is to affirm the view that Scripture is *not* God's Truth once delivered for all time, that it *cannot* be interpreted with certainty, that some sort of experiential ephemeral "Jesus" (who should not be confused with the Jesus of Scripture) is the ground of our being and the primary authority for our faith and practice. Consequently, in their view, it is fallacious to write down individual or collective interpretations as guidelines for engaging in joint religious activities or voluntary mission work among otherwise autonomous Baptist churches. Additionally, with this set of epistemological convictions, they have no basis for assuming that the Gospel applies to anyone else, especially when engaging in mission work to adherents of other world religions. Hence, we have no Story to tell the nations, only stories from our own relative experiences. The ground for missionary activity is removed because we cannot interpret, with any degree of conviction, Christ's words as recorded in the New Testament, at least not beyond one's own individual life circumstances.

> Our words are culture-bound, provincial, and particular. Such human constraint militates against our making magisterial declarations for a universal audience. . . .
> Yet this does not weaken our witness, for the most convincing word we share is the story we tell about our own discovery of light.[24]

No wonder R. Keith Parks asserts that Baptists should rally around the cause of missions in lieu of doctrine. Since doctrinal convictions are supposed to be relative and individualized, we should simply skip discussion of them and go on to do what we think is mission or evangelistic work, with no basis for defining such work apart from our subjective experiences and assumptions. This is remarkably similar to living in a house with no foundation. It may look solid to the naked eye, but it will likely not withstand the gathering storm of secular encroachment.

NOTES

1. R. Keith Parks, "An Afterword of Warning" in *Stand With Christ: Why Missionaries Can't Sign the 2000 Baptist Faith and Message,* ed. Robert O'Brien (Macon: Smyth & Helwys, 2002), 151.

2. For the context of the document, see its preamble on pp. 193–99 of this volume.

3. For development of the historic position of Baptists on the inerrancy of the Bible, see L. Russ Bush and Tom J. Nettles, *Baptists and the Bible: The Baptist Doctrines of Biblical Inspiration and Religious Authority in Historical Perspective* (Chicago: Moody, 1980).

4. *Christianity Today,* "Baptists Fire Missionaries: Thirteen Missionaries Fired and Twenty Resign Over the Baptist Faith and Message," 47, no. 7 (June 2003), 24.

5. For a polemical justification of this argument, see Robert O'Brien, ed., *Stand With Christ: Why Missionaries Can't Sign the 2000 Baptist Faith and Message* (Macon: Smyth & Helwys, 2002).

6. See David J. Hesselgrave, *Paradigms in Conflict: 10 Key Questions in Christian Missions Today* (Grand Rapids: Kregel, 2005), 20. Hesselgrave poignantly emphasizes this significant point: "Although changes there must and will be, the future of Christian missions will depend more on changes that are not made than it will on changes that are made."

7. Gal. 1:6–9.

8. What are now termed "unreached people groups" have been variously defined. For present purposes, a functional definition provided by the Lausanne Committee for World Evangelization Strategy Working Group is "a significantly large sociological grouping of people who perceive themselves to have a common affinity for one another. . . . From the viewpoint of evangelization, this is the largest possible group within which the Gospel can spread without encountering barriers to understanding or acceptance." Cited by Samuel Wilson, "Peoples, People Groups," *Evangelical Dictionary of World Missions,* ed. A. Scott Moreau (Grand Rapids: Baker, 2000), 744–46.

9. Matt. 24:14, 28:19–20; Mark 16:15; Luke 24:46–49; John 20:21; and Acts 1:8. Christ made commissioning statements in several places and on a number of occasions in the days prior to His ascension. This lends weight to the argument that the task of the Church is clearly delineated until He returns and that the Great Commission was not a passing footnote to His message. The coverage and scope of the commission is also clear—to all, everywhere, in any given era.

10. For a case study of this phenomenon, see Thom Rainer, "Evangelism and Missions, *BF&M* Article 11," in "An Exposition from the Faculty of the Southern Baptist Theological Seminary on *The Baptist Faith and Message 2000,*" www.sbts.edu/pdf/bfmexposition.pdf, 33–34; accessed 18 January 2007. For further discussion, see Timothy K. Beougher, "Life-

style Evangelism," *Evangelical Dictionary of World Missions*, ed. A. Scott Moreau (Grand Rapids: Baker, 2000) 578–79.

11. Rom. 10:13–15 clearly establishes the literal requirement for communicating the Gospel intentionally and objectively.

12. Eph. 4:15.

13. See note 9 above for commands laying the foundation for engaging in the global proclamation of the Gospel.

14. For articulation of the worship-based motivation for missionary activity, see John Piper, *Let the Nations Be Glad!* (Grand Rapids: Baker, 1993).

15. Mark Wingfield, "El Paso Missionary Recalls Rankin Pledged No Signing," *The Baptist Standard*, 8 April 2002; www.baptiststandard.com/2002/4_8/ pages/rankin.html; accessed on 9 January 2006.

16. Earl R. Martin, "Why Some Missionaries Won't Sign A Creed," in *Stand With Christ: Why Missionaries Can't Sign the 2000 Baptist Faith and Message,* ed. Robert O'Brien (Macon: Smyth & Helwys, 2002), 123–36.

17. For discussion of the nuances and background of the SBC's transformation, which has been in process since 1979 and remains so to this day, see Nancy Tatom Ammerman, *Baptist Battles: Social Change and Religious Conflict in the Southern Baptist Convention* (New Brunswick: Rutgers University Press, 1990).

18. Ron Hankins and Lydia Barrow-Hankins, "Open Letter," May 30, 2003; see www.mainstreambaptists.org/letters/hankins2.htm; accessed 29 December 2005.

19. See William L. Lumpkin, *Baptist Confessions of Faith*, revised (Valley Forge: Judson, 1969).

20. For description of how the Mullins tradition developed after 1925 in the SBC, see R. Stanton Norman, *More Than Just a Name: Preserving Our Baptist Identity* (Nashville: Broadman & Holman, 2001). For the theological methodology reflected by R. Keith Parks, past president of the IMB, see note 1 above.

21. See Tom Nettles, *Ready for Reformation: Bringing Authentic Reform to Southern Baptist Churches* (Nashville: Broadman & Holman, 2005), 8. Nettles adeptly describes the experiential basis for religious knowledge and interpreting the Bible extant in many academic settings on the eve of the Conservative resurgence in 1979. Today, it seems to be resurfacing under the guise of postmodernity.

22. T. D. F. Maddox, "Scripture, Perspicuity, and Postmodernity," *Review and Expositor* 100 (2003), 568–69.

23. Robert P. Sellers, "A Baptist View of Missions for Postmodernity," *Review and Expositor* 100 (2003), 645.

24. Sellers, "A Baptist View," 666–67.

•Article XII•

Education

Steve W. Lemke

$\mathscr{F}$ew confessional statements of any faith community include a separate statement on education. However, all three *Baptist Faith and Message* statements (1925, 1963, and 2000) contain an article on education (Article XX in 1925; Article XII in 1963 and 2000). Even before the 1925 version of the *Baptist Faith and Message* was written, E. Y. Mullins in 1912 (then president of the Southern Baptist Theological Seminary) included a separate section on education in his *Baptist Beliefs*,[1] though noting how unusual it was to include education as a doctrine. Raising education to the level of a confessional statement, particularly since little wording of the education article has been changed since the 1920s, flies in the face of the stereotype of Southern Baptists as rural, undereducated, and anti-intellectual. In fact, Southern Baptists have demonstrated a greater commitment to Christian higher education than almost any other American denomination. Southern Baptist state conventions have founded and maintain about fifty Baptist colleges and universities; and the Southern Baptist Convention's six seminaries are among the largest accredited seminaries in North America.

Why do Southern Baptists, whose roots were in poorly educated persons in the rural South, place such a high value on education? Primarily, Baptists understand Christian education as obedience to the Great Commission given by Jesus Christ before His ascension to "make disciples" of all nations by teaching them the truths of the faith (Matt. 28:19–20). The Great Commission is cited among the Scriptures supporting Article XII; Herschel Hobbs cited the Great Commission as a rationale for Baptist education in his commentary on the 1963 version of the *Baptist Faith and Message,* and in *Baptist Beliefs* E. Y. Mullins also specifically refers to the Great Commission as undergirding the imperative of education.[2] Article XII of the *Baptist Faith and Message 2000*

121

draws a direct practical connection between educational preparation and the effective kingdom of God, particularly the work of missions and benevolence.

Honing and sharpening an axe takes time, but that investment pays great dividends because a sharp axe can cut more wood more effectively in a shorter period of time than a dull one. God used many uneducated men such as James and John to achieve His work in exceptional ways, but He used the well-educated apostle Paul to make the greatest impact on the first-century world. As a rule, better-educated missionaries and ministers ordinarily make greater contributions and enjoy larger opportunities for service than dedicated servants of God who lack training.

In addition to its role in fulfilling the Great Commission, Mullins identified five distinctive Baptist doctrines that require an educated church.[3] First, a regenerate church membership requires education to grow in grace in sanctification. Second, our non-sacramental view of the ordinances requires that Baptists be instructed in the proper meaning and practice of these observances to understand their significance fully. Third, the democratic process through which Baptist polity functions according to the priesthood of all believers is greatly enhanced by an educated church membership. Fourth, better education can foster a more accurate interpretation of the Word of God. Fifth, knowledge and wisdom are essential to Christian leaders in order to discern the most effective means by which to extend the kingdom of God.

A biblical appreciation for education is grounded in the very nature of God. God the Father is the *source* of all truth (Ps. 31:5; Isa. 65:16). Since God created all things, all truth is God's truth.[4] All the treasures of wisdom and knowledge are in Him and His Son, Jesus Christ (Col. 2:3). Jesus Christ *embodies* the truth (John 1:14, 14:6; Col. 1:15–17, 2:2–9). Jesus is Truth incarnate. However profound the sum of all the learning of mankind, it is incomplete without Christ, for all things fit together in Him (Col. 1:17). Any worldview of which Jesus is not the key component has a fatal flaw. All truths are merely half-truths unless they are grounded in Him who is Truth (Col. 2:8–9). The Holy Spirit *leads* us to truth (John 14:16–17,26, 15:26, 16:7–14; 1 John 4:6, 5:6). The Spirit indwells believers and teaches us God's truth, particularly giving testimony to the truth of God made manifest in Jesus Christ (John 15:26; 16:14). The Spirit was instrumental in the inspiration of Scripture (2 Pet. 1:21). God's Word is the God-given *guideline* for truth (John 17:17; 2 Cor. 4:2; Heb. 4:12; 2 Tim. 2:15, 3:14–17; 2 Pet. 1:21). The Bible, inspired by God, is the plumbline or measuring stick by which we may discern the truth (2 Tim. 3:14–17).

Scripture places a high premium on the inherent and practical benefits of wisdom. While all three versions of the *Baptist Faith and Message* cite numerous biblical references affirming godly wisdom (Job 28:28; Prov. 3:13–26, 4:1–10, 8:1–7,11, 15:14; Eccles. 7:19; 1 Cor. 1:18–31; James 1:5, 3:17), the *Baptist*

Faith and Message 2000 includes four sentences at the beginning of the article from the 1925 version (which had been omitted in the 1963 version) explicitly praising the value of wisdom and knowledge. These statements identify Christianity as "the faith of enlightenment and intelligence" because in Christ "abide all the treasures of wisdom and knowledge." Far from the obscurantist position with which Baptists are sometimes stereotyped, the statement affirms "all sound learning" as "a part of our Christian heritage," and asserts that believers are uniquely positioned to learn because the new birth opens their faculties of understanding more fully and enhances their thirst for knowledge. Scripture often contrasts the pseudo-wisdom of the world from godly wisdom and warns believers against being deceived by false teachers (1 Cor. 1:18–31; 1 Tim. 1:3–7; James 3:17).

Two important means commended in Scripture for obtaining wisdom are instruction by godly teachers and prayerful reflection on God's Word. Because godly wisdom is highly valued in Scripture, the position of teacher is regarded as a sacred trust. As Hobbs notes in his commentary on the 1963 version of the *Baptist Faith and Message,* godly leaders are commanded in both the Old and New Testament to "teach," "instruct," and "edify" the people of God.[5] Many Scripture references cited in support of Article XII refer to this teaching ministry (Deut. 4:1,5,9,14, 6:1–10, 31:12–13; Matt. 4:2, 28:19–20; Eph. 4:11–16; 1 Tim. 1:3–7). Some of the Scriptures cited refer to the teaching ministry of outstanding godly leaders such as Moses (Deut. 4:5,14), Ezra (Neh. 8:1–8), and Jesus (Matt. 5:2). A teaching ministry is listed among the gifts of the Spirit (Eph. 4:11–16) as godly pastor-teachers edify the people of God through their teaching. Other Scriptures affirm the value of individual prayerful meditation on God's Word (Pss. 1:1–2, 19:7–14, 119:11; Phil. 4:8; 2 Tim. 2:15, 3:14–15; James 1:5). Godly teaching and meditation are focused on the principles, teachings, and admonitions of God's Word (Pss. 19:7–14, 119:11; Matt. 7:24–27; 2 Tim. 2:15, 3:14–17). The purpose of godly teaching and meditation is not to achieve a mystical experience, as in the case of some other religions, but for disciples to achieve life transformation and godly living (Deut. 4:1–14, 6:1–10; Pss. 19:7–14, 119:11; Prov. 3:13–26; Matt. 7:24–27, 28:19–20).

Christian education begins in the home. Parents have the primary responsibility for nurturing their children in godly instruction (Deut. 4:9, 6:2,7; Prov. 4:1–10; Eph. 6:4). All further instruction is supplementary to parental instruction. Local churches provide Christian education to complement and reinforce parental instruction. Discipleship is one of the crucial functions of a New Testament church (Acts 2:42). Even in the Old Testament era, the Word of God was read in public settings to people of all ages—men and women, adults and children (Deut. 4:1–14, 6:1–10, 31:11–13; Neh. 8:1–8). Christian churches have used a variety of means through the years to provide religious instruction.

Although Sunday School and small group Bible study are now a commonplace component of Baptist church life, it was not always so. The Sunday School movement was initiated by Robert Raikes in Gloucester, England, in the 1780s to provide Christian training for the poor children who worked all week long in the factories. The Sunday School movement was soon popularized in America with the encouragement of famous Americans such as Francis Scott Key and Daniel Webster. Despite its importance through the past century, however, Sunday School is just one tool in Christian education. Christian training can also be done effectively in cell groups, home Bible studies, weekend retreats, individual study, Vacation Bible School, and a variety of other venues.

Recognizing the significance of schools in the lives of children, many Baptist churches have begun their own schools to provide a Christian environment and instruction for their children's education. Article XII affirms that "an adequate system of Christian schools is necessary to a complete spiritual program for God's people." The statement in no way denigrates the value of secular education, but recognizes that secular education alone is not sufficient to meet all the needs of the church. We need dedicated Southern Baptist laypersons to be salt and light in the secular schools of our nation. However, Christian schools offer a distinctive contribution to the life of the church. As Mullins notes, "Christian education is not necessarily in conflict with education by the state," for in fact "they mutually supplement each other." However, "Christian ideals and the Christian type of civilization are dependent upon education under Christian auspices. Other things being equal, therefore, the denomination of Christians which most widely and most thoroughly promotes education will most deeply impress the world."[6]

Early in their history, Baptists realized the need for education beyond home and church, so Baptist colleges were established to provide higher-level training. J. P. Greene, president of William Jewell College for three decades, argued for Baptist schools in the original edition of *Baptist Why and Why Not*:

> Why education in Baptist colleges? Because when we own the colleges we can make them positively Christian. The word "Baptist" is dear to us, but not so dear as the word "Christian." We want our children to be Baptists, but Christians first. A Baptist college in name only will not please us. It must also be animated by the Spirit of Christ. The main reason for having our own colleges is that we may have Christian schools where we can educate our children.[7]

The pragmatic value of training lay leaders and ministers for Baptist churches was cited often as a major rationale for Baptist colleges. Confronted by a prominent Baptist layman who referred to a Baptist college "as a hopeless and needless institution" that could not compete with state colleges, renowned Baptist theologian and seminary professor A. T. Robertson reminded the layman that the majority of denominational leaders (both ministers and laypersons) were graduates of Baptist colleges rather than state colleges, and that Baptists could not succeed without an educated leadership.

> When the matter is thought through, it becomes plain that the question at bottom is one of denominational efficiency. . . . Without properly trained leadership no denomination can make headway today. It is immaterial what the cost to the denomination may be. It must have its denominational school or go out of business as a serious factor in modern life. This is not the whole case for the denominational college, of course, but it is the heart of it.[8]

J. P. Greene also praised the value of a denomination training its own young people, especially its young ministers.

> It is absolutely necessary that our young ministers be educated in Baptist colleges. . . . Some of the friends of "the new learning" think that preachers should be educated in secular schools, away from denominational traditions, and among young men of other callings. There is nothing in this. We would as well take a child away from his family, and thus save him from family traditions. . . . What is the matter with our denominational traditions? God gave us these preachers—they were begotten in these traditions. Unbelief is not producing any preachers, and therefore is not competent to educate ours. . . . Our colleges must be "feeders" for the seminaries. This is the natural order: The Baptist college and then the Baptist seminary! It is well to remember also that secular learning does not like the theological seminary any better than it likes a denominational college. It would abolish Christian education entirely. It would have a "divinity school" of its own, divorced from creed and from the Bible.[9]

This pragmatic rationale did not lessen the academic quality of Baptist education, but on the contrary reinforced high scholarly standards. As Robertson asserted, Baptist collegians should not "receive an inferior grade of culture," for "nothing but the best can meet the demands for Baptist culture in the South today."[10] Baptist institutions thus were not created to be just like secular schools; they were created to provide "added value"—providing quality education from within a distinctively Christian perspective. Institutions which bear the name "Christian" or "Baptist" are pledging to their denomination, donors, students, and parents that they will provide a Christian environment for their students, and instruction from within a Christian worldview.

As our students are confronted by competing and hostile worldviews in our pluralistic, secular society, the recovery of a Christian foundation or worldview is a crucial task of Christian education. Worldviews address such questions as: "Where did we come from? Who are we? What has gone wrong with the world? What solution can be offered to fix it?"[11] That God is Creator of all things (Gen. 1:1) and that all reality coheres in Christ (Col. 1:17) are two fundamental building blocks of the Christian worldview. As David Dockery notes, the Christian worldview points "to a unity of knowledge, a seamless whole because all true knowledge flows from the one Creator to his one creation."[12] Faith and learning are thus compatible and mutually supportive, and Christian presuppositions can inform every discipline. In addition to deepening students' appreciation of the Christian worldview, Christian colleges should train students to think in a distinctively Christian way. As T. S. Eliot asserted, "A Christian education must primarily teach people to be able to think in Christian categories."[13] The New Testament calls believers to love God with all their minds (Matt. 22:37–40), to achieve life transformation by the renewing of their minds (Rom. 12:2), to focus their thoughts on godly things (Phil. 4:8), and to take every thought captive to Christ (2 Cor. 10:5). If all things cohere in Christ (Col. 1:17), only those with Christian presuppositions have the proper frame of reference to comprehend fully how everything fits together.

In our increasingly secularized world, Christian presuppositions are often disdained.[14] This devaluation of Christian thought is expressed compellingly but disturbingly by Isaac Kramnick and L. Laurence Moore in an aptly entitled article, "The Godless University," in *Academe*, a publication of the American Association of University Professors. "Without a doubt," they write, "we live in an intellectual world where committed theism, but not atheism, is presumed to get in the way of learning."[15] Most Christian colleges have felt in the middle of a tug-of-war between academic excellence (as defined by the secular world) and Christian doctrinal distinctives (as defined by the church). While this bifurcation may arise from a false dichotomy, the pressure of being dismissed as irrelevant by one's scholarly guild is very real to any reputable scholar.[16] Such pressure has led many institutions founded by Christian denominations to abandon their denominational identity in order to become academically oriented private colleges.[17] George Marsden summarizes the pattern of colleges shedding their Christian identity as documented in James Burtchaell's landmark work *The Dying of the Light*, which traces the abandonment of church affiliation in colleges associated with seven different faith traditions.

> Yet in all but a few cases the colleges have moved inexorably from strong denominational identities to non-sectarian Christian identities, to an essentially deistic religious humanism, to a "respect" for their religious heritage (or being "rooted" in it) and an emphasis on "values." What makes Burtchaell's accounts delightful is his ear for the vapid rhetoric that covers up the abandonment of

central Christian teachings. Invariably the administrators who oversee the major transitions assure supporters and alumni that they are actually strengthening their heritage by emphasizing its spirit over its letter. Such "elegant and earnest inanity" (51), he concludes, is "more delusional than deceitful" (850), but all the more persuasive because it is sincerely meant. Once the substance of Christianity is removed from the rhetoric, it is left for the next generation to demote the original denominational sponsors to a "heritage" and to point to things like open-mindedness, a respect for persons who differ, or to wheelchair ramps as evidence that the heritage is still intact.[18]

Some of the best academic institutions in America were founded by Baptists as fruits of the First and Second Great Awakenings, including Brown University, Bucknell University, the University of Chicago, Colgate University, Rochester University, Temple University, Colby College, and Vassar College.[19] Unfortunately, all these schools completely abandoned their Baptist identity decades ago. Beginning with Baylor University in 1990, the last two decades have witnessed nearly another dozen formerly Baptist-related colleges sever or significantly redefine their relationship with the Baptist state convention which birthed and funded them with millions of dollars—including Averett University, Georgetown College, Grand Canyon University, Mercer University, Meredith College, Palm Beach Atlantic University, the University of Richmond, Stetson University, Wake Forest University, and William Jewell College. Three additional institutions (namely, Missouri Baptist University, Belmont University, and Shorter College) have attempted unsuccessfully to escape Baptist ownership. In most cases, the colleges moved to be autonomous of their Baptist state conventions by amending their charters to create self-perpetuating boards of trustees (including non-Baptists) rather than continuing to have trustees elected by the Baptist state convention. Although some of these schools continue to speak of their Baptist heritage, the lengths to which they have gone to sever their relationships with their sponsoring state Baptist entities make it clear that they view continued close association with Baptists as repugnant. As Carl F. H. Henry has remarked, "For one reason or another, Baptists seem often unable to preserve their academic institutions for the mission for which their founders established them."[20]

How can Baptists keep their institutions committed to the integration of faith and learning? In a study funded by the Lilly Endowment, Michael Beaty and Larry Lyon, two faculty members of Baylor University, studied how Christian institutions approach the integration of faith and learning. Beaty distinguished several approaches to the role of religious commitments at a Christian university.[21] The first position is a secularized "minimalist" perspective that understands faith and learning to be "separate and largely antagonistic areas of interest," with the very idea of a Christian university to be "an oxymoron" and "an anachronism."[22] A second position also perceives faith and learning to be two separate realms, and limits the role of faith from being integrated fully into the institution's life. Both faith and learning are seen as having value in this "two spheres view," but "mingling religious and academic commitments simply makes for confusion."[23] The role of faith is limited to the caring environment of the school, to private or public extracurricular religious expressions, or to a handful of courses in religion or ethics. In a third perspective, faith and learning are not perceived as separate areas, but rather they stand in some organic relation to one another. The school's religious commitment is integrated into the entire curriculum and throughout the life of the institution.

According to Beaty, the "two spheres" understanding of the relation between faith and learning, which bifurcates religious beliefs and academic pursuits into two separate spheres and tends to limit the role of faith to a caring environment on campus, is the majority view at Baylor and other Christian universities.[24] In this two spheres perspective, Beaty observes, a Christian university does "everything a state university did and more" by offering "the best possible education in a Christian or at least caring environment."[25] The danger of this approach, according to Beaty, is that "the less relevant religious beliefs become to the definitive tasks of a university, the more universities truncate and marginalize the influence of such beliefs. If such beliefs have a role at all, it is safely on the periphery of university life, relegated to the extracurricular. . . . Put more forcefully, the two spheres view cannot be a solution to Baylor's crisis, because in an important way it is a symptom of that crisis."[26]

The Christian faith dimension of a Baptist institution should not be marginalized to merely providing a caring environment, encouraging private spiritual experiences, or offering personal extracurricular religious activities. Baptists offer care for students, spiritual encouragement, and extracurricular religious activities on virtually *every* college campus in America (both secular and church-related) through Baptist Campus Ministry programs, so offering various extracurricular spiritual activities on a Baptist college campus offers little beyond what is available at secular universities. If a college's relationship to its denomination amounts to nothing more than treating students with respect or providing a few extracurricular activities, Baptists might rightly wonder whether their gifts of many millions of dollars through the years were a wise investment.

Several recent proposals require more from Baptist institutions than merely a Christian atmosphere on campus,[27] a denominationally committed administration, a Bible course in the curriculum, or even a confessional statement.[28] The "something more" of these proposals converges on the need for a genuine integration of faith and learning at Baptist institutions of higher education. John Kuykendall, president of Methodist-related Davidson College voiced this expectation of "something more" from a Christian institution in his commencement address to the class of 1990:

> Has anyone ever come right out and told you that this is a Christian college? Not "church-related," but Christian? . . . Have we told you that Davidson means to be Christian—that Davidson College stands within a living tradition which intends to hold together the things of the mind and the things of the spirit; with the conviction stated in our constitutional document that "Jesus Christ" is the central fact of history, giving purpose, order, and value to the whole life; and that God is "the source of all truth." . . . Have we told you that you have an obligation as a member of this community—an obligation which continues into alumni status—to deal seriously with that truth both in your intellectual life and in your moral life?[29]

Although Baptists expect their colleges to reflect Christian standards and beliefs, they expect even higher standards from Baptist seminaries. From their earliest days, Baptist seminaries have taken confessional statements seriously. James P. Boyce delivered a famous inaugural address, entitled "Three Changes in Theological Institutions," to the trustees of Furman University at the inception of a seminary within the college which eventually became the Southern Baptist Theological Seminary.[30] The three changes Boyce proposed were to (1) maximize the number of trained ministers by creating a multitiered system of theological education that allowed for admission of students who did not have a classical education; (2) provide exceptional quality of education such that the best Baptist scholars could develop their own theology without dependence on theological traditions alien to Baptist beliefs; and (3) assure doctrinal integrity by all the faculty affirming a confessional statement.[31] If it seems unusual that Baptists, who so proudly call themselves "people of the Book," would see benefits in utilizing a confession in this way, one should keep in mind that many Baptists in Boyce's day were led astray by Alexander Campbell and his slogan, "No creed but the Bible."[32] We can appropriate the Bible's truths fully only when God's Word is interpreted properly (2 Tim. 2:15–18). Confessions outline boundaries of proper interpretation within which faculty members can teach.

At the inception of the Southern Baptist Theological Seminary, Boyce led the faculty to adopt the "Abstract of Principles," which predated the first *Baptist Faith and Message* and remains a doctrinal confession both for that seminary and for Southeastern Baptist Theological Seminary. At its founding in 1917, the faculty of New Orleans Baptist Theological Seminary likewise wrote a confessional statement known as the "Articles of Religious Belief." All faculty members in the seminary's history have signed this doctrinal confession, and subsequently the *Baptist Faith and Message* as well. All the Southern Baptist seminary faculties have pledged to teach according to the *Baptist Faith and Message 2000.*

The motivation for writing each of the three versions of the *Baptist Faith and Message* arose in part from concerns about doctrinal orthodoxy at Baptist seminaries. The issue of Darwinism was a significant concern in the 1920s, the publication of Ralph Elliot's commentary on Genesis was a concern in the 1960s, and the Peace Committee identified doctrinal concerns at several seminaries in the 1980s. A number of steps were taken to address these concerns, including the presidents of all six Southern Baptist seminaries signing the Glorieta Statement in 1986 in concert with the Peace Committee,[33] and signing the "One Faith, One Task, One Sacred Trust" statement before the messengers of the Southern Baptist Convention in 1997, both of which pledged to maintain doctrinal orthodoxy at the seminaries.

> Let the churches of the Southern Baptist Convention know that our seminaries are committed to theological integrity and biblical fidelity. Our pledge is to maintain the confessional character of our seminaries by upholding those doctrines so clearly articulated in our confessions of faith; by teaching the authority, inspiration, inerrancy, and infallibility of the Bible; by maintaining the purity of the Gospel and affirming the identity of Jesus Christ, by whose blood we have been redeemed and in whose name alone salvation is to be found; and by proclaiming with boldness the precious and eternal truths of God's Word.[34]

In no way do these confessional commitments limit faculty or students from exploring the full dimensions of all fields of learning. One can study a controversial issue and discuss all perspectives on that issue fairly without advocating non-Christian perspectives. In fact, it is crucial for Christian apologists to comprehend fully the strengths and weaknesses of non-Christian perspectives.

Christian institutions of higher learning walk a delicate line between Christian doctrinal parameters and academic freedom. The *Baptist Faith and Message 2000* retains the three sentences on academic freedom and responsibility that were added to the 1963 version's article on education, which call for "a proper balance between academic freedom and academic responsibility," noting that freedom "is always limited and never absolute." The *Baptist Faith and Message* lists three limitations on the academic freedom of teachers in its schools: "the pre-eminence of Jesus Christ," "the authoritative nature of the Scriptures," and "the distinct purpose for which the school exists." All freedom is indeed limited and balanced by responsibility. We have many freedoms as Americans, such as the freedoms to drive cars and to speak freely. However, all of these freedoms have limitations. We can drive cars only if we pass driving tests, drive responsibly, and do not violate hundreds of traffic regulations, which could lead to the revocation of our license. Likewise, our freedom of speech is strictly limited so that slanderous or perjurious speech is not permitted. The three limitations on academic freedom stated in the *Baptist Faith and Message* are certainly modest. No one worthy of the name "Christian" could teach contrary to the pre-eminence of Jesus Christ or the authoritative Word of God. Teaching "for the distinct purpose for which the school exists" means to teach according to its purpose, mission statement, and confessional commitments. Can well-qualified Christian teachers with excellent academic credentials be found who will teach within these boundaries? J. P. Greene answered with a resounding "Yes, for every department of learning . . . !" because these persons prefer to teach in Christian schools:

> The "liberty" there offered them is the kind they desire. In unChristian schools they are fettered. Their unbelieving colleagues may assail the Christian religion, and be upheld on the plea of "liberty of investigation," but if they say a word for Christ they are called "sectarian." It would be a joy to their hearts to work with pious associates in a college where the Spirit of Christ reigns.[35]

Such doctrinal parameters are not unusual for a theological institution. A policy statement on academic freedom adopted by the national accreditation agency for theological institutions of all denominations, the Association of Theological Schools (ATS),[36] notes that "the freedom of the person of faith always involves a commensurate responsibility toward God and neighbor. It is never the freedom merely to be left alone or to ignore basic obligations."[37] The statement also notes that "freedom has specific import in the context of a religious confession of faith," "theological schools may acknowledge specific confessional adherence as laid down in the charters and constitutions of the schools," and both institutions and their faculties should "respect this confessional loyalty."[38] The ATS statement on "Principles of Academic Freedom" affirms that faculty members should be "free to teach, carry on research, and publish" and should "have freedom in the classroom to discuss the subjects in which they have competence . . . without harassment or limitations."[39] However, the statement continues, "In pursuit of the inquiry for truth, a theological school which has a confessional or doctrinal standard may expect that its faculty subscribe to that standard, and the requirement for such subscription should be mutually understood at the time of their affiliation with the institution," and cautions faculty members that their public statements at least imply "the tacit representation of their institution in whatever is said."[40] The *Baptist Faith and Message* statement on academic freedom and responsibility is thus perfectly compatible with the ATS guidelines.

As Baptists enter the twenty-first century, we are confronted by many challenges. We need great Christian colleges and seminaries to train the next generation of Southern Baptists. We must recover a vision of Baptist higher education for this century that openly embraces both educational excellence and the scandal of the cross. Jimmy Draper envisions this kind of Baptist university:

> In that university, you seek truth because you have already found it in Jesus Christ. In that university, you have freedom of thought because you have already submitted every thought captive to Jesus Christ as the source of all truth. In that university, you study complexity because you have already found simplicity in Jesus Christ. In that university, you gain wisdom because you have embraced the foolishness of the cross. It is in embracing the scandal of the cross that you find the dignity of learning.[41]

May God find us faithful in this sacred task!

NOTES

1. E. Y. Mullins, *Baptist Beliefs* (Louisville: Baptist World, 1912), 74–76.

2. Herschel H. Hobbs, *The Baptist Faith and Message,* reprint (Nashville: Convention, 1996), 97–100; Mullins, *Baptist Beliefs,* 74–76.

3. Mullins, *Baptist Beliefs,* 74–76.

4. For a fuller discussion of this claim, see Arthur Holmes, *All Truth Is God's Truth* (Grand Rapids: Eerdmans, 1977).

5. Hobbs, *The Baptist Faith and Message,* 97.

6. Mullins, *Baptist Beliefs,* 76.

7. J. P. Greene, "Why Education by Baptist Schools," in *Baptist Why and Why Not,* ed. J. M. Frost (Nashville: Sunday School Board of the Southern Baptist Convention, 1900); rev. ed., ed. Timothy and Denise George (Nashville: Broadman & Holman, 1999), 84. Lest Greene be accused of being merely an obscurantist anti-intellectual preacher, it should be noted that he was a vigorous proponent of academic excellence—for example, he was a charter member of the Western Philosophical Association. Tragically, the very college that Greene led for three decades has now forsaken its Baptist identity.

8. A. T. Robertson, "Baptist Colleges Are Essential (April 26, 1923)," in *The Best of A. T. Robertson,* ed. David Dockery, Denise George, and Timothy George (Nashville: Broadman & Holman, 1996), 227–28.

9. Greene, "Why Education by Baptist Schools," 81–84.

10. Robertson, "Baptist Colleges Are Essential," 228.

11. These worldview questions are posed by Gregory Alan Thornbury in "The Lessons of History," in *Shaping a Christian Worldview: The Foundation of Christian Higher Education,* ed. David Dockery and Gregory Alan Thornbury (Nashville: Broadman & Holman, 2002), 40–60.

12. David S. Dockery, "The Great Commandment as a Paradigm for Christian Higher

Education," in *The Future of Christian Higher Education*, ed. David S. Dockery and David P. Gushee (Nashville: Broadman & Holman, 1999), 12.

13. T. S. Eliot, *Christianity and Culture* (New York: Harcourt Brace, 1940), 22.

14. This secularist disdain for Christian thought and some of its consequences are well documented in Allan Bloom, *The Closing of the American Mind* (New York: Simon and Schuster, 1987); Stephen L. Carter, *The Culture of Disbelief: How American Law and Politics Trivialize Religious Devotion* (New York: Anchor, 1993); Christopher Jencks and David Riesman, *The Academic Revolution* (Garden City: Doubleday, 1968); George M. Marsden, *The Soul of the American University: From Protestant Establishment to Established Nonbelief* (New York: Oxford University Press, 1994), *The Outrageous Idea of Christian Scholarship* (New York: Oxford University Press, 1997); Mark A Noll, *The Scandal of the Evangelical Mind* (Grand Rapids: Eerdmans, 1995); and Douglas Sloan, *Faith and Knowledge: Mainline Protestantism and American Higher Education* (Louisville: Westminster/John Knox, 1994).

15. Isaac Kramnick and L. Laurence Moore, "The Godless University," *Academe* 81, no. 6 (November–December 1996), 21.

16. Michael Beaty recounts an early example of this challenge confronting Baylor University when a faculty member of the new University of Texas in 1890 described church-related colleges as "pious frauds" and called for their closure since the state had begun its own secular universities. See Michael Beaty, Todd Buras, and Larry Lyon, "Christian Higher Education: An Historical and Philosophical Perspective," *Perspectives in Religious Studies* 24, no. 2 (Summer 1997), 150–52. Stunned by this criticism, trustee president B. H. Carroll delivered an eloquent defense at the next convention of Texas Baptists. See "Report of the Board of Trustees of Baylor University at Waco," in *Proceedings of the Baptist General Convention of Texas, held at the First Baptist Church, Waxahachie, Texas, October 10–13, 1890* (Fort Worth: Mail, 1890), 31–38.

17. James Tunstead Burtchaell, *The Dying of the Light: The Disengagement of Colleges and Universities from Their Christian Churches* (Grand Rapids: Eerdmans, 1998).

18. George Marsden, review essay for *The Dying of the Light*, by James Burtchaell, in *Christian Scholar's Review* 29, no. 1 (1999), 177–78.

19. For more on how these Baptist-founded institutions abandoned their Baptist heritage, see Beaty, Buras, and Lyon, "Christian Higher Education," 144–65; Burtchaell, *The Dying of the Light*; Timothy George, "The Baptist Tradition," in *Theological Education in the Evangelical Tradition*, ed. D. G. Hart and R. Albert Mohler Jr. (Grand Rapids: Baker, 1996), 17–44; Carl F. H. Henry, "Baptists and Higher Education," in *Baptist Why and Why Not*, ed. Denise George, Timothy George, and Richard D. Land (Nashville: Broadman & Holman, 1997), 83–98; H. I. Hester, *Partners in Purpose and Progress: A Brief History of the Education Commission of the Southern Baptist Convention* (Nashville: Education Commission, 1977); William E. Hull, "The Crisis in Baptist Higher Education: An Historical Perspective," *Journal of the South Carolina Baptist Historical Society* 18 (November 1992), 2–13; Charles P. Johnson, *Higher Education of Southern Baptists: An Institutional History, 1826–1954* (Waco: Baylor University Press, 1955); Leon McBeth, *The History of Southern Baptist Higher Education* (Nashville: Education Commission, 1966); and Gregory Alan Thornbury, "The Lessons of History," in *Shaping a Christian Worldview*, 40–60.

20. Henry, "Baptists and Higher Education," 83.

21. Beaty and his collaborators actually developed several different typologies through the study to describe various approaches to faith in learning. One version of the three-tier typology is in Michael Beaty and Larry Lyon, "Integration, Secularization, and the Two-Spheres View at Religious Colleges: Comparing Baylor University with the University of Notre Dame and Georgetown College," *Christian Scholar's Review* 29, no. 1 (September 1999), 73–112. The three categories, as the title suggests, are (a) secularization, (b) the two-spheres view, and (c) integration of faith and learning. A similar three-tier typology with (a) the "minimalist conception," (b) the "minimalist-plus conception," and (c) an integrated conception is developed in Michael D. Beaty, "An Apology for the Christian University," available online at www3.baylor.edu/~Michael_Beaty/typology.html. A fourth category is added in Michael Beaty and Larry Lyon, "Religion and Higher Education: A Case Study of Baylor University," a preliminary report for the Lilly Endowment, available online at www3.baylor.edu/~Michael_Beaty/Lilly_Report.html, with the four categories being (a) total separation and antagonism of faith and learning, (b) faith and learning as separate and irrelevant to each other, (c) faith and learning as separate but equal, and (d) integration of faith and learning. This typology is expanded to seven categories in Michael Beaty, Larry Lyon, and Todd C. Ream, "Faith and Learning: Toward a Typology of Faculty Views at Religious Research Universities," *Christian Higher Education* 3 (2004), 349–72 to include (a) faith and learning as separate and independent; (b) limited integration of faith and learning in the campus environment, but not curricular; (c) integration of faith and learning limited to individual and private expressions, but not curricular; (d) integration of faith and learning limited to individual and public expressions, but not curricular; (e) integration of faith and learning limited to a very limited place in the curriculum; (f) faith and learning limited and specified in the curriculum; and (g) integration of faith and learning. In all these typologies, there is one secularist and one integrationist perspective, all the other iterations being varieties of the two-spheres perspective.

22. Beaty and Lyon, "Religion and Higher Education," 4; cf. Beaty, "An Apology for the Christian University," 1–2; Beaty, Lyon, and Ream, "Faith and Learning," 355–56; and Beaty and Lyon, "Integration, Secularization, and the Two-Spheres View at Religious Colleges," 73–75.

23. Beaty and Lyon, "Religion and Higher Education," 4–7; cf. Beaty, "An Apology for the Christian University," 1–2; Beaty, Lyon, and Ream, "Faith and Learning," 356–65; Beaty and Lyon, "Integration, Secularization, and the Two-Spheres View at Religious Colleges," 74–101; and Beaty, Buras, and Lyon, "Christian Higher Education," 154–64.

24. Beaty traces the articulation of this two spheres view as far back in Baylor University history as President S. P. Brooks (1902–1931), who asserted that Baylor served two independent yet equally important goals—the "material sphere" of human learning in the classrooms and the "spiritual sphere" to be cultivated through various extracurricular activities. See Beaty, Buras, and Lyon, "Christian Higher Education," 154–58.

25. Beaty and Lyon, "Religion and Higher Education," 6.

26. Beaty and Lyon, "Religion and Higher Education," 6–7.

27. Several excellent proposals, some of which are rather comprehensive and interdisciplinary, are in Dockery and Gushee, eds., *The Future of Christian Higher Education*; Dockery and Thornbury, eds., *Shaping a Christian Worldview*; Hart and Mohler, eds., *Theological Educa-*

tion in the Evangelical Tradition; Arthur Holmes, *The Idea of a Christian College* (Grand Rapids: Eerdmans, 1975); William E. Hull, "The Crisis in Baptist Higher Education" as well as "Christian Higher Education at the Crossroads," *Perspectives in Religious Studies* 19, no. 4 (Winter 1992), 441–43; and Harry Lee Poe, *Christianity in the Academy: Teaching at the Intersection of Faith and Learning* (Grand Rapids: Baker, 2004).

28. Although encouraging diligence in maintaining doctrinal fidelity and accountability, Gregory Thornbury's warning should be heeded: "Confessions alone, however, do not suffice to preserve the Christian character of the university if not utilized and remembered. To those institutions unwilling either to place or use the . . . confessions in the governing documents of the school, a warning: your identity as a Christian organization is as close to theological amnesia as a new president, dean, department chair, or influential faculty member (see Exod. 1:8)." Thornbury, "The Lessons of History," 58.

29. John Kuykendall, "Commencement Address," in *Davidson Journal* (Summer 1990), 18; cited in Michael Beaty, "An Apology for the Christian University."

30. James P. Boyce, "Three Changes in Theological Education (July 31, 1856)," in *Treasures from the Baptist Heritage,* ed. Denise and Timothy George (Nashville: Broadman & Holman, 1996), 103–38. Boyce was one of the founders and the first president of the Southern Baptist Theological Seminary, and also served nine times as president of the Southern Baptist Convention.

31. Boyce, "Three Changes," 103–38.

32. Timothy George, introduction to Boyce, *Treasures from the Baptist Heritage,* 5–6.

33. "Southern Baptist Convention Peace Committee," report in *Annual of the Southern Baptist Convention 1987* (Nashville: Southern Baptist Convention, 1987), 232–42; the Glorieta Statement is included on p. 235. The report is also available online at www.baptist2bap tist.net/b2barticle.asp?ID = 65.

34. "Proceedings, Southern Baptist Convention, Dallas, Texas, June 17–19, 1997," in *Annual of the Southern Baptist Convention 1997* (Nashville: Southern Baptist Convention, 1997), 86. The "One Faith, One Task, One Sacred Trust" statement is often included on the websites and publications of the seminaries. For example, *The Tie* (a publication of the Southern Baptist Theological Seminary) 65, no. 4 (August 1997), 2; Golden Gate Baptist Theological Seminary, *2002–2003 Catalog,* 117–18; Midwestern Baptist Theological Seminary, *Academic Catalog 2002–2004,* 81–82; and Southeastern Baptist Theological Seminary, *Academic Catalog 2003–2004,* 173.

35. Greene, "Why Education by Baptist Schools," 86.

36. "Academic Freedom and Tenure," a statement adopted as advice and counsel by ATS in 1976, in *Bulletin of the Association of Theological Schools in the United States and Canada* 46 (2005): 41–43; also available online at the ATS website.

37. *Bulletin of the ATS,* 41.

38. *Bulletin of the ATS,* 42.

39. *Bulletin of the ATS,* 42.

40. *Bulletin of the ATS,* 42–43.

41. Jimmy Draper, "A Vision for a Christian Baptist University," in *The Future of Christian Higher Education,* 22–23.

• Article XIII •

Stewardship

Barry K. Creamer

$\int$tewardship is not on the face of it a controversial subject. Still, every charitable organization dependent on continuing financial donations needs to state its understanding of stewardship. Such statements may take a variety of forms, but they all serve a pragmatic end. If nothing else, they remind donors—and potential donors—that their resources are something for which they ought to be grateful and which they ought to share. And, while statements on stewardship serve this pragmatic end in Southern Baptist life, they also do more. For, as Article XIII of the *Baptist Faith and Message* makes clear, the matter of stewardship touches on various theological and doctrinal matters as well as issues of discipleship.

EXPOSITION

It seems appropriate, then, to begin with an overview of the content of the *Baptist Faith and Message 2000*'s article on stewardship. Stewardship involves relations between an owner, a steward, a resource, and the purpose for which that resource is to be used. So Article XIII naturally divides into statements about these relations. It first addresses the relation between the Creator and His creation. It then moves to the relations between believers and the world, their material resources, the purpose of those resources, and finally their specific obligations and methods of giving. Of course, each part of the article is informed by the biblical passages included in the list of references at its conclusion.

God toward Humanity

God is the source of each good thing and therefore its ultimate owner. This fact serves as a basis for the article. Insofar as material wealth is a blessing, God is its source. But the article goes well beyond such wealth, claiming that God is the source of "all blessings." This echoes James 1:17, which tells us that God is the giver of every good gift.[1] So, as the Apostle Paul indicates in his address on Mars Hill, God's blessings extend beyond material wealth to life, breath, and all things.[2] The point is that, since God is the source of *all* good things and thus their owner, good stewardship concerns itself not only with material resources such as money but also with every other blessing from God—even life itself.

Humanity toward God

That all good things come from God gives rise to obligations associated with them. Of course, a host of underlying assumptions come into play here— assumptions which, though the article itself does not justify them, are nonetheless warranted. For instance, regarding humanity, it is assumed that with privileges and rights come responsibilities; regarding nature, it is assumed that a thing's purpose is determined by its origin. So if God provides a particular blessing, it is He who determines that blessing's purpose. Rom. 6:6–22, 12:1–2, and 1 Cor. 6:19–20—each of which is included in the list of references at the end of the article—undergird these assumptions. Such references, which appeal to the obligation of the redeemed to offer to God the fruits of their redemption, move us from the universal blessings bestowed upon all to the specific blessings bestowed upon the redeemed alone.

Believers toward the World

The first mention of a specific obligation in the article concerns the believer's responsibility to the world. While this responsibility is directed toward the world, its grounding comes from God Himself. Its source is the divine will. Specifically, Christians' responsibility to the world, rooted in their debt to God, is expressed as a "holy trusteeship in the gospel." As this implies, trusteeship involves first and foremost stewardship of the gospel itself. By putting the gospel first among resources for which Christians must give a good account as stewards, the article accomplishes a significant task in two ways. That task is to make clear that Southern Baptists hold evangelism (broadly construed) as their highest priority. It makes this clear by implying that God, whose ownership of the resources defines their purpose, has made reaching the lost world such a priority. But it also makes clear the importance of evangelism by implying that Christians' stewardship of *all* their resources ought to be aimed in one way or another to the ultimate purpose of reaching the unredeemed. Believers' responsibility regarding the gospel corresponds to God's desire concerning the unredeemed; the significance of stewarding all their resources corresponds to the significance of the task toward which God wishes to direct those resources—namely, saving those who are lost.

Believers toward Material Gifts

The article next turns to a more specific statement of the kinds of resources entrusted to the stewardship of Christians (namely, "time, talents, and material possessions") for their service to God. In referring to Matt. 25:14–29, the article puts a burden not only on the faithful who would use their resources to serve God but also on the unfaithful who would simply neglect their resources. Such neglect amounts to disobedience. Christians ought actively to seek ways to invest what God has given them in this world for the advancement of Christ's kingdom. To leave a resource unused is to misuse it.

Believers toward God and Man

Alms are almost certainly the best-known way of expressing selflessness with material resources. In fact, secular businessmen speak in terms of giving back to the community that has given so abundantly to them. But the *Baptist Faith and Message* allows no secularization. Even alms are understood so that faithful stewardship involves nothing less than a believer's commitment to Jesus' great commandments. Those commandments have two objects—love of *both* God *and* man. So the ultimate purpose for which a resource is entrusted to a believer is similarly twofold—*both* to glorify God *and* to help man.

By this point in the article it is also clear that references to passages like Matt. 19:21, Acts 2:44–47 and 20:35 invoke not only the importance for Christians of serving others with their material possessions, but also the importance of not being entrapped by self-serving materialism. The article obviously eschews serving material interests in favor of using material resources for the kingdom's sake.

Believers toward the Redeemer and Redemption

The article's last sentence contains the only change in it from the 1925 version to the 1963 one—the addition of the phrase, "According to the Scriptures," at the beginning of that sentence. As the biblical references listed at its end presumably attest, the entire article is "according to the Scriptures." So the 1963 version apparently deemed it necessary to make explicit the dependence of the point made in its last sentence—to wit, that believers should give to kingdom work "cheerfully, regularly, systematically, proportionately and liberally"— on Scripture. The sentence's short list of characteristics makes clear the importance of the giver's attitude. It appeals directly to some of the most oft-mentioned passages on stewardship in the New Testament (such as 1 Cor. 16:1–3 and 2 Cor. 9).

ISSUES AND CONTROVERSIES

Although little controversy attaches to the topic of Christian stewardship in general, some arises with regard to the particular form and strength of the steward's obligation. Among Southern Baptists, a disconnect seems to exist between what is commonly regarded as the benchmark of Christian giving, the tithe, and what can be justifiably required of the giver according to Scripture. Many thoughtful Southern Baptists not only tithe themselves but also expect others to do so as well, though they seldom provide warrant for this expectation from the New Testament. Article XIII refers to both the Old Testament passages usually taken to establish the tithe as the standard of giving (namely, Gen. 14:20, Lev. 27:30–32, and Mal. 3:8–12) and the New Testament passage usually taken as extending that standard into the Christian era (namely, Matt. 23:23). Ironically, however, the tithe itself is mentioned neither explicitly nor implicitly.

That the article on stewardship raises little controversy should not be construed as a sign that its topic is insignificant. Certainly, the authors of the various versions of the *Baptist Faith and Message* see stewardship as critically important, a fact underscored by their devoting an entire article to it. In his exposition of the confession's 1963 version, Herschel Hobbs explains its purpose:

> Baptists emphasize the soul's competency before God, freedom in religion, and the priesthood of the believer. However, this emphasis should not be interpreted to mean that there is an absence of certain definite doctrines that Baptists believe, cherish, and with which they have been and are now closely identified. It is the purpose of this statement of faith and message to set forth certain teachings which we believe.[3]

Hobbs thus understands the *Baptist Faith and Message*'s primary purpose to be the articulation of distinctively Baptist doctrines. Since such doctrines can be rightly understood only in the context of those commitments which all orthodox Christians share, however, the statement also articulates doctrines which Baptists take to be fundamental to Christian orthodoxy. In light of this, the inclusion in the confession of an article on stewardship indicates that its authors see the topic as either distinctively Baptist (and thus an important part of Baptist identity) or fundamental to that faith once for all delivered over to the saints (and thus an important part of Christian orthodoxy).

There are at least a couple of reasons for the doctrine's importance. First, stewardship concerns the disposition of private property. From the eighth commandment, "Thou shalt not steal," to John Locke's right to life, liberty, and property,[4] it has long been held that property brings with it both rights as well as responsibilities. As Article XIII implies, good stewards recognize that rights and responsibilities derive from God, to whom all things ultimately belong. So, then, the theological basis for the doctrine of stewardship is twofold. On one hand, God is the ultimate owner of all things; on the other hand, He has entrusted us with possessions with respect to which we have both privileges and obligations. And, in Article XIII, that twofold basis manifests itself in two significant ways. It first recognizes one's responsibility to use material possessions rightly (in accordance with God's will for them); it then recognizes the discretionary nature of stewardship (so that, within the context of the responsibility to use them rightly, one has freedom to dispose of one's possessions as one sees fit). The voluntary nature of stewardship accounts for the opposition to communism of many conservative Christians who nonetheless recognize the biblical precedent of believers having all things in common.[5] In Baptist circles in particular, "having all things in common" means *voluntarily* sharing all things. Second, the doctrine of stewardship is also important because how one uses one's possessions provides a measure of faith and faithfulness.[6] For, of course, the love of money is "the root of all evil,"[7] and unfaithfulness with respect to it points to unfaithfulness in other areas of life as well.[8]

But why does so little controversy attach to Article XIII? Here an answer is not difficult to find. The *Baptist Faith and Message* seeks to identify the distinctive commitments of Southern Baptists. And, as indicated above, one of the most deeply held commitments among Southern Baptists concerns missions both at home and abroad. Indeed, one could rightly describe Baptists' primary self-understanding with the phrase, "Bible and mission." We are certainly "a people of the book"; and we are just as surely a missional people. Great mission efforts, however, require great stewardship. This fact puts stewardship at the center of Southern Baptist life and thus explains its relatively uncontroversial standing there. Perhaps not surprisingly, Southern Baptists seem quite successful when it comes to stewardship. Even the convention's detractors recognize the success of its efforts to send and support missionaries in the field. Indeed, the Southern Baptist Convention has experienced undeniable success in these areas and has developed the premier missions agencies in the world today.[9]

Curiously, however, its success in these areas may explain the need for the recent conservative resurgence within the convention. For success can lead to complacency, and in Christian work that can lead to bureaucratic entrenchment and doctrinal laxness. Whether such laxness takes the form of theological disinterest (which neglects orthodox doctrine) or desertion (which abandons it altogether) makes no difference. The result is a people adrift, without doctrinal moorings. Likewise, bureaucratic entrenchment can easily lead a denomination to forget—and subsequently neglect—the purposes for which it was founded.

The stability of the article on stewardship across various versions of the *Baptist Faith and Message* testifies to the undiminished commitment of Southern Baptists to work together for the advancement of Christ's kingdom. But the adjustments and revisions in many of the confession's other articles testify to the need for doctrinal diligence. For the commitment to work together for our Lord's kingdom will be effectual only in a context which affirms that faith once for all delivered over to the saints—which faith is, in the end, the message which Baptists have historically proclaimed.

NOTES

1. Interestingly, James 1:17 is not included among the passages listed at the article's end.

2. See Acts 17:16–31.

3. Herschel H. Hobbs, *The Baptist Faith and Message* (Nashville: Convention, 1971), 242–43.

4. Cf. John Locke, *The Second Treatise of Government*, ed. Thomas P. Peardon (New York: MacMillan, 1952), 5.

5. See Acts 4:32.

6. See Heb. 13:5–6.

7. See 1 Tim. 6:6–10.

8. See Luke 16:10–13.

9. Cecil and Susan Ray, *Cooperation: The Baptist Way to a Lost World* (Stewardship Commission of the Southern Baptist Convention, 1985), 103.

·*Article XIV*·

Cooperation

Chad Owen Brand

$\mathcal{O}$ne of the most complicated issues that has faced Christian churches over the centuries has been the question of cooperation. This was already an issue at the end of the first century. As the Apostles were dying off, churches began to face the question of how to handle disputes between congregations over doctrinal and practical matters. In some cities, a single bishop was appointed to govern all of the churches (which were often house-churches), and so became the court of appeal in such disputes. These bishops eventually assumed a greater and greater degree of authority, so that in time they held essentially apostolic authority in their own regions. This ensured, ideally, a kind of conformity and uniformity of churches in a particular area on matters of doctrine and practice, with local churches submitting to the bishop.

In actuality, it was not always quite so neat. Sectarian movements arose in some parts of the empire, such as the Donatists of North Africa. They resisted the evolving "catholic" consensus and appointed their own bishops, so that by around the year A.D. 400 they were nearly equal in numbers to the older tradition and had about as many bishops. But the Donatists considered "catholicism" to be spiritually corrupt and the "Catholics," for their part, saw the sectarians as schismatics who had divided the body of Christ. Throughout the centuries, then, the debate over cooperation has raged unabated.

CHURCH POLITY IN THE NEW TESTAMENT

The New Testament offers some real insights on the degree of cooperative ministry in the earliest churches. At the same time, it delineates for us an approach to ecclesiological concerns that fences off some possible approaches to cooperation. Even further, it features warnings about the potential dilution of the Christian message, a dilution that is all the more deadly when different churches band together and hold beliefs contrary to the Word of God.

New Testament churches were autonomous bodies under the Lordship of Christ, but they also engaged in significant cooperative ministry with one another. That these churches were not under the jurisdiction of some kind of "mother church" or of a body of key leaders is easily demonstrated from various texts. In Acts 6:3 the Twelve Apostles urge the Jerusalem church to "seek out from among you seven men of good reputation" (NKJV) to care for the Hellenistic widows. The church at Antioch sensed a command from the Holy Spirit to send missionaries to Galatia (Acts 13:1–3). The church did not consult with the Apostles or the Jerusalem church before embarking on this action, but simply sent out the men the Spirit led them to appoint for the task. It would not have been inappropriate to consult with the Apostles, of course, since they were men who had authority over all the churches, but it was not necessary for a local church to seek outside authorization to carry out its ministry. Ministry, then, is the responsibility of local congregations.

Local churches also have the responsibility to discipline members, ordain leaders, baptize new believers, and carry out other works of service within their own orbit of ministry. Discipline is a local church responsibility. In 1 Cor. 5, Paul rebukes the Corinthian church for failing to discipline a man living in gross sin. He grudgingly carries out a pronouncement of discipline from a distance since the Corinthians failed to do so in their own church life. The Apostle also reminds Timothy not to neglect the gift that was bestowed on him by the "laying on of hands by the presbytery" (1 Tim. 4:4). This "presbytery" was not some extra-ecclesial body governing the affairs of local churches from the outside, but was rather the elders appointed to govern local congregations from within (Acts 14:23). Baptism was also under the auspices of the local church. Paul makes this point clear by noting that he baptized only a handful of the Corinthians when he began his ministry there; doubtless the rest were baptized by newly appointed elders or deacons saved in the early days of that congregation. Local churches also have the responsibility to discern true teaching from false (2 Tim. 3:1–9), and to expel false teachers when they are discovered (1 John 2:19). Other responsibilities could be added to the list.[1] What is clear from these passages is that the local church carries out its own works of ministry and is fully qualified to do so since it is itself the body of Christ (1 Cor. 12).[2]

Some scholars have argued, on the other hand, that the Bible contains evidence of extra-ecclesial bodies exercising jurisdiction over local churches. These scholars are to be found largely in the Presbyterian and the Reformed denominations, especially in Great Britain and America, but also in parts of the

Continent. The major text adduced in defense of this position is Acts 15, where the Jerusalem church met with Paul and Barnabas to discuss the issue of Gentile evangelism. Some have argued that this is the first "presbytery" meeting mentioned in the NT, and that this passage supports the view that local churches are not autonomous, but instead are in some ways under the direction of such presbyterial bodies.[3] They further contend that these bodies comprise representatives from the various churches under their guidance, so that this constitutes a kind of representative body in many ways similar to the United States Senate. Representatives are sent up, and then rulings are passed down. A careful reading of Acts 15 will show, however, that this is a misinterpretation. If this were to be a representative body, delegates from all of the churches should have been present. But they are not. There is no one present from the other Judean churches, the Silician churches (other than Antioch), or the Galatian churches. This is a meeting of the church of Jerusalem, also attended by Paul and Barnabas from Antioch. No presbytery here.

Still others argue for another model in which persons and institutions outside or "higher" than the local church govern the affairs of local congregations. In this model, a system of bishops exercises oversight of churches within a region, or diocese. There is a wide diversity of types of this system, some being fairly simple with only a single level of such administrators scattered about in different localities, while others are multilayered, with archbishops ministering at a still higher level than the bishops, and in some cases with a single bishop at the top managing the entire structure. Roman Catholicism and the various Eastern Orthodox communions are examples of the latter, with Pope and Patriarchs, respectively, sitting at the highest level of governance. The Anglican Church also fits this description, and it is governed by the sitting monarch of England, with the Archbishop of Canterbury in the highest ecclesiastical position. Other "episcopal" denominations include Methodism and several Pentecostal and Holiness groups, such as the Church of God (Holiness) and the Church of God (Pentecostal). All of these have a system of bishops, but their structure is much simpler than the older and larger bodies.

Oddly enough, those who hold to such an ecclesiology often do not argue their case exegetically. Rather, they contend that this form of church order is the natural evolution from the apostolic churches of the first century.[4] When the Apostles died off, there was need for a new generation of apostolic leaders, and so "bishops" took over that role as the successors to the Apostles. This provided for both efficient solutions to disputes between churches and the settling of doctrinal questions. That the original Apostles might never have considered or condoned such a "solution" is not important, since the system itself has worked so well. That, of course, is the question, a question raised by those who have argued that there is no hint of such an arrangement in the NT. In other words, the NT nowhere states that bishops are to be successors to the Apostles. But that is not to say that we do not know just where "bishops" fit in to the system. The NT is actually clear on this; a "bishop" (literally, "overseer," from the Greek *episkopos*) is the same office as that of elder and of pastor. This is clear from passages such as 1 Pet. 5:1–5 where the terms overseer, elder, and pastor are used interchangeably about the same individual leaders. The office of bishop is not superior to that of elder or pastor, but is rather the same office.

My point is simple. Neither presbyterial nor episcopal structures of church order can be found in the NT. On the other hand, we do have many examples of congregational polity—that is, ministry done by local congregations under the Lordship of Jesus Christ. Cooperation between churches in ministry must not, therefore, be governed by authoritarian structures which place bishops, presbyteries, general assemblies, conventions, or any other organized structures or individuals above or from outside the authority of the local congregation. The question before us now is this: What kinds of cooperation between churches are to be found in the NT?

COOPERATIVE MINISTRY
IN THE NEW TESTAMENT

There was a considerable amount of cooperative ministry between churches and individuals in the early church. Peter and John were sent by the Jerusalem church to assist Philip the evangelist in his work among the Samaritans (Acts 8). This was not a case of the Jerusalem church intruding, but rather one in which this church offered glad assistance in the new work. The Apostles did not remain there to manage the work, but very soon returned to their own church to tell the good news of the salvation of the Samaritans.

A new Gentile mission was later begun in Antioch, and soon the Jerusalem church sent Barnabas to see what was happening (Acts 11:21). It was a wise decision to send Barnabas since he was a Cypriot Jew (Acts 4:36–37) and would have more sensitivity to a Gentile Christian work than some others from Jerusalem might have had. Barnabas saw an opportunity for a great work, and so traveled to Tarsus to ask Paul to come and join the new work in Antioch, and the two of them ministered there for a year. Certainly Barnabas was sent by the Jerusalem Christians, but they did not manage the situation. Nor would the Apostles have been likely to have recommended that Barnabas include Paul as an assistant in this work, since he still had a less than stellar reputation in that city (Acts 9:26). The point is that these two men went and offered their services, and the Antiochenes welcomed them and before long made them "members" of that church, from which Paul would carry out a wider ministry for many years.[5]

Other cooperative efforts included several examples of financial support for churches that were struggling. Paul mentions offerings for churches, especially for the Jerusalem church (Rom. 15:26; 1 Cor. 16:1–2; 2 Cor. 8–9). In Acts 11 Paul and Barnabas took an offering to the Christians in Jerusalem, an event that probably occurred in A.D. 46, since Josephus mentions a famine that hit Judea especially hard that year. In Rom. 15:26 Paul mentions a gift that was given by the Macedonian and Achaian Christians, calling it a "fellowship." On his third missionary journey Paul made repeated references to the needs of the Jerusalem Christians and encouraged the Romans and Corinthians especially to help out.

There was also considerable ministry sharing between early churches. Timothy was from Lystra, but even before he traveled with Paul there is evidence that he had ministered in nearby Iconium as well as his home church. During Paul's second missionary journey he enlisted Timothy's assistance in his itinerant ministry so that through their joint efforts, "the churches were being strengthened" (Acts 16:5). At Troas, Luke joined Paul's team, and after traveling with him to Macedonia, the Apostle left Luke in Philippi in order to help encourage this new church for a period of time (Acts 17:1).[6] More examples could be assembled, but this should make it clear that churches assisted one another in joint, mutually agreeable, cooperative efforts in ministry.

POTENTIAL PITFALLS OF COOPERATION

Christian churches must face the question of just what kinds of cooperation are appropriate and which ones are not. Certainly it would be unacceptable to be engaged in ministry with non-Christian groups, though some would find it acceptable to join hands with some such groups in moral or humanitarian causes. Our focus here, though, has to do with ministry issues related to eternal salvation and to the truths of the faith.

Throughout the history of the church Christians have had to face the problem of heresy or false teaching. "Heresy" has generally been defined as holding to false teachings on the major doctrinal issues Christians hold dear, especially those doctrinal issues outlined by the early creeds—Trinity, the deity of Christ, redemption by Christ, the fact of the Second Coming, and so on. Joining with heretical movements that deny these cardinal truths is unwise, since they essentially teach "another gospel." Likewise, churches and movements that have been seduced by the theological relativism associated with liberalism are also moving in a theological vortex that is outside the pale of biblical faith.

There is also the issue of "levels" of cooperation. Churches that hold to different kinds of polity (such as congregational and presbyterial) might be able to work together in an area evangelistic effort, if they both hold to the faith once delivered to the saints, but would probably not be able to work together more closely within the same associational or denominational structure since their ecclesiology is so different. It would also be difficult to imagine how Christians who hold strong, opposing convictions about what the Bible teaches on such matters as, e.g., infant baptism/believers' baptism could work and minister together in the same congregation. It is important to be able to affirm our common faith in Christ, even if we cannot walk hand in hand in every venture.

STEWARDS OF A COMMON WORK

Southern Baptist churches have long had a commitment to work together to carry out the work of mission and evangelism in our world. They have been passionately committed to mission, and to everything that goes into making mission possible for a very long time. Since 1925, they have also been committed to a method for carrying out that work with other Southern Baptist churches, a method known as the Cooperative Program. Churches usually send a percentage of their revenues to the state conventions, and those conventions then send a percentage to the SBC Executive Committee. These monies are used by state conventions and the SBC in carrying out the various mandates of mission, education, benevolence, and other ministries.[7] In this way, Southern Baptists have done much valuable work in furthering kingdom causes. Though struggles still persist over how "cooperation" works even between Southern Baptist churches, they continue to commit themselves to the task of reaching a world for Christ through cooperation in ministry at every level.

NOTES

1. For a more complete treatment, see Chad Owen Brand and David E. Hankins, *One Sacred Effort: The Cooperative Program of Southern Baptists* (Nashville: Broadman & Holman, 2005), 43–52.

2. In 1 Corinthians one of Paul's major points of concern is division within the congregation. He argues in chapter 12 that this division is unacceptable since the body of Christ is one. That point obviously entails that each individual congregation is in a sense the body of Christ in itself. It is also true that the entirety of Christ's people compose his body, a point

Paul seems to be making in Col. 1:18. In other words, it is the case both that each congregation is the body of Christ (in microcosm) and that all believers compose the body of Christ at one and the same time.

3. See, for example, Robert L. Reymond, *A New Systematic Theology of the Christian Faith* (Nashville: Nelson, 1998), 895–900.

4. Paul F. M. Zahl, "The Bishop-Led Church," in *Perspectives on Church Government: Five Views of Polity*, ed. Chad Owen Brand and R. Stanton Norman (Nashville: Broadman & Holman, 2004), 214–43.

5. See the discussion on this series of events in Brand and Hankins, *One Sacred Effort*, 65–66.

6. The point here is that the last half of Acts 16 is written in the first person, as Luke was with Paul. But beginning in 17:1, Luke writes in the third person, until 18:5 where Paul again appears at Philippi and Luke rejoins the team, writing again in the first person.

7. See Brand and Hankins, *One Sacred Effort*, 110–17, 126–59.

• *Article XV* •

The Christian and the Social Order

C. Ben Mitchell

$\mathcal{W}$illiam Faulkner once said that being a Southern Baptist was an "emotional condition that has nothing to do with God or politics or anything else."[1] Had the eminent Mr. Faulkner known his history better, he would have known that Southern Baptists have had a social consciousness since their founding in 1845. After all, one of the impetuses of the founding of the Southern Baptist Convention (SBC) was the controversy over whether missionaries could own slaves. Even though our forbears were on the wrong side of that particular issue, slavery was, and still is, a social issue.[2]

THE HISTORY OF SOUTHERN
BAPTIST SOCIAL ENGAGEMENT

It is also true, however, that beyond slavery, social concerns were not high on the agenda in the nascent denomination. Missions, both foreign and domestic, took precedence over nearly everything else. The preamble to the constitution of the SBC states that messengers gathered in Augusta, Georgia, in 1845 "for the purpose of carrying into effect the benevolent intention of our constituents, by organizing a plan for eliciting, combining, and directing the energies of the whole denomination in one sacred effort, for the propagation of the Gospel."[3] Nevertheless, one phrase in that original constitution proved to be a harbinger of things to come: "It shall be the design of this Convention to promote Foreign and Domestic Missions, and *other important objects connected with the Redeemer's kingdom.*"[4] The final clause in that sentence made clear that the mission of the convention had entailments that might lead to projects additional to missions *per se.* That is not to argue, of course, that local congregations were not already engaged in social ministry of some sorts. The Baptist churches that inaugurated the SBC had been in existence for some time, and doubtless they were as active in their own communities as other churches, but their social engagement is beyond the scope of this chapter.

The institutional history of Southern Baptist engagement in social concerns is long and interesting. A few highlights must suffice. From its genesis to the turn of the twentieth century, Southern Baptist social and ethical concern focused primarily on temperance, despite the fact that in 1888 James P. Boyce, the founder of the Southern Baptist Theological Seminary and the then president of the SBC, ruled out of order two resolutions on temperance as not germane to the work of the denomination.[5] From 1900 to 1914, Southern Baptist social concern began to take shape. During this period, on a motion by George Hillyer of Georgia, the Committee on Civic Righteousness was formed under the chairmanship of A. J. Barton, who had held positions with both home and foreign mission boards, three state convention offices, and pastored in Tennessee, Arkansas, Texas, Louisiana, and North Carolina. In other words, he was well known and trusted by his peers.[6] The Committee made its first report to the denomination at the annual meeting in 1908.[7] The report began with a somewhat populist declaration: "Strong men with statesman principles have proven that the masses of the people will eagerly support righteous leaders for noble ends"; a somewhat postmillennial theological affirmation: "Civic Righteousness and the kingdom of God are bound up in each other. We are learning anew that Christ's commission to his followers is not primarily to increase the census of heaven, but to make down here a righteous society in which Christ's will shall be done, his kingdom come"; and a clarion call for Southern Baptists to "resist the encroachments of evil upon our body social and body political, and to enlist ourselves as aggressive builders of the new order. . . ."[8] Even though this statement seems to invoke a broad social agenda, the convention's efforts during this first decade of the new century actually centered almost exclusively on opposition to alcohol. In fact, at the 1908 convention a standing Committee on Temperance, led by A. J. Barton, was formed. "We will preach temperance, practice temperance, pray for temperance, and vote for temperance," declared the committee.[9]

Southern Baptist social concern expanded and broadened from 1914 to 1953. In 1913, J. N. Prestridge, who had made the 1908 report on temperance, moved the formation of a standing committee that might enjoy success fighting problems other than alcohol. In 1914, the Convention created the Committee on Social Services, which absorbed the Committee on Temperance. Nevertheless, the Committee on Social Services embraced a much more comprehensive ambit than its parent. Giving the first report of the Committee, W. L. Poteat, then president of Wake Forest College, opined that the kingdom of God is "the organic expression of the Will of God in human relations, an all-embracing social ideal to be realized in . . . the early life of man . . . the will of God operative and controlling in the individual and social life."[10] As Southern Baptist historian Leon McBeth points out, several sections of the report are remarkable for their scope: "upon business the church must impose its enobling restraints. It must check private greed and compose class antagonisms. It must erect the Christian standard in the marketplace, and insist that the labor of women and children be regulated . . . that the industrial system provide a minimum of necessary working hours with the maximum of wholesome life conditions, and that the workers have a fair share in the prosperity they produce."[11] Moreover, observes McBeth, "The report insists that 'the Christian Church is directly responsible for the right solution of social problems' such as war, alcohol, vice, and disease. The report emphasizes the sanctity of personal health and urges more attention to public sanitation" and calls on the church "to provide for the poor, the sick, and the defective, and what is more important, to provide against them."[12]

On May 16, 1920, the year Prohibition went into effect, George W. Truett, a member of the Social Services Committee and pastor of the First Baptist Church of Dallas, delivered from the east steps of the nation's Capitol his famous sermon on "Baptists and Religious Liberty" to 15,000 onlookers.[13] J. B. Gambrell said of the sermon,

> Since Paul spoke before Nero, no Baptist speaker ever pleaded the cause of truth in surroundings so dignified, impressive and inspiring. The shadow of the Capitol of the greatest and freest nation on earth, largely made so by the infiltration of Baptist ideas through the masses, fell on the vast assembly, composed of Cabinet members, Senators and members of the Lower House, Foreign Ambassadors, intellectuals in all callings, with peoples of every religious order and of all classes.
>
> The subject was fit for the place, the occasion and the assembly. The speaker had prepared his message. In a voice clear and far-reaching he carried his audience through the very heart of his theme. History was invoked, but far more, history was explained by the inner guiding principles of a people who stand today, as they have always stood, for full and equal religious liberty for all people.
>
> There was no trimming, no froth, no halting, and not one arrogant or offensive tone or word. It was a bold, fair, thorough-going setting out of the history and life principles of the people called Baptists. And then, logically and becomingly, the speaker brought his Baptist brethren to look forward and take up the burdens of liberty and fulfill its high moral obligations, declaring that defaulters in the moral realm court death.

Truett's sermon maintains that, while whoever "believes in Christ as his personal Saviour is our brother in the common salvation, whether he be a member of one communion or of another, or of no communion at all," Baptists have a particular stake in protecting "the priceless principle" of religious liberty and preserving "a free church in a free state." Since Baptists submit to the absolute Lordship of Christ, affirm that the Bible alone is the rule of faith and practice, and believe in liberty of conscience before God, they repudiate, said Truett, "any attempt to force the conscience, or to constrain men, by outward penalties, to this or that form of religious belief. Persecution may make men hypocrites, but it will not make them Christians." He declared to the throng:

> God does not raise up a nation to go strutting selfishly, forgetful of the high interests of humanity. National selfishness leads to destruction as truly as does individual selfishness. Nations can no more live to themselves than can individuals. Humanity is bound up together in the big bundle of life. The world is now one big neighborhood. There are no longer any hermit nations. National isolation is no longer possible in the earth. The markets of the world instantly register every commercial change. An earthquake in Asia is at once registered in Washington City. The people on one side of the world may not dare to be indifferent to the people on the other side. Every man of us is called to be a world citizen, and to think and act in world terms. The nation that insists upon asking that old murderous question of Cain, "Am I my brother's keeper?" the question of the profiteer and the question of the slacker, is a nation marked for decay and doom and death. The parable of the Good Samaritan is Heaven's law for nations as well as for individuals. Some things are worth dying for, and if they are worth dying for they are worth living for.

Things worth dying for, Truett maintained, include "the sanctity of womanhood," "the safety of childhood," "the integrity of one's own country," and "the freedom and honor of the United States."

Finally, he called his hearers to be "the right kind of Christians"—Christians who support informed democracy, reinvigorate Christian schools, win souls unto salvation, and, who, with Wesley, see that "the world is my parish."

In that same year, 1920, the Committee on Temperance and Social Service report included a statement on race relations and a change in the name of the committee to the Social Services Commission. Thirteen years later, in 1933, Edwin McNeill Poteat called for an expansion of the committee's agenda to include "a more comprehensive and direct leading with the great social issues of the South." Bogged in controversy, the report from the committee three years later was tabled.

The World War II years were formative in the life of the Social Services

Commission. A. J. Barton died in 1943, and J. B. Weatherspoon, a professor at the Southern Baptist Theological Seminary, was elected as chairman. Alcohol, race relations, and war and peace became dominant themes. Under his leadership a "new rationale" was fashioned for the Commission, moving it beyond a mere reporting agency to "a genuine and forthright concern for the social, political, and economic procedures in whose creation and direction our nation and our God have committed to us the responsibility of sharing."[14] On a recommendation from the Executive Commission of the SBC, an initial budget of $10,000 from the Cooperative Program was offered to the Social Services Commission, which immediately hired a full-time professional staff.

The Commission's first executive secretary was Hugh A. Brimm, a doctoral graduate in social ethics from the Southern Baptist Theological Seminary and the head of the Department of Sociology and Social Ethics at Mercer University.[15] Brimm focused on writing and conferencing, establishing the Ridgecrest conferences, and speaking on a wide variety of social concerns. As historian John Lee Eighmy points out, Brimm came under fire when he advocated some unpopular social ideas in *Light,* the publication he founded. "He denounced the concentration of wealth, supported cooperatives, and condemned unfair labor practices; and he repeatedly complained about racial discrimination and backed the proposals of Truman's civil rights committee."[16] In 1952, Brimm took a teaching position at the Carver School of Missions at Southern Seminary in Louisville, and A. C. Miller was elected head of the Commission, which was relocated to Nashville. In 1953, its name was changed yet again, this time to the Christian Life Commission (CLC).

A. C. Miller's legacy included an emphasis on the importance of the biblical witness, insisting that "the work of the Commission was biblical, not merely social."[17] When, in 1954, the Supreme Court ruled that the "separate but equal" doctrine in education was unconstitutional, the Commission under Miller supported the decision, insisting "that every man is embraced in the love of God; every man has value in the sight of God; and every man is included in the plan of God."[18] Although the Commission's voice was clearly prophetic, it was not always appreciated, even among its own constituency. This was true throughout the troubled 1960s, 1970s, and 1980s when the Christian Life Commission's message was mixed at best.

Foy A. Valentine took the reins of the CLC in 1960. Dr. Valentine was a stalwart defender of racial justice and the civil rights movement of the 1960s. He fought courageously against racial discrimination, despite the fact that at times he was nearly a lone voice among Southern Baptists. But his leadership could also be faulted by its moderate agenda in other arenas. During his tenure with the CLC, Valentine was a trustee and chairman of the executive committee of Protestants and Other Americans United for Separation of Church and

State, now Americans United for the Separation of Church and State, with fifty-plus years of involvement with the organization. He was appointed by President Carter to the President's Commission for a National Agenda for the Eighties. He also served on the Baptist World Alliance's Commission on Religious Liberty and Human Rights and was a trustee and board president of the Baptist Joint Committee on Public Affairs (now the Baptist Joint Committee for Religious Liberty). He also served on the executive committee of the National Temperance League's board of directors. Efforts were made at the annual meetings of the Southern Baptist Convention in 1965, 1967, and 1970 to defund the Commission and close its doors. But Valentine remained at the helm until his retirement in 1987, after which the very turbulent presidency of Nathan Larry Baker lasted only from 1987 to 1988.

Richard D. Land became the president of the CLC in 1988, leading the charge for the commission's most recent name change to the Ethics & Religious Liberty Commission (ERLC) in 1997. Prior to becoming the ERLC's president, Dr. Land served as Vice-President of Academic Affairs for the Criswell College in Dallas, Texas. From 1980 until 1988, Dr. Land hosted a syndicated weekly radio program, *Issues of the Eighties,* which generated an enthusiastic response among listeners in many cities. While on a leave of absence from the Criswell College, Land served from January 1987 to May 1988 as Administrative Assistant to the Honorable William P. Clements Jr., Governor of Texas. He was the governor's senior advisor on church-state issues and areas relating to "traditional family values" as well as anti-drug, anti-pornography, and anti-abortion legislation. In addition to these issues, Dr. Land had senior staff responsibility in the areas of public higher education, mental health and retardation, the physically handicapped, and AIDS.

In 1998, Land began cohosting a thirty-minute nationally syndicated weekday radio talk show, *For Faith & Family,* as well as a daily radio commentary, *For Faith & Family Insight,* sponsored by the ERLC. The broadcast began with 120 stations; as of 2006, it was heard on approximately 600 stations by more than 1.5 million listeners. He also began a syndicated live, three-hour, caller-driven radio program, *Richard Land Live!*

In July 2005, Senate Majority Leader Bill Frist (R-TN) appointed Land to the U.S. Commission on International Religious Freedom (USCIRF), an independent and bipartisan federal agency. Frist's senatorial appointment marked Dr. Land's third term of service to the USCIRF. President George W. Bush selected Dr. Land for his two previous terms (lasting from September 2001 to September 2004). In February 2005, Land was featured in *Time* magazine as one of "The Twenty-five Most Influential Evangelicals in America" that year.

The budget of the ERLC grew from $1,035,600 in 1987/88 to

$3,141,653 in 2004/05. Land also led the commission to purchase its first permanent offices in Washington, D.C., in 1993. Named Leland House, it honors John Leland, a seventeenth-century Baptist pastor who helped James Madison win Virginia's battle for religious liberty. James A. Smith Sr. was the commission's first full-time staffer in D.C. While not a lobbying organization *per se,* the Washington office has helped the ERLC participate in coalitional activities and has greatly assisted in helping to inform elected officials about Southern Baptist moral, social, and policy concerns.

ARTICLE XV: THE CHRISTIAN
AND THE SOCIAL ORDER

The exegesis of Article XV is actually quite straightforward. The article begins, like its predecessors in the 1925 and 1963 versions of the *Baptist Faith and Message,* with an affirmation of the Christian's duty to make the will of Christ supreme both in his or her own life and in the life of the larger society. This affirmation is grounded in the Bible's call to personal holiness and the confession of Jesus that Christians are the salt of the earth and the light of the world (Matt. 5:13–15).

Likewise, Article XV observes that the means of "improvement" of both humanity and society are only enduring when they are wed to a regenerate person. That is, the article affirms that key to lasting change among individuals and among individuals living in community is what older theologians called "experimental religion." In this sense, the article is an evangelical affirmation. Here I am using University of Sterling historian David Bebbington's definition of evangelicalism as conversionist, activist, biblicist, and crucicentrist.[19] As conversionists, Southern Baptists believe that personal regeneration is necessary for holiness and assurance. As activists, Southern Baptists are committed to incarnational living, viz., they are to embody the teachings of the incarnate Christ. As biblicists, Southern Baptists affirm the final authority of the Old and New Testaments for faith and practice. As crucicentrists, Southern Baptists understand that the cross of Christ is the means by which the Christian life is possible.

Southern Baptists confess in Article XV that certain moral duties are entailed in obedient Christian discipleship. Both the 1925 and 1963 statements begin, as does the 2000 statement, with the negative duties. Opposition to "every form of greed, selfishness, and vice" is universally maintained in all three statements. Apparently, every generation of Southern Baptists has found this expression sufficiently comprehensive. The *Baptist Faith and Message 2000,* however, adds to these general negative duties opposition to both racism and "all forms of sexual immorality, including adultery, homosexuality, and pornography." This expression testifies to the timeliness of statements of faith. That is, especially with respect to orthopraxy, a statement must reflect some of the particular concerns of its own cultural context. The painful reality of racism and the epidemic nature of sexual immorality in the early twenty-first century make it necessary for the statement of faith to point to the acuity of these vices.

The positive duties are elucidated next. In 1925, these included provision for "the orphaned, the aged, the helpless, and the sick." In 1963, a general class of "the needy" was added—"the orphaned, the needy, the aged, the helpless, and the sick." By 2000, another class of concern was addressed—"the orphaned, the needy, the abused, the aged, the helpless, and the sick." Anyone familiar with contemporary cultural crises will see the necessity of addressing the needs of victims of wife abuse, child abuse, and minister abuse.

Significantly, the *Baptist Faith and Message 2000* also includes an affirmation of the sanctity of human life. Since human life is to be respected as sacred, Southern Baptists affirm that they "should speak on behalf of the unborn and contend for the sanctity of all human life from conception to natural death." Like some other religious groups, Southern Baptists' first significant foray into bioethics was in response to the practice of abortion. While the convention would modify its position on abortion almost immediately, its first resolution on abortion in 1971 was consistent with what was later codified as law in *Roe v Wade* (1973) and its companion ruling *Doe v Bolton* (1973).

> WHEREAS, Christians in the American society today are faced with difficult decisions about abortion; and
>
> WHEREAS, Some advocate that there be no abortion legislation, thus making the decision a purely private matter between a woman and her doctor; and
>
> WHEREAS, Others advocate no legal abortion, or would permit abortion only if the life of the mother is threatened;
>
> Therefore, be it *Resolved,* that this Convention express its belief that society has a responsibility to affirm through the laws of the state a high view of the sanctity of human life, including fetal life, in order to protect those who cannot protect themselves; and
>
> Be it further *Resolved,* That we call upon Southern Baptists to work for legislation that will allow the possibility of abortion under such conditions as rape, incest, clear evidence of severe fetal deformity, and carefully ascertained evidence of the likelihood of damage to the emotional, mental, and physical health of the mother.

While the resolution invoked a "high view" of the sanctity of human life as its guiding theological principle, at the same time it allowed for what would be regarded by subsequent Conventions as overly expansive exceptions. The 1974

Convention essentially reconfirmed the previous resolution, but in 1976 significant nuances were added.

> WHEREAS, Southern Baptists have historically held a biblical view of the sanctity of human life, and
>
> WHEREAS, Abortion is a very serious moral and spiritual problem of continuing concern to the American people, and
>
> WHEREAS, Christians have a responsibility to deal with all moral and spiritual issues which affect society, including the problems of abortion, and
>
> WHEREAS, The practice of abortion for selfish non-therapeutic reasons destroys fetal life, dulls our society's moral sensitivity, and leads to a cheapening of human life,
>
> Therefore be it *Resolved*, that the messengers to the Southern Baptist Convention meeting in Norfolk in June, 1976, reaffirm the biblical sacredness and dignity of all human life, including fetal life, and
>
> Be it further *Resolved*, that we call on Southern Baptists and all citizens of the nation to work to change those attitudes and conditions which encourage many people to turn to abortion as a means of birth control, and
>
> Be it further *Resolved*, that in the best interest of our society, we reject any indiscriminate attitude toward abortion, as contrary to the biblical view, and
>
> Be it further *Resolved*, that we also affirm our conviction about the limited role of government in dealing with matters relating to abortion, and support the right of expectant mothers to the full range of medical services and personal counseling for the preservation of life and health.

By 1977, Southern Baptists were becoming more sensitive, articulate, and conservative on the issue of abortion. The 1977 resolution on abortion not only reaffirmed word-for-word the 1976 resolution, but added the following prefatory clause: "Resolved, that this Convention reaffirm the strong stand against abortion adopted by the 1976 Convention, and, in view of some confusion in interpreting part of this resolution we confirm our strong opposition to abortion on demand and all governmental policies and actions which permit this." Resolutions on abortion continued to evolve, including resolutions in 1978 and 1979, until, in 1980, the Convention adopted a resolution favoring legislation prohibiting abortion "except to save the life of the mother." In 1982, abortion, infanticide, and euthanasia were linked in a resolution that stated, "Social acceptance of abortion has begun to dull society's respect for all human life, leading to growing occurrences of infanticide, child abuse, and active euthanasia," and called for "legislation and/or a constitutional amendment which will prohibit abortions except to save the physical life of the mother" and "legislation which will prohibit the practice of infanticide." Landmark bioethics cases and literature were breaking during the decade from

1973–1983. These phenomena affected the entire American culture, including Southern Baptists.

Southern Baptist attitudes toward abortion and abortion-related policy continued to grow more conservative. The 1984 convention resolution on abortion opined that abortion was "a national sin" and that an unborn child is "a living individual human being," while the 1988 resolution stated, "Human life, from fertilization until natural death, is sacred and should be protected, not destroyed." Every subsequent resolution on abortion to date extends that assertion. For instance, in 1993 Southern Baptists passed a resolution against the Freedom of Choice Act and another resolution criticizing President Clinton's abortion policies. In 1995, the Convention passed a resolution against the nomination of Dr. Henry Foster as Surgeon General of the United States. The following year, Southern Baptists passed resolutions favoring the Partial-Birth Abortion Ban and a resolution requesting that all political parties include a pro-life platform. Finally, in 2003, messengers passed a resolution saying: "That we lament and renounce statements and actions by previous Conventions and previous denominational leadership that offered support to the abortion culture."

At the other end of life, Southern Baptists have addressed euthanasia and assisted suicide through their resolutions process. A resolution "On Assisted Suicide" was passed in 1996. The resolution begins by citing recent developments in law and social practice related to assisted death, including two U.S. Courts of Appeals decisions striking down laws prohibiting assisted suicide, Jack Kevorkian's persistent assistance in the suicide of his patients, and the erosion of the medical consensus against assisted death.

> WHEREAS, Two U. S. Courts of Appeals have voted for the first time in American history to strike down laws prohibiting physician assisted suicide; and
>
> WHEREAS, Michigan courts have consistently acquitted Dr. Jack Kevorkian of any criminal wrong-doing in assisting individuals to end their own lives by suicide; and
>
> WHEREAS, A University of Pennsylvania survey recently found that 20 percent of nurses polled had performed euthanasia or assisted in the suicide of a patient; and
>
> WHEREAS, Western medicine has heretofore followed both the Judeo-Christian tradition and the over 2,500 year-old Hippocratic tradition forbidding physicians to assist in the death of their patients; and
>
> WHEREAS, The Bible teaches that God created all human life in His own image and declares human life to be sacred from conception until natural death (Genesis 1:29:6 [sic] and following); and
>
> WHEREAS, The Bible likewise teaches that murder, including self-murder, is immoral (Exodus 20:13); and
>
> WHEREAS, American society seems to be embracing the "culture of death."

Be it therefore RESOLVED, that we the messengers of the Southern Baptist Convention, meeting in New Orleans, Louisiana, June 11–13, 1996, affirm the biblical and Hippocratic prohibitions against assisted suicide; and

Be it further RESOLVED, that we commend and encourage medical science in its efforts to improve pain management techniques, thus removing one major impetus toward assisted dying; and

Be it further RESOLVED, that we call upon physicians, nurses, hospice workers, individual Christians and local churches to make emotional, psychological, and spiritual care of suffering patients a priority, thereby relieving the sense of isolation and abandonment some dying patients feel; and

Be it further RESOLVED, that we vigorously denounce assisted suicide as an appropriate means of treating suffering; and

Be it finally RESOLVED, that we call on federal, state, and local governments to prosecute under the law physicians or others who practice assisted suicide.

Lastly, Article XV and its progenitors of 1925 and 1963 observe that Christians are to seek to bring every sphere of social life—"industry, government, and society as a whole"—under the "sway" of the principles of "righteousness, truth, and brotherly love." To achieve this, Christians should work with others of good will, as long as doing so does not compromise loyalty to Christ. Thus, the spirit of cooperation works both within Southern Baptist life and among Southern Baptists' cultural cobelligerents.

CONCLUSION

This study of the *Baptist Faith and Message 2000*'s Article XV and the history of social engagement represent only the *institutional* history of Southern Baptist social engagement. The real story is the way local congregations bring applied Christianity to bear upon their local communities. The *congregational* history would require a vast library to record. Local Southern Baptist churches and associations routinely speak prophetically into the church and culture and minister in priestly ways to those in their communities in need. Both the International and North American Mission Boards extend social ministry to a hurting world. While there is clearly more to be done, Southern Baptists continue to develop a more sensitive and comprehensive social consciousness.

NOTES

1. Cited in John Lee Eighmy, *Churches in Cultural Captivity: A History of the Social Attitudes of Southern Baptists* (Knoxville: University of Tennessee Press, 1972), ix.

2. A fact which, among other things, occasioned a resolution in 1995 lamenting Southern Baptists' racist past. See "Resolution on Racial Reconciliation on the 150th Anniversary of the Southern Baptist Convention," which can be accessed online at www.sbc.net/resolutions/amResolution.asp?ID = 899.

3. *Annual,* Southern Baptist Convention, 1845, p. 3, emphasis added.

4. Article II, Constitution of the Southern Baptist Convention, *Annual* (1845), p. 3.

5. Leon McBeth, "Origin of the Christian Life Commission," *Baptist History and Heritage,* 1 (October 1966), 29.

6. "Eight to Eighty: Some Christian Life Commission Highlights from 1908–1980," *LIGHT* (June–July 1980), 1.

7. Other members of the committee included S. P. Brooks, president of Baylor University; J. B. Gambrell, former president of Mercer University and later editor of the *Baptist Standard,* Southwestern Seminary faculty member, and president of the Southern Baptist Convention; P. E. Burroughs, pastor of First Baptist Church, Temple, Texas and later of Broadway Baptist Church, Ft. Worth, and finally educational secretary of the Sunday School Board; and W. T. Lowery, president of Blue Mountain College and later Mississippi College. "Eight to Eighty," 1.

8. *Annual,* Southern Baptist Convention, 1908, p. 35–36.

9. *Annual* (1908), p. 36. Cited in McBeth, "Origin of the Christian Life Commission," 31.

10. *Annual,* Southern Baptist Convention, 1914, p. 37.

11. Cited in McBeth, "Origin of the Christian Life Commission," 32.

12. McBeth, "Origin of the Christian Life Commission," 32.

13. George W. Truett, "Baptists and Religious Liberty," available at www.biblebelievers.com/truett_baptist_religious.html; accessed 4 July 2006.

14. *Annual,* Southern Baptist Convention, 1948, p. 336.

15. "Eight to Eighty," 4.

16. Eighmy, *Churches in Cultural Captivity,* 183.

17. Eighmy, *Churches in Cultural Captivity,* 183.

18. Eighmy, *Churches in Cultural Captivity,* 183.

19. See David W. Bebbington, *Evangelicalism in Modern Britain: A History from the 1730s to the 1980s* (London: Routledge, 1989) and his *Evangelicalism: Comparative Studies of Popular Protestantism in North America, the British Isles and Beyond, 1700–1990* (Oxford: Oxford University Press, 1994).

· Article XVI ·

Peace and War

E. David Cook

$\mathcal{I}$n examining the *Baptist Faith and Message 2000*, it is vital to see the clear link and progression from what is said about the Christian and the social order in Article XV and what follows on peace and war in Article XVI. As the former article makes clear, Baptists base their social, moral teaching firmly on biblical principles, especially those of righteousness, truth, and brotherly love. By righteousness is meant a right and proper relationship with God and the doing of His will in terms of right and proper relationships with all other human beings (Dan. 9; Ezra 9; Matt. 5:20, 6:1; Phil. 1:11). Jesus Christ fully embodied, exemplified, and taught such righteousness, most of all in His law of love. We are not only to love God and our neighbour as ourselves, but we are also to love one another as Christ loved us (John 15:12).

The history of Baptists and Anabaptists is fraught with opposition from and to the various forms of government that tried to require Baptists to conform to state religious practices and beliefs. In their nonconformity, there was always an uneasy relationship with and attitude toward the State. Like Paul in Rom. 13, Baptists regard the State as God's instrument in controlling and restraining evil as well as supporting and encouraging what is good. It is no accident that, both in terms of social order and peace and war, Baptists are encouraged to work with all men of righteousness and of good will in any good cause. It is also no surprise that the list of good causes includes working for the poor and needy and putting an end to war.

Baptists have always upheld the freedom of the individual conscience, holding that the State has no right to require its members to do what is against their God-given conscience. This has been expressed historically by conscientious objection, which recognized the freedom of the individual not to engage directly in war if an individual's conscience forbade the use of force or violence. Of course, there might follow some penalty like imprisonment for taking such a stance. In a way, the acceptance of such a penalty was a form and means of upholding the validity of the State and its role in ordering society for the restraint of evil and rewarding of goodness.

Article XVI is interesting in its brevity and order of priority. It does not begin with the reality and awfulness of war, but with the search for peace. The history of Baptists is not only of a refusal to conform to State religion but also often a refusal to bear arms at all. Pacificism had many Baptistic roots and supporters based on the specific teachings of Christ, the Prince of Peace (Matt. 5:39,44). It is only the gospel of our Lord which is able to overcome the spirit of war in the hearts and minds of humanity.

The focus of the article is very much on the coming kingdom of Christ whose reign will usher in the end of war and the rule of love. Interestingly, there is only one specific Old Testament reference at the end of Article XVI (Isa. 2:4), with no explicit mention of the transformation in the rule of Christ by which swords are beaten into ploughshares and spears into pruning hooks (cf. Mic. 4:3).

Article XVI begins with a recognition that Baptists are under an obligation and have a specific duty. This is not an optional extra, but a basic requirement of following Christ. It is to seek peace with all men. This implies some active effort rather than expecting peace simply to come along. It has to be worked for in the fulfilment of Christian responsibility. Peace, however, is not the mere absence of conflict. When reference is made to 'peace,' the rich and full meaning of the Hebrew idea of "shalom" is the intention and the aim. It is fullness, wholeness, flourishing, and harmony. It is right relationships between God and humanity, between all human beings, and between women and men. All of humanity is to experience and enjoy the "shalom" peace of Christ. Likewise, peace is also restored with the world itself and the animal kingdom (Isa. 35, 34:14). The key here is that the Fall is put right and God's original pattern of right relationships restored in the new heaven and the new earth. But this is not fully our experience until Christ returns; thus we are called to seek peace built of the principles of righteousness, recognizing that being right with God is the only way we can hope to live peaceably with each other and with the created order.

The only pattern for such right relationships is found in the person and teaching of Jesus Christ. He is the Prince of Peace and the model for peaceful relations. Paul urges in Gal. 6:16–26 that Christians keep in step with the Spirit, and so the *Baptist Faith and Message* urges Christians to do everything in their power to put an end to war. War is an aberration and was no part of God's original intention or plan for human beings. It arises from sin and is part of the curse of sin and its effects on the world and human beings. In Christ, who makes all things new, we are summoned to live, act, and work together differently.

The Sermon on the Mount (Matt. 5–7) is the focal point of Jesus' teaching and expression of how Christians are to live in love. Even our feelings and attitudes are to be transformed, as they are indicators of the seriousness of sin and the need for salvation and change. The spirit of war can only be replaced by the gospel and good news of Christ. He alone has the power to change hearts, minds, attitudes, actions, and behavior.

No attempt is made to offer a plan of action for getting rid of war. Instead there is a reiteration that what the world needs is the acceptance of Christ and His teaching. Christ alone is the answer to the warring spirits in humanity. He breaks the power of sin and replaces it with new life, attitudes, and actions. What is true of the individual is also true of everyone—the whole of humanity.

The danger is that we read the *Baptist Faith and Message* merely as a call to individuals to seek peace. It is a summons to the Baptist community as a community to work for peace "in all the affairs of men and nations." This is not some pious, vague hope, but a clarion call for "the practical application of His law of love." Baptists are called to "destroy" their enemies by loving them to death. This is a summons for creative ways of showing communal love in situations where the natural human response is to fight, kill, and make war.

In setting up the Truth and Reconciliation Commission in South Africa, a forum was created in which the victims addressed, confronted, and ultimately worked toward forgiving those who had done great evil and were willing to recognize their responsibility, confess their wrongdoing, repent, and seek forgiveness. This was no easy task, but it created an alternative to retaliation killings and allowed the South African community to move beyond the past, to recognize and deal with evil done, to acknowledge truth, and to embrace and practice forgiveness.

The real world of politics can be transformed when the practical love of Christ is matched by creative strategies of peacemaking and building, which do not deny or conceal evil, but name it and show how the power of Christ's transforming love can enable a society and individuals to move beyond their pain and to restore righteous relationships.

Such transformation comes only through prayer and prayer is at the heart of Article XVI. All Christians throughout the world are called to pray not so much for the ideal of peace as for the active "reign of the Prince of Peace." This recognizes that human effort alone will not solve the world's problems, far less prevent and end wars. This requires divine intervention and human beings have a key role in pleading with God that the full reign of Christ will take control of all nations and communities. When we pray that God's will be done on earth as it is in heaven, we are then working toward and looking for a time when God will bring His perfect peace in human relationships and the world will be as God created it to be and is working His purposes out to be. This is when Christ returns and reigns supreme. The pictures from the prophets Isaiah and Micah as well as the final chapters of the book of Revelation give us a glimpse of what that will be like (Isa. 35; Mic. 4; Rev. 21–22). However, this still leaves the hard question for Baptists of the moral permissibility of war.

PACIFISM

There is a long tradition among Anabaptists that all war is wrong and that the teaching of Jesus does not allow the use of force. This view takes the Sermon on the Mount and the Love Commandment of Jesus as requiring all Christians to love their enemies, to turn the other cheek, and not to respond to force with any form of violence. War can never be justified in this view and peacekeeping and peacemaking are the only options for followers of Christ.

Others regard the Sermon on the Mount as dealing with how individuals should seek to live their lives in their personal relationships. Love and turning cheeks cannot and ought not to be expected of governments, whose God-given function is the control and restraint of evil and the rewarding of goodness. The moral standards required of nations must fit with the thrust of the whole of Scripture, including the reality that God instituted wars against evil, that Jesus never condemned soldiers for their work and indeed used appropriate force in the cleansing of the Temple (Matt. 21:12–16; Mark 11:15–18; Luke 19:45–48; John 2:13–16). In addition, Paul stressed the legitimate use of force in his teaching concerning the role and function of the State (Rom. 13:1–6) and the book of Revelation (Rev. 9, 11:12–18, 20:7–15) depicts a final battle between good and evil where Satan and all his power will be utterly defeated. On these kinds of grounds many Christians support their government and nation when it seems that war is the only option.

JUST WAR

Southern Baptists are among the most loyal American supporters of their nation and its armed forces. They recognize that governments have a key role to play in constraining evil and reinforcing what is good. The legitimate use of force is part and parcel of the restraint of evil. Jesus Himself used force to drive out the moneychangers who had changed the Temple—His Father's house—from a place of prayer and healing into a "den of thieves." This was no loss of control; on the contrary, a careful reading of the various Gospels' accounts of what happened, and especially of what occurred before and after, shows that Jesus engaged in a careful, considered, and appropriate use of force to restore God's original intention and pattern (Matt. 21:12–17). Likewise, Rom. 13 argues that governments are under the authority of God, to Whom they are answerable, and are entitled to use appropriate force in their God-given task of restraining evil and rewarding good. Thus, many Southern Baptists both fight for their country and support their government when it goes to war to restore justice and restrain evil. This, however, does not mean that every war is morally justified and that governments have no obligation to explain the moral case for going to and continuing in a war.

When Constantine became a Christian and the Holy Roman Empire was founded, Christians, freed from the curse of Emperor worship, joined the military and many acknowledged that God had called them to work for justice and peace. The church recognized that in this present age war would be inevitable, as Christ had predicted (Mark 13). Given the inevitability of war, the question arose, what limits if any could be placed upon nations going to and pursuing war? This question led to the just war tradition, which tries to set down rules about what should be done before going to war as well as for the conduct of war once hostilities have broken out. These are *jus ad bellum* and *jus in bello*— rules about going to war and rules for the conduct of war.

It is important to note that the assumption for Christians is that they will live in peace with others. If however that peace is impossible, then going to war requires some kind of moral justification. We do not just fight whenever we want and over whatever we wish. Moral justifications are required before we go to war and moral rules about the way we conduct war. We cannot do anything and everything we feel like doing. Anger, the spirit of war, and fighting need to be controlled and the resort to force morally justified.

BEFORE GOING TO WAR

A war may only be declared by a legitimate, properly constituted authority. It must be the last resort, only undertaken when all else has failed. It must have a just cause, which usually is taken to mean that it is in self-defense or else in response to an act of aggression. It must have a just intention, i.e., to seek a just, lasting, and honorable peace. It is clear that even with a formal declaration of war the ultimate aim is peace. That peace is not just an absence of conflict, but rather a restoration of what is good and right. In this sense, the just war tradition clearly upholds and reinforces the aim of bringing about the reign of the Prince of Peace and the shalom where all relationships will be as God intended, with the result of harmony and well being for all.

In recent days an attempt has been made to include another ground for going to war, namely, a preemptive strike to prevent evil before it has a chance to gain a foothold. This is hotly debated as it could be broadened to include any, even vaguely, possible threat on some indefinite timescale.

What is clear is that war is never to be undertaken lightly or without good moral reasons. Part of the democratic process is that the public have a right to know why a government thinks that war is necessary and the justification for such a serious move. Inevitably, there will be discussion and debate about the validity of such grounds, but that is fruitful and necessary if a government wishes to have the full support of those it seeks to serve.

RULES FOR THE CONDUCT OF WAR

Rules for just war deal also with the conduct of war. This finds expression today in the call for nations to abide by the Geneva Convention and its rules about the treatment of prisoners and non-combatants. The damage and evil done in war must be less than that which exists under the present and continuing situation. The use of force must be proportional to the risk and danger from the opposition. There is to be no overkill or excessive use of force. Non-combatants are to be protected as far as possible. This was one reason that Saddam Hussein used schoolchildren as a shield to protect his palaces from Allied bombing, knowing that it would breach the moral rules of war by targeting innocent people if discriminate bombing had been used.

Such rules show that even in war there are some marks of human decency and attempts to limit and restrain the evil that men do to each other. It also shows a concern for the weak and defenseless. With both the protection of the innocent and the proportionate use of force, the aim is clearly to limit harm, protect the innocent, and avoid the escalation of evil and violence. It seems odd to stress that even in war levels of human control are expected. Nevertheless, such control is expected of both nations and all those who serve in the military. Discipline is a requirement, not an optional extra.

The just war aims at setting limits to the amount of force used and the way that force is used. It seeks, even in wartime, a sense of proportion and discrimination. The search for a just and lasting peace is a clear responsibility of all involved in conflict as is the duty to protect the innocent and vulnerable. No one pretends that fulfilling such requirements and applying such rules is easy, but that there is a common acceptance of the need for and appropriateness of such rules is important. For those who ignore all such standards are regarded as barbaric, evil, and beyond deserving of a place in the human community.

Governments still appeal to these standards as they try to persuade public opinion to support their efforts in waging war.

Yet even the fact of such rules, the necessity for them, and the appeal to and attempts at applying them all point to the same conclusion—namely, that war is never the end and purpose in itself. The aim of war is peace and justice. Genuine peace—the shalom of the Old Testament and the promise of the fully transforming presence of the Prince of Peace in His reign—rests in the nature, presence, and power of Christ.

It is no accident therefore that the *Baptist Faith and Message* puts Christ at the heart and center of how evil can be controlled, wars ended, and righteousness fulfilled and expressed in every relationship among people.

CONCLUSION

In a world of nuclear and biological threats from terrorists and rogue nations, Baptists must avoid confusing their faith with blind patriotism. The *Baptist Faith and Message 2000* reminds and obliges us to make the pursuit of peace the center of all our efforts. That cannot be done by purely human effort, but requires the grace and power of Christ, the Prince of Peace. This pursuit of peace means both a challenging of governmental authority to justify any use of force as a genuine means of seeking and making a just and lasting peace. This also means debating vigorously whether any particular war or use of force is justified. The ways in which wars are conducted and the behavior of troops toward both combatants and those who are clearly innocent must also be subject to scrutiny—and punishment when wrongdoing is established.

In the Early Church, dying was not considered the worst thing that might happen to one; the belief in eternal life and the good providence of God enabled people to forgive enemies and face even death as Stephen does in Acts 6. Bringing the standards of Christ to bear in wartime must certainly mean distinguishing the use of force for legitimate peaceful ends from the use of violence. War reveals the fallen, twisted nature of human beings and their need for salvation from such aggression as well as the spirit of war and the evil that drives us. Thanks be to God Who in Christ can free us to be like our Lord and Master!

Being part of the blessed peacemaking community also means that, as both individuals and a community, we must seek active ways of bringing peaceful solutions to difficult personal, national, and international problems and conflicts. Transformed communities show transformed relationships. Our call is to show such transformation in our relationships by the practical application of the law of Christ's love and to pray for the reign of the Prince of Peace within and between every nation.

• *Article XVII* •

Religious Liberty

Jerry A. Johnson

$\mathcal{W}$hat is the proper relationship between church and state? The question is asked perpetually in America, if not the rest of the world. Baptists have always had a unique answer. The *Baptist Faith and Message* answers the question with Article XVII, which concerns religious liberty. The last sentence of the article summarizes well the Baptist position: "A free church in a free state is the Christian ideal, and this implies the right of free and unhindered access to God on the part of all men, and the right to form and propagate opinions in the sphere of religion without interference by the civil power." This essay will briefly explore what religious liberty means for Baptists, what it does not mean, why Baptists have historically emphasized it and how it is needed especially today.

RELIGIOUS LIBERTY MEANS GOD ALONE IS LORD OF THE CONSCIENCE

Article XVII is built upon the opening affirmation, "God alone is Lord of the conscience." Believing that true religion is about a personal relationship with God, Baptists deny the state any role in matters of the soul, the spirit, or the conscience. This is especially true about salvation. According to the apostle Paul, the gospel of salvation is "that Christ died for our sins in accordance with the Scriptures, that he was buried, that he was raised on the third day in accordance with the Scriptures" (1 Cor. 15:3–4). As believers testify to this message, the Spirit of God alone convicts sinners and draws them to Christ, and all who believe in Jesus as Savior and Lord are miraculously "born again" (John 3:3,16). There is no role for the government here.

For this reason, the article asserts, "The gospel of Christ contemplates

171

spiritual means alone for the pursuit of its ends." The church must rely on the sword of the Spirit, not the sword of Caesar, for the conversion of souls and the redemption of the culture. Accordingly, the *Baptist Faith and Message* places a limitation on what the church should expect from the state: "The church should not resort to the civil power to carry on its work." It is instructive to note that the ultimate symbol of Christianity, the cross, serves as a powerful reminder that the state's only role in the gospel story was as the executing authority that carried out the crucifixion of Jesus. This fact foreshadowed a tension between church and state that remains to this day.

Before explaining more of what religious liberty is, it is important to note that the opening statement implies from the beginning what it is not. Religious liberty is not an absolute license to believe or do anything one desires and still call oneself a Baptist—or, for that matter, a Christian. To the contrary, the introductory sentence assumes the "Lord of the conscience." The "Lord" is certainly not the state; nor is He the individual. Instead, God alone is Lord of the conscience. On a personal and spiritual level, the conscience should be bound in loving obedience to the will and word of God, under the Lordship of Christ. Whatever may be affirmed under the banner of religious liberty, it cannot be used to negate the Christian responsibility to follow the Master. In fact, the true follower of the Lord Jesus Christ is obligated to obedience and a conscience bowed down before the written word of God.

RELIGIOUS LIBERTY MEANS UNBIBLICAL CREEDS HAVE NO AUTHORITY

However, the *Baptist Faith and Message* article is primarily addressing the individual vis-à-vis the public square. Here the human conscience should be "free from the doctrines and commandments of men." There should be no forced groupthink or mind control in matters of religious thought or speech. In this article, God as "Lord of the conscience" is juxtaposed to the "commandments of men," especially those that are "contrary to His word, or not contained in it."

On one hand, this means religious freedom from both anti-biblical and extra-biblical notions. Early Christians rightly felt no obligation to profess, "Caesar is Lord," even if the Roman government demanded it, because the commandment is "contrary to His word." Likewise, present day Christians should feel no obligation to affirm unbiblical "dogma" that is "not contained in" the Bible, even if some ecclesiastical authority demands it.

On the other hand, one can infer from this biblical qualifier that the principle of religious liberty allows churches to adopt confessions of faith, provided they are not "contrary to His word." The very existence of the *Baptist Faith and Message* statement presupposes that Christians and churches are free to articulate their biblical beliefs and define who they are for purposes of fellowship and cooperation in ministry. The article does not prohibit churches from formulating scriptural statements of faith. Instead, the article places limitations on the state and false ecclesiastical authorities, especially when they attempt to violate the conscience with beliefs that are forced or false.

RELIGIOUS LIBERTY MEANS NO STATE CHURCH AND NO CHURCH STATE

The article continues, "Church and state should be separate." The church should be separate and free from the state. In other words, there should be no state church. In no sense should the state operate or govern the affairs of the church. As the Baptist understanding of the church rules out a state church, it also rejects the notion of a church state. Article XVII stands for "a free church in a free state." While a church-based state may not seem like an immediate threat to the West or to America in the twenty-first century, the paradigm has past, present, and future significance. History is rife with examples of religious groups attempting to establish or control the state. Herschel Hobbs urged Baptists to recall "that the papacy has never relinquished its claim to authority over both church and state."[1] Today "Christian" Reconstructionist and Theonomist movements, albeit marginal, seek to establish some kind of utopian theocratic government. In addition, pseudo-Christian cult movements continue to spring up with their own land, laws, and cultural norms, such as polygamous marriage. And the world faces the future specter of a growing number of Islamic Republics in which clerics rule the state. Although Baptists would stand against many of these movements because they are not Christian, they should also oppose these government arrangements in principle, because they amount to "church-states." Even when "Christian" in name, this misguided paradigm compromises the true nature and mission of the church as well as the spiritual nature of salvation.

RELIGIOUS LIBERTY MEANS THE STATE HAS OBLIGATIONS TO THE CHURCH

While the state must not own the church, and the church must not run the state, there are some things the state owes the church. For instance, Article XVII states, "The state owes to every church protection and full freedom in the pursuit of its spiritual ends." Again, the church should expect from the state neither funding nor endorsement of it or its message. However, the state owes the church the protection of religious liberty, including accommodation of an individual's right to religious expression. Christians are increasingly denied this protection today. In Western democracies, almost anything is acceptable in public under the Orwellian guise of tolerance, except mentioning the name of Jesus in a public statement or prayer. The government should protect the rights of citizens to talk about Christ or any other religious theme anywhere, anytime. Even with this protection, the article wisely cautions, "no ecclesiastical group or denomination should be favored by the state more than others." All Baptists seek here is a level playing field.

Likewise, it is wrong when governments discriminate against churches in other matters. When building permits for new churches are denied in the name of "city planning," when existing church buildings are shut down under the rule of "eminent domain," when homeless shelters are closed for the sake of "public health," and when neighborhood Bible studies are banned under the pretense of "traffic ordinances," we have started down a steep and well-greased slippery slope. These government intrusions are harbingers of more ominous threats to religious liberty. In Europe, Canada, and California, the right of preachers to proclaim the biblical teaching about homosexuality (Rom. 1:18–32) has been challenged by civic authorities. Baptists believe the government has no business censoring the pulpit.

RELIGIOUS LIBERTY MEANS THE CHURCH HAS OBLIGATIONS TO THE STATE

Not only does the state owe protection to the church, but the church also owes something to the state. Article XVII states the obligation: "Civil government being ordained of God, it is the duty of Christians to render loyal obedience thereto in all things not contrary to the revealed will of God." Even if the church does not owe the state a coronation of its king, a scriptural mandate for citizenship remains. Here the biblical evidence—from Jesus, Paul, and Peter—is telling.

First, Christians owe a secular debt to the government. According to Jesus, Christians are under authority in matters belonging to the state. "Render to Caesar," he says, "the things that are Caesar's" (Matt. 21:21). The apostle Paul affirms this principle in his exhortation to "be subject to the governing authorities" (Rom. 13:1). Paul applies the teaching by adding "taxes to whom taxes are owed, revenue to whom revenue is owed, respect to whom respect is owed, honor to whom honor is owed" (Rom. 13:7). Likewise, Peter states,

"Be subject for the Lord's sake to every human institution, whether it be to the emperor as supreme, or to governors." In general, his readers are told, "Honor the emperor" (1 Pet. 2:13–17). Any attempt by Christians to avoid government rule under the mantra of religious liberty is misguided. Christians ought to obey the law, pay taxes, and say "your honor" to the judge and "yes sir" to the policeman.

Second, Christians also owe a spiritual debt to the government. The church owes the state prayer to God on its behalf. Paul instructs Timothy, "I urge that supplications, prayers, intercessions, and thanksgivings be made for all people, for kings and all those in authority" (1 Tim. 2:1–2). In order that we might live in peace and the gospel might go forth, the church is commanded to pray for government leaders.

Third, it should be added that American Christians, and others who live under representative government, have a special obligation. Here Christians owe the state both a voice and a vote. Jesus said, "You are the salt of the earth . . . You are the light of the world" (Matt. 5:13–16). The United States *Constitution* begins with "We the people . . ." and, in Lincoln's language, envisions a government "of the people, by the people and for the people." This means that Christians must do their civic duty as "citizen Christians."[2] Ultimately, along with all other citizens in our democratic republic, citizen Christians are "Caesar" and they are "in authority" as they cast their ballots and speak through their elected representatives. The church owes the state obedience, taxes, honor, submission, prayer, salt, light, a voice, and a vote.

RELIGIOUS LIBERTY MEANS CIVIL DISOBEDIENCE IS SOMETIMES REQUIRED

Obedience to the state is not without exception. Article XVII calls for "loyal obedience . . . in all things not contrary to the revealed will of God." Baptists in Europe and America were historically willing to be ostracized, and even persecuted unto death, over this exception. For instance, Baptists accept the Great Commission from Jesus as the "revealed will of God." The evangelistic command in Matt. 28:19–20 is four-fold: go, make disciples, baptize, and teach. Baptists have been willing to obey the state except when it says they may not preach or practice believers' baptism. Early Baptists paid a high price for this conviction and their civil disobedience.

It is important to note that Jesus' command is prefaced by the statement, "All authority in heaven and on earth has been given unto me" (Matt. 28:18). The authority of Jesus trumps the authority of Caesar. It is always right to speak about Jesus anywhere, anytime, no matter what the government may say. This is the pattern of the early church in the book of Acts. When first-generation Christians got arrested for witnessing in Jerusalem, the authorities "charged them not to speak or teach at all in the name of Jesus" (Acts 4:17). Peter and John responded with refusal and the rhetorical challenge: "Whether it is right in the sight of God to listen to you rather than God, you must judge, for we cannot but speak of what we have seen and heard" (v. 19). Later, when arrested again and reminded by the council that they were commanded "not to teach in this name," Peter and the apostles answered, "We must obey God rather than men" (Acts 5:29). The pattern of these early Christians has been the pattern of Baptists. This is not a carte blanche excuse for Christians to disobey government just because *they think* God might not approve of something. In matters strictly secular or not addressed by Scripture, believers are to be in submission to the government, period. However, when the state tries to forbid the church from obeying the Great Commission, there is a higher authority. Ultimately, Christ is Lord.

RELIGIOUS LIBERTY IS A
DISTINCTIVE OF BAPTISTS

Along with the doctrine of "The Church," one of the most distinctively Baptist articles found in the *Baptist Faith and Message* is Article XVII. To be sure, there are articles in the confession that various denominations have historically affirmed in substance (such as those on God and Stewardship). On other matters, Baptists have provided singular leadership during times of crisis. Note, for instance, how Southern Baptists have recently reaffirmed the authority, inspiration, inerrancy, and sufficiency of Scripture in a prophetic way. Yet there was an era when most Presbyterians and Methodists upheld such a view of Scripture. However, the articles concerning the church and religious liberty are different. They are uniquely Baptist; and they are also necessarily linked.

To illustrate how the twin ideas of religious liberty and the church are linked for Baptists, one need go no further than the *Baptist Faith and Message* article on the Church. It states, "A New Testament church of the Lord Jesus Christ is an autonomous local congregation of baptized believers . . . governed by His laws . . . seeking to extend the gospel to the ends of the earth." A state church would be governed by secular law, not "His laws," and could not be called "autonomous." Moreover, it could hardly be "local." Similarly, a church state would charge government with the Great Commission. Baptists, however, believe the church, rather than the state, is "to extend the gospel to the ends of the earth."

To show how Article XVII is uniquely Baptist, a simple contrast will suffice. It is an interesting fact of history that one may find examples of civil governments that have been officially Lutheran, Anglican, Congregational, Presbyterian, Roman Catholic, Orthodox Christian, Shia Muslim, Sunni Muslim, or even Atheist. However, no civil government has ever been officially "Baptist." This is no accident. By definition, no government could ever be genuinely Baptist, because Baptists reject the notion of an official state church or an official church state.

RELIGIOUS LIBERTY IS A
CONTRIBUTION FROM BAPTISTS

Having said that there has never been a Baptist state, it is important to note the contribution Baptists have made to the American model of church-state relations. While Baptists like Thomas Helwys and John Merton were faithful defenders of soul liberty in England, they bore unique witness only as dissenters in a country that still has a state church to this day. In contrast, Baptists like Roger Williams, Isaac Backus, and John Leland shaped the unique character of American church-state relations. Southern Baptist church historian Robert Baker makes a strong and straightforward claim, stating, "The Baptist people led America toward religious liberty."[3]

While most of the early American colonies had official denominations, the Baptists worked with Thomas Jefferson and James Madison to oppose state churches and to enshrine religious liberty in the *Bill of Rights*. John Leland was the most outspoken Baptist on religious liberty and exercised considerable influence on both Jefferson and Madison. This preacher's support of Jefferson's stand against established churches in New England was obvious. In a July 5 anniversary oration celebrating American independence, Leland stated, "May the combination of rulers and priests, church and state, be dissolved, and never re-unite."[4] Leland was clearly opposed to an official state church. His argument was theological. "Finally," he states, "religion is a matter between God and individuals: the religious opinions of men not being the objects of civil government, nor in any way under its control."[5]

Notwithstanding Leland's rejection of an established church, he did not see religious liberty as opposed to Christian involvement in political affairs. To the contrary, Leland publicly supported both Jefferson and Madison for office, campaigned for them vigorously, and often preached on political themes. In fact, a plausible case has been made that Leland's influence on Madison led the Father of the *Constitution* to include the *Bill of Rights* as amendments to it, and to include in the First Amendment a guarantee of religious freedom. Leland was relentless in his critique of official state churches.[6] He reflected on his accomplishments in this area: "The plea for *religious liberty* has been long and powerful; but it has been left for the United States to acknowledge it a right inherent, and not a favor granted. . . ."[7] This language echoes the Jeffersonian maxim in the *Declaration of Independence* that "liberty" is a God-given right of everyone—meaning that freedom, especially religious freedom, is not something government can grant or take away. One may even infer a Baptist influence on the 1948 *Universal Declaration of Human Rights*, inasmuch as Baptists like Leland influenced Jefferson and Madison, and to the degree that the United Nations *Declaration* draws on the United States *Declaration of Independence* and the *Bill of Rights'* First Amendment:

> Article 18. Everyone has the right to freedom of thought, conscience and religion; this right includes freedom to change his religion or belief, and freedom, either alone or in community with others and in public or private, to manifest his religion or belief in teaching, practice, worship and observance.[8]

The phrase "freedom to change his religion" is important. While the *Declaration* and *Bill of Rights* only imply the right to convert from one religion to another, current global challenges to religious liberty make an explicit statement of that right necessary.

RELIGIOUS LIBERTY IS A CAUSE YET TO BE FULLY REALIZED

Nevertheless, governments have historically tried to infringe on religious freedom and still do so today. Article XVII takes a realistic stance on this point. "A free church in a free state," it affirms, "is the Christian ideal." Sadly, however, the ideal has rarely been realized. For this reason, the Baptist intellectual leader Carl F. H. Henry suggests "Religious Liberty as a Cause Celebre" for our generation.[9] All nations, including Western democracies, need a fresh understanding and appreciation of the Baptist distinctive of religious liberty.

Throughout the world, a wave of persecution challenges religious liberty. The *Baptist Faith and Message 2000* speaks out against this trend, stating, "The state has no right to impose penalties for religious opinions of any kind." Henry laments official policies that allow or sanction the execution of Christians in states like Saudi Arabia, China, North Korea, and Egypt. In addition, other nations considered to be U.S. allies, such as Israel and Turkey, discriminate against Christians and prohibit evangelism as a matter of public policy. Henry's solution to these problems is to use the *Universal Declaration of Human Rights*, with its religious liberty clause in Article 18, as a litmus test for some aspects of U.S. foreign policy.[10] Henry calls for change:

We need to protest discrimination directly to foreign leaders and their embassies in Washington and elsewhere. We ought to press for sanctions against those who routinely violate religious liberty principles. Other than emergency relief and survival assistance, we ought to oppose American financial and military aid to governments guilty of gross human rights violations.[11]

While some Baptists will be reticent to give up their support for the state of Israel because of a United Nations declaration, and others might argue that U.S. foreign policy should be controlled only by national security interests, Henry's call for action urges Baptists to take religious liberty seriously and to do something about it.

In addition to challenges throughout the world, religious liberty is being threatened by a growing "wall of separation" in the West. While the *Declaration of Independence* and the United States *Constitution* never speak of a "wall of separation" between church and state, Americans have been seduced into believing the urban legend that government may not acknowledge God in any way.[12] To be sure, Article XVII prohibits government from establishing an official church or denomination, as does the First Amendment to the *Constitution*. And, according to both documents, the government may not force personal religious beliefs upon anyone. However, none of these limitations should keep the state from acknowledging the Jeffersonian "self evident" truths referred to in the *Declaration*, such as the reality of the "Creator" and God-given rights bestowed by the Creator on all, such as the right to life and liberty.[13] The law may also recognize other moral demands made by God, especially those made known to all peoples at all times through general revelation.

Furthermore, none of these limitations prohibit church and state from free and voluntary cooperation on projects where the interests of the state and the church can both be advanced, e.g., faith-based initiatives to feed the poor. While the *Baptist Faith and Message* rightly warns that the "state has no right to impose taxes for the support of any form of religion," it is possible that church and state have a cause in common that does not involve state support of religion *per se*. However, even in such cases, churches should be very cautious about accepting government money if doing so might lead to government control. Indeed, government shekels may lead to government shackles. Such entanglement should be avoided at all costs.

Even more controversial, neither document prohibits the government from acknowledging the Judeo-Christian worldview that is undeniably the heritage of American law and culture. Article XVII's claim that "no ecclesiastical group or denomination should be favored by the state more than others" deserves special notice. It does not concern the Judeo-Christian worldview in general. This point is especially important in a pluralistic world. Cultural and legal norms will draw on either the Judeo-Christian worldview, the Islamic worldview, or the atheistic-humanistic worldview that exalts man as the measure of all things. There can be no naked public square.[14] Interestingly, insofar as the Baptist view of religious liberty prevails in the public square, complete liberty for Muslims and atheists to believe, practice, and teach their religion in public follows. If either the Muslim or atheistic worldview were to prevail, however, it does not follow that Christians would be free to believe, practice, and teach their religion in public. In fact, Christians cannot do so today in Muslim Saudi Arabia or atheistic China.

In conclusion, the stakes are high for everyone, not just Baptists, when it comes to the *Baptist Faith and Message 2000*'s understanding of religious liberty. Religious liberty protects the gospel from corruption by the secular state. For, as Article XVII states, "The gospel of Christ contemplates spiritual means alone for the pursuit of its ends." Religious liberty protects the mission of the church. For, as the article maintains, "The church should not resort to the civil power to carry on its work." Religious liberty protects the church from state-control and the state from church-control. "Church and state," the confession affirms, "should be separate." Religious liberty protects individual freedom—the right of everyone "to form and propagate opinions in the sphere of religion without interference by the civil power." Religious liberty is thus good for the gospel, good for the church, good for the state, and good for the individual.

NOTES

1. Herschel H. Hobbs and E. Y. Mullins, *The Axioms of Religion*, rev. ed. (Nashville: Broadman, 1978), 128.

2. Richard D. Land, "Citizen Christians Have Rights Too" in Richard D. Land and Louis A. Moore, *Citizen Christians: The Rights and Responsibilities of Dual Citizenship* (Nashville: Broadman & Holman, 1994), 6. Land, Southern Baptists' point man on issues of religious liberty, explains the unusual word order: " 'Why Citizen Christians and not Christian Citizens?' The answer is that we did that purposely, deliberately, and with much forethought. We wanted to put the emphasis on the noun. We are Christians, and the adjective 'citizen' is to modify the noun 'Christian,' and not the other way around. We are Christians first, foremost, and always."

3. Robert A. Baker, *The Baptist March in History* (Nashville: Convention, 1958), 128.

4. John Leland, *Writings of the Late Elder John Leland*, ed. L. F. Greene (New York: G.W. Wood, 1845), 270.

5. Leland, *Writings*, 181.

6. Leland, *Writings*, 177–92. This is a classic address from 1791 by Leland on religious liberty. Note the terminology found in both the *Declaration of Independence* and the *Baptist Faith and Message* in the title as well as the humor of the subtitle: "The Rights of Conscience

Inalienable, and Therefore Religious Opinions not Cognizable by Law; or, The High-Flying Churchman, Stripped of His Legal Robe, Appears a Yaho."

7. Leland, *Writings*, 39.

8. *Universal Declaration of Human Rights* (1948), Article 18. It is instructive to note that the First Amendment to the United States *Constitution* provides a categorical pattern for Article 18 of the U.N. *Declaration of Human Rights*: compare (1) "right" to "rights"; (2) "freedom of speech" to "freedom . . . in teaching"; (3) "free exercise" to "freedom, either alone or in community . . . in public . . . practice . . . worship . . . observance"; and (4) "religion" to "religion." One will search in vain for this kind of correspondence in other comparable documents, such as France's 1789 *Declaration of the Rights of Man and of the Citizen*, which merely forbids persecution for opinions in general, "even religious ones," and then only if they "do not disturb the public order" (Article 10).

9. Carl F. H. Henry, "Religious Liberty as a Cause Celebre" in Land, *Citizen Christians*, 64–77.

10. Henry, "Religious Liberty," 64–77. Henry explicitly applies the "United Nations *Universal Declaration of Human Rights'* commitment to freedom of religion" to the specific cases of granting U.S. military aid to Saudi Arabia (68), electing a U.N. Secretary General (70), and giving financial aid to Egypt (71). In addition, Henry implicitly applies this principle to "billions of dollars in credit and aid" for Israel (71–73) and "Most-Favored Nation Trade Status" for China (73).

11. Henry, "Religious Liberty," 75.

12. Philip Hamburger, *Separation of Church and State* (Cambridge: Harvard University Press, 2002). Hamburger conclusively exposes the "wall of separation" myth, documenting it as a recent development in America, invented because of Protestant fears about growing Catholic influence, and later propagated by secularists who desired to muzzle Christianity in general.

13. Gary T. Amos, *Defending the Declaration: How the Bible and Christianity Influenced the Writing of the Declaration of Independence* (Brentwood: Wolgemuth & Hyatt, 1989). Amos shows that the "rights" language used by Jefferson in the *Declaration of Independence* presupposes the Judeo-Christian worldview. For a similar treatment of the *Constitution*, see John Eidsmoe, *Christianity and the Constitution: The Faith of Our Founding Fathers* (Grand Rapids: Baker, 1987).

14. Richard J. Neuhaus, *The Naked Public Square: Religion and Democracy in America* (Grand Rapids: Eerdmans, 1984).

The Family

Dorothy Kelley Patterson

$\mathcal{D}$uring the 1997 Southern Baptist Convention in Dallas, the following motion was made by Charles Lawson from Maryland:

> That the President of the Southern Baptist Convention appoint a committee to review the *Baptist Faith and Message* of May 9, 1963, for the primary purpose of adding an Article on The Family, and to bring the amendment to the next convention for approval.

In response, President Thomas D. Elliff appointed the Baptist Faith and Message Study Committee: Anthony Jordan, Executive Director-Treasurer of the Baptist General Convention of Oklahoma; Bill Elliff, then pastor of the First Baptist Church, Little Rock, Arkansas, and now pastor of The Summit Church, North Little Rock, Arkansas; Richard Land, President of the Ethics and Religious Liberty Commission of the Southern Baptist Convention; Mary Mohler, a homemaker and the Director of the Seminary Wives Institute of the Southern Baptist Theological Seminary in Louisville, Kentucky; Dorothy Patterson, a homemaker and then Professor of Women's Studies at Southeastern Baptist Theological Seminary and now Professor of Theology in Women's Studies at Southwestern Baptist Theological Seminary; Damon Shook, then pastor of Champion Forest Baptist Church, Houston, Texas, and now retired; and John Sullivan, Executive Director-Treasurer of the Florida Baptist Convention. The committee, in turn, reported back with a draft of the article on the family to the 1998 annual meeting of the Southern Baptist Convention in Salt Lake City, Utah.

BACKGROUND

Keenly aware of the sacred trust placed in their hands by President Elliff at the instruction of the Convention, the Baptist Faith and Message Study Committee proceeded with its work over a year's time. The *Baptist Faith and Message* had not been amended since Herschel H. Hobbs and others called for a statement of faith for Southern Baptists in 1963. That resulting confession had stood the test of time as a clear declaration of what Southern Baptists held dear in doctrinal commitments. The assignment to produce a concise, clear statement expressing the beliefs generally held by Southern Baptists concerning the nature of the family and its relationships was a daunting one. The committee, therefore, approached its responsibility with prayer, diligence, and humility. This work was done well enough that when the revision of the entire 1963 document was ordered and subsequently adopted during the presidency of Paige Patterson, this article was adopted in its original form as part of the entire document.

Richard Land reminded the men and women beginning this task that such calls for adding or revising a document of this importance do not arise in a vacuum. Just as in 1963, when concerns over modernism prompted the Southern Baptist Convention to appoint a committee to draft a revised statement, so in these years approaching the turn of the century, because the family has been under assault in a unique and overwhelming way, the need for clarifying and expressing a biblical perspective on the family becomes necessary. The covenant of marriage was being broken on personal whim; the investment of time in rearing a child was too often rejected for the sake of convenience or what appeared to be a more important expenditure of time and resources; the home of nurture and fellowship had been turned into a house of affluence and materialistic indulgence. Husbands and wives were going their separate ways, pursuing individual dreams and goals and personal career aspirations; parents were accepting their responsibilities as only temporary and unworthy of full energies and creativity, and they seemed to be searching the marketplace for surrogates to whom their mundane duties could be assigned; children were becoming a law unto themselves, ever seeking new and better entertainment and demanding more and more things to compensate for less and less parental involvement in their lives. Marriage could be easily dismissed with a piece of paper; life in the womb could be snuffed out for whatever reason seemed appropriate to the mother. Unquestionably there is trouble in the land, and families are bearing the brunt of these destructive forces.

No better way to approach a problem of this magnitude could be found than to look to Scripture for divine wisdom and heavenly solutions! What was needed first and foremost then, as well as for generations to come, was a clear understanding of the Creator's design for marriage and the home.

The committee went to work on its task by first going to Scripture. The Southern Baptist statement on the family is thoroughly biblical. Every line is deeply rooted in the clear teachings of Scripture. Its theological nature is in keeping with the language of the earlier versions of the *Baptist Faith and Message*. The committee sought to use words and phrases that would carry the same timelessness as the 1925 and 1963 statements. The article on the family is articulated from a positive perspective. Its intent is to declare what is believed rather than to describe what is not believed, following the pattern set by Southern Baptists' earlier statements of faith.

While the family statement stands firmly on its own, perhaps an extended commentary will enhance knowledge and expand an understanding of the underpinnings or foundation for these truths found in Scripture. The commentary will be a useful tool for those who seek to comprehend what Southern Baptists believe the Scripture teaches regarding the family and relationships therein.

COMMENTARY

The family is defined by God as the foundational institution of human society.[1] From the beginning, God has used the family as the primary classroom and as the foremost object lesson for teaching His people about Himself and challenging them to embrace the holy lifestyle He demands. Before there were civil governments or communities or assemblies of worship, God established the home by creating the man and the woman and bringing them together in the Garden of Eden to engage in spiritual ministry through companionship, dominion, procreation, and worship.

Marriage

God's purpose for marriage was introduced in the creation order (Gen. 2:24) and then reaffirmed in the Gospels (Matt. 19:5; Mark 10:7–8) and the Pauline epistles (Eph. 5:31). This biblical principle for marriage transcends time and culture. It is not dependent upon perfect people, right choices, or optimum circumstances. Marriage, according to Scripture, is a covenant commitment to the exclusive, permanent, monogamous union of one man and one woman, and thus this union cannot be defined as a flexible contract between consenting human beings. Rather, the strong and enduring bond of marriage, pledged in the presence of God Himself, is enriched by the couple's unconditional love for and acceptance of one another and empowered by their unconditional commitment to be obedient to God.

God's plan for marriage, inaugurated in Genesis and reaffirmed in the New Testament (Gen. 2:24; Matt. 19:5; Mark 10:6–8; Eph. 5:31) has three parts:

- leaving father and mother, the public proclamation of commitment, the wedding celebration of the exclusive union that takes priority over every other earthly relationship;
- cleaving or clinging to one another, the personal development of growing in love and commitment to each other;
- the climactic one-flesh sexual and physical union; the highest intimacy, which is to be shared only by husband and wife.

The very nature of the plan affirms its monogamy and permanence. Assignments were made to the husband and wife by God. Spiritual efficiency marked the new union as distinct assignments were linked with equal worth.

Believers must resist any claims of legitimacy for sexual relationships that have been declared illicit or perverse in Scripture, lest they fall prey to an accommodation to the spirit of the age. Deviation from God's plan for marriage mars the image of God (Gen. 1:27) and distorts the oneness God intended in the sexual union established between one woman and one man after they have committed themselves to one another in an exclusive, lifetime commitment. The perversion of homosexuality defies even the continuation of the generations, since it renders natural conception impossible (Rom. 1:18–32). Fornication does irreparable damage to the beautiful sexual union in God's plan for marriage. Such blatant immorality, too, affects adversely the next generation, since the exclusivity of the divinely designed union is marred and the pattern for God's perfect plan is pushed aside, replaced by human whim.

In marriage, two people physically become one flesh (Gen. 2:24); two families are socially grafted together; and the husband and wife portray spiritually the relationship between Christ and the Church (Eph. 5:23–27). The union is designed to provide a lifetime of spiritual and emotional support (Deut. 24:5), to offer a channel for the mutual satisfaction of sexual desires, and to present the best setting for conceiving and nurturing the next generation. The complementary relationship between husband and wife is presented as part of the perfect pre-Fall setting (Gen. 2:8–25), and then that sacred relationship is carefully defined within the canon of Scripture for succeeding generations after the Fall (Eph. 5:21–33; Col. 3:18; 1 Pet. 3:1–7). God's perfect plan for marriage cannot be marred or damaged by changing cultures or sinful human beings. Human implementation of God's plan most certainly will be flawed as a result of sin, but His standard can always be trusted as the right and best pattern for marriage.

Marriage, according to God's plan, is a lifelong commitment. The breaking of its bonds brings hurt not only to the man and woman whose union is torn asunder but also to their extended family, especially their own children, and even to friends and acquaintances; and every effort ought to be made for marital reconciliation and restoration (Mal. 2:16). Jesus clearly did not advocate divorce but called attention in a positive way to His design for marriage presented "in the beginning" at creation (Gen. 2:24), while noting that the "hardness" of the human heart could occasionally circumvent that plan (Matt. 5:31–32; 19:3–9; Mark 10:6–12; Luke 16:18; Rom. 7:1–3; 1 Cor. 7:1–16).

The Fall introduced distortions into the relationships between men and women just as it brought chaos and tragedy throughout the world. The husband's humble, loving, servant headship has often been replaced with domination or passivity. The wife's voluntary and willing submission to her husband's leadership has often been exchanged for usurpation or servility. Redemption in Christ would call for husbands to forsake harsh or selfish leadership and to extend loving care to their wives (1 Pet. 3:7) and for wives to forsake resistance to the authority of their respective husbands and to practice willing, joyful submission to that leadership (1 Pet. 3:1–2).

Husbands

At the dawn of God's creative activity, before the creation of the woman, the man received his initial assignments. He was charged to provide (Gen. 2:15), protect (v. 15), and lead (the important spiritual instruction concerning the forbidden fruit was entrusted to him, vv. 16–17). The importance of these responsibilities was affirmed when, after the disobedience of the first couple, the Lord confronted Adam (rather than Eve, who first took the fruit, ate it, and gave it to Adam) as the one responsible for spiritual leadership as well as protection and provision. Adam was judged for listening to his wife and acquiescing to her directives rather than taking responsibility for reminding Eve of the Lord's mandate.

God commands husbands to love their wives as Christ loves the church (Eph. 5:25). This love, which is protective, nurturing, serving, and edifying, is not replaced with, but accompanied by, headship. This headship calls the husband to a loving servant leadership in which he cares responsibly for his wife's spiritual, emotional, and physical needs.

As defined in Scripture, the husband's headship was established by God before the Fall; it was not the result of sin (Gen. 2:15–17; see also Num. 1:2–3,17–19). His responsibility is to be assumed with humility and administered with a servant's heart; it is not a right to be demanded with unbridled pride or pursued with oppressive tyranny. The wife is to respond with submission to her husband's loving headship and with honor and respect for his God-given leadership (Eph. 5:21–22,33; 1 Pet. 3:1–4).

Servanthood does not nullify leadership but rather defines and refines its outworking. The balance between servanthood and leadership is beautifully portrayed in Jesus Himself (Luke 22:26; Heb. 13:17), who modeled servant leadership for the husband and selfless submission for the wife (Eph. 5:23–27; Phil. 2:5–8). Not only did Jesus model the Creator's plan for these different roles, but He also affirmed the equality in Christ of the husband and the wife (Gal. 3:28; 1 Pet. 3:7). As the wife submits herself to her husband's leadership, the husband humbles himself to meet his wife's needs for love and nurture (Eph. 5:25–29; 1 Pet. 3:7).

Wives

Wives, on the other hand, were created to be "helpers" to their husbands (Gen. 2:18). The term "helper," which is also used by God to identify Himself (Exod. 18:4; Deut. 33:7), describes the woman God created to become a partner with the man in the overwhelming task of exercising dominion over the world and extending the generations (Gen. 1:28; 2:18). When you call upon God to be your "Helper," you are not suggesting that He divest Himself of His deity and supernatural powers. Rather you ask Him to come to your aid *with* the powers of His divine person. There is no hint of inferiority in the term. It describes function (what she does) rather than worth (who she is). As the man's "helper," the woman complements him through her own unique function in the economy of God; she brings to that assignment her giftedness, creativity, and energies. However, as one "comparable to him," she, too, is created "in the image of God" (Gen. 2:18). Both the woman and the man bear God's image fully, but each respectively expresses that image in God-ordained ways through manhood or womanhood. Thus, distinctions in masculine and feminine roles are ordained by God as part of the created order (Gen. 1:27). Their differing roles in relating to one another provide a picture of the nature of God and the way He relates to His people. As the realities of headship and submission are enacted within loving, equal, and complementary male-female roles, the image of God is properly reflected as well. The wife is created in God's image; she, together with her husband, is a joint-heir of the gospel; but she was given her own unique assignment as both husband and wife assumed responsibility for dominion of the world.

A wife's submission to her husband does not decrease her worth but rather enhances her value to both her husband and the Lord (1 Pet. 3:4). This humble and voluntary yielding of a wife to her husband's leadership becomes a resource for evangelism (1 Pet. 3:1–2), an opportunity for glorifying God (1 Pet. 3:4–6), a channel for spiritual growth as ultimately the wife trusts herself to the Lord, and a means for bringing honor to His Word (Titus 2:3–5). Grammatically and etymologically, submission (Gk. *hupotasso*, "line up under") indicates a choice. Submission is above and beyond obedience; it is resting, leaning, trusting, abandoning yourself and your desires and rights. Submission is void of stubbornness or rebellion. Of course, a woman, as every human being, has rights. But she can choose to lay down those rights, as did Jesus (Phil. 2:5–7). A woman can be coerced, but the word used here in Scripture clearly indicates the making of a choice. Otherwise, the action is meaningless. A wife who wants to honor Christ will choose to stand under her husband's authority—not because of his merit but because she wants to be obedient to Christ. Ultimately, when a wife submits to her husband, she casts herself simply and completely upon the providence of God.

A wife's model for submission is Jesus Himself, who had no other purpose than to do the Father's will (Heb. 10:7; Ps. 40:7–8), not considering His own will (John 5:30). Her submission is "as unto the Lord" (1 Pet. 3:5). If genuine, it is voluntary (as her choice, an act of the will, not grudgingly but with joy), complete (with an attitude that spills over into every area of life, "in everything," Eph. 5:24), and continual (being consistently practiced through every season of life). Submission should be a wife's natural response to her husband's love and a prerequisite to his headship.

Parents and Children

The family is the natural setting for molding and nurturing a child in the ways of the Lord (Prov. 22:6). Parents are admonished to take seriously their responsibility for the spiritual formation of their children by introducing them to God (salvation) and teaching them His Word (discipleship). Fathers and mothers are given these assignments:

- to model biblical manhood and womanhood through incarnational living so that children are able to observe the sanctification process in the lives of their parents (Deut. 6:4–9,20–25; Josh. 4:6–7);
- to teach their children moral values from Scripture (Deut. 6:4–9); and
- to lead them to love and serve the Lord through consistent discipline (Ps. 78:4–8).

The boundaries of a young child are established by his parents (Prov. 3:12; 13:24; 22:6; 23:13–14; 29:15,17; Eph. 6:4). However, the ultimate goal of parents is to move the child first to parental obedience, then to personal account-ability, and finally to God-honoring obedience (Ps. 119:9–11). The child ideally moves from parent-control to self-control to God-control.

Childless couples, as well as single men and women, have the opportunity to pass on a godly legacy through their interaction with the children in their extended family circles, in their churches, and in their respective communities. Rearing up the next generation unto the Lord is an awesome privilege and weighty responsibility.

CONCLUSION

Doctrine and practice, whether in the home or the church, are not to be deter-mined according to modern cultural, sociological, and ecclesiastical trends or according to personal emotional whims; rather, Scripture is to be the final authority in all matters of faith and conduct (2 Tim. 3:16–17; Heb. 4:12; 2 Pet. 1:20–21). God chose to reveal Himself to His people through family language: He used the metaphor of the home to describe the heavenly dwelling where believers will join Him for eternity. He selected the analogy of family relation-ships (husband/wife and parent/child) to illustrate how believers are to relate to Him: God identifies Himself as the Husband and Israel as His wife (Hos. 2:19–20). God calls Himself Father, and Jesus is the Son; Jesus is the Bride-groom, and the Church is the Bride; believers are brothers and sisters in Christ, having been adopted by the heavenly Father as His children. The most basic and consistent spiritual teaching, character development, and discipleship train-ing should occur within the family circle (Deut. 6:4–9). A Christ-centered family has the potential to give a "word about God" to a world indifferent to spiritual truths. Those within the family circle have a unique opportunity to study the Bible and to learn theology through object lessons built into the very structure of the family.

Godly families help build the church just as churches ought to help build godly families. Scripture makes frequent connections between the life of the family and the life of the church (1 Tim. 3:5; 5:1–2). Leadership patterns in the family are consistently reflected in the church as well (1 Tim. 2:9–14; 3:1–7; Titus 1:5–9). Believers would do well to affirm heartily and to commit themselves devotedly to upholding the concept of the family as God's original and primary means of producing godly offspring. Thus, forevermore they ought to develop in their own hearts a holy passion and devoted commitment to pass on godly values from generation to generation (Deut. 6:4–9; Ps. 78:5–7).

NOTES

1. Notice that the article's understanding of the family, as "composed of persons related to one another by marriage, blood, or adoption," makes no provision for deviant sexual behavior such as homosexuality or lesbianism. The importance of natural biological ties and the extended family are affirmed.

Comparison of 1925, 1963, and 2000 Baptist Faith and Message

Preamble to the 1925 Baptist Faith and Message

The report of the Committee on Statement of Baptist Faith and Message was presented as follows by E. Y. Mullins, Kentucky:

REPORT OF THE COMMITTEE ON BAPTIST FAITH AND MESSAGE

Your committee beg leave to report as follows:

Your committee recognize that they were appointed "to consider the advisability of issuing another statement of the Baptist Faith and Message, and report at the next Convention."

In pursuance of the instructions of the Convention, and in consideration of the general denominational situation, your committee

Preamble to the 1963 Baptist Faith and Message

Committee on Baptist Faith and Message

The 1962 session of the Southern Baptist Convention, meeting in San Francisco, California, adopted the following motion:

"Since the report of the Committee on Statement of Baptist Faith and Message was adopted in 1925, there have been various statements from time to time which have been made, but no over-all statement which might be helpful at this time as suggested in Section 2 of that report, or introductory statement which might be used as an interpretation of the 1925 Statement."

"We recommend, therefore, that the president of this Convention be requested to call a meeting of the men now serving as presidents of the various state conventions that

Preamble to the 2000 Baptist Faith and Message

The 1999 session of the Southern Baptist Convention, meeting in Atlanta, Georgia, adopted the following motion addressed to the President of the Convention:

"I move that in your capacity as Southern Baptist Convention chairman, you appoint a blue ribbon committee to review the *Baptist Faith and Message* statement with the responsibility to report and bring any recommendations to this meeting next June in Orlando."

President Paige Patterson appointed the committee as follows: Max Barnett (OK), Steve Gaines (AL), Susie Hawkins (TX), Rudy A. Hernandez (TX), Charles S. Kelley, Jr. (LA), Heather King (IN), Richard D. Land (TN), Fred Luter (LA), R. Albert Mohler, Jr. (KY), T. C. Pinckney (VA), have decided to recommend the New Hampshire Confession of Faith, revised at certain points, and with some additional articles growing out of present needs, for approval by the Convention, in the event a statement of the Baptist faith and message is deemed necessary at this time.

The present occasion for a reaffirmation of Christian fundamentals is the prevalence of naturalism in the modern teaching and preaching of religion. Christianity is supernatural in its origin and history. We repudiate every theory of religion which denies the supernatural elements in our faith.

As introductory to the doctrinal articles, we recommend the adoption by the Convention of the following statement of the historic Baptist conception of the nature and function of confessions of faith in our religious and denominational life, believing that some such statement will clarify the atmosphere and remove some causes of misunderstanding, friction, and apprehension. Baptists approve and circulate confes-

would quality as a member of the Southern Baptist Convention committee under Bylaw 18 to present to the Convention in Kansas City some similar statement which shall serve as information to the churches, and which may serve as guidelines to the various agencies of the Southern Baptist Convention. It is understood that any group or individuals may approach this committee to be of service. The expenses of this committee shall be borne by the Convention Operating Budget."

Your committee thus constituted begs leave to present its report as follows:

Throughout its work your committee has been conscious of the contribution made by the statement of "The Southern Baptist Faith and Message" adopted by the Southern Baptist Convention in 1925. It quotes with approval its affirmation that "Christianity is supernatural in its origin and history. We repudiate every theory of religion which denies the supernatural elements in our faith."

Nelson Price (GA), Adrian Rogers (TN), Roger Spradlin (CA), Simon Tsoi (AZ), Jerry Vines (FL). Adrian Rogers (TN) was appointed chairman.

Your committee thus constituted begs leave to present its report as follows:

Baptists are a people of deep beliefs and cherished doctrines. Throughout our history we have been a confessional people, adopting statements of faith as a witness to our beliefs and a pledge of our faithfulness to the doctrines revealed in Holy Scripture.

Our confessions of faith are rooted in historical precedent, as the church in every age has been called upon to define and defend its beliefs. Each generation of Christians bears the responsibility of guarding the treasury of truth that has been entrusted to us [2 Timothy 1:14]. Facing a new century, Southern Baptists must meet the demands and duties of the present hour.

sions of faith with the following understanding, namely:

1. That they constitute a consensus of opinion of some Baptist body, large or small, for the general instruction and guidance of our own people and others concerning those articles of the Christian faith which are most surely conditions of salvation revealed in the New Testament, viz., repentance towards God and faith in Jesus Christ as Saviour and Lord.

2. That we do not regard them as complete statements of our faith, having any quality of finality or infallibility. As in the past so in the future Baptists should hold themselves free to revise their statements of faith as may seem to them wise and expedient at any time.

3. That any group of Baptists, large or small, have the inherent right to draw up for themselves and publish to the world a confession of their faith whenever they may think it advisable to do so.

Furthermore, it concurs in the introductory "statement of the historic Baptist conception of the nature and function of confessions of faith in our religious and denominational life. . . ." It is, therefore, quoted in full as a part of this report to the Convention:

"(1) That they constitute a consensus of opinion of some Baptist body, large or small, for the general instruction and guidance of our own people and others concerning those articles of the Christian faith which are most surely held among us. They are not intended to add anything to the simple conditions of salvation revealed in the New Testament, viz., repentance towards God and faith in Jesus Christ as Savior and Lord.

"(2) That we do not regard them as complete statements of our faith, having any quality of finality or infallibility. As in the past so in the future, Baptists should hold themselves free to revise their statements of faith as may seem to them wise and expedient at any time.

New challenges to faith appear in every age. A pervasive anti-supernaturalism in the culture was answered by Southern Baptists in 1925, when the *Baptist Faith and Message* was first adopted by this Convention. In 1963, Southern Baptists responded to assaults upon the authority and truthfulness of the Bible by adopting revisions to the *Baptist Faith and Message*. The Convention added an article on "The Family" in 1998, thus answering cultural confusion with the clear teachings of Scripture. Now, faced with a culture hostile to the very notion of truth, this generation of Baptists must claim anew the eternal truths of the Christian faith.

Your committee respects and celebrates the heritage of the *Baptist Faith and Message*, and affirms the decision of the Convention in 1925 to adopt the *New Hampshire Confession of Faith*, "revised at certain points and with some additional articles growing out of certain needs. . . ." We also respect the important contributions of the 1925 and 1963 editions of the *Baptist Faith and Message*.

With the 1963 committee, we have been guided in our work by the 1925 "statement of the historic Baptist conception of the nature and function of confessions of faith in our religious and denominational life. . . ." It is, therefore, quoted in full as a part of this report to the Convention:

(1) That they constitute a consensus of opinion of some Baptist body, large or small, for the general instruction and guidance of our own people and others concerning those articles of the Christian faith which are most surely held among us. They are not intended to add anything to the simple conditions of salvation revealed in the New Testament, viz., repentance toward God and faith in Jesus Christ as Saviour and Lord.

(2) That we do not regard them as complete statements of our faith, having any quality of finality or infallibility. As in the past so in the future, Baptists should hold themselves free to revise their statements of faith as may seem to them wise and expedient at any time.

"(3) That any group of Baptists, large or small, have the inherent right to draw up for themselves and publish to the world a confession of their faith whenever they may think it advisable to do so.

"(4) That the sole authority for faith and practice among Baptists is the Scriptures of the Old and New Testaments. Confessions are only guides in interpretation, having no authority over the conscience.

"(5) That they are statements of religious convictions, drawn from the Scriptures, and are not to be used to hamper freedom of thought or investigation in other realms of life."

The 1925 Statement recommended "the New Hampshire Confession of Faith, revised at certain points, and with some additional articles growing out of certain needs. . . ." Your present committee has adopted the same pattern. It has sought to build upon the structure of the 1925 Statement, keeping in mind the "certain needs"

4. That the sole authority for faith and practice among Baptists is the Scriptures of the Old and New Testaments. Confessions are only guides in interpretation, having no authority over the conscience.

5. That they are statements of religious convictions, drawn from the Scriptures, and are not to be used to hamper freedom of thought or investigation in other realms of life.

of our generation. At times it has reproduced sections of that Statement without change. In other instances it has substituted words for clarity or added sentences for emphasis. At certain points it has combined articles, with minor changes in wording, to endeavor to relate certain doctrines to each other. In still others—e.g., "God" and "Salvation"—it has sought to bring together certain truths contained throughout the 1925 Statement in order to relate them more clearly and concisely. In no case has it sought to delete from or to add to the basic contents of the 1925 Statement.

Baptists are a people who profess a living faith. This faith is rooted and grounded in Jesus Christ who is "the same yesterday, and today, and forever." Therefore, the sole authority for faith and practice among Baptists is Jesus Christ whose will is revealed in the Holy Scriptures.

A living faith must experience a growing understanding of truth and must be continually interpreted and related to the needs of

(3) That any group of Baptists, large or small, have the inherent right to draw up for themselves and publish to the world a confession of their faith whenever they may think it advisable to do so.

(4) That the sole authority for faith and practice among Baptists is the Scriptures of the Old and New Testaments. Confessions are only guides in interpretation, having no authority over the conscience.

(5) That they are statements of religious convictions, drawn from the Scriptures, and are not to be used to hamper freedom of thought or investigation in other realms of life.

Baptists cherish and defend religious liberty, and deny the right of any secular or religious authority to impose a confession of faith upon a church or body of churches. We honor the principles of soul competency and the priesthood of believers, affirming together both

each new generation. Throughout their history Baptist bodies, both large and small, have issued statements of faith which comprise a consensus of their beliefs. Such statements have never been regarded as complete, infallible statements of faith, nor as official creeds carrying mandatory authority. Thus this generation of Southern Baptists is in historic succession of intent and purpose as it endeavors to state for its time and theological climate those articles of the Christian faith which are most surely held among us.

Baptists emphasize the soul's competency before God, freedom in religion, and the priesthood of the believer. However, this emphasis should not be interpreted to mean that there is an absence of certain definite doctrines that Baptists believe, cherish, and with which they have been and are now closely identified.

It is the purpose of this statement of faith and message to set forth certain teachings which we believe.

our liberty in Christ and our accountability to each other under the Word of God.

Baptist churches, associations, and general bodies have adopted confessions of faith as a witness to the world, and as instruments of doctrinal accountability. We are not embarrassed to state before the world that these are doctrines we hold precious and as essential to the Baptist tradition of faith and practice.

As a committee, we have been charged to address the "certain needs" of our own generation. In an age increasingly hostile to Christian truth, our challenge is to express the truth as revealed in Scripture, and to bear witness to Jesus Christ, who is *"the Way, the Truth, and the Life."*

The 1963 committee rightly sought to identify and affirm "certain definite doctrines that Baptists believe, cherish, and with which they have been and are now closely identified." Our living faith is established upon eternal truths. "Thus this generation of

Southern Baptists is in historic succession of intent and purpose as it endeavors to state for its time and theological climate those articles of the Christian faith which are most surely held among us."

It is the purpose of this statement of faith and message to set forth certain teachings which we believe.

Respectfully Submitted,

The Baptist Faith and Message Study Committee Adrian Rogers, Chairman

1925 Baptist Faith and Message Statement

I. The Scriptures

We believe that the Holy Bible was written by men divinely inspired, and is a perfect treasure of heavenly instruction; that it has God for its author, salvation for its end, and truth, without any mixture of

1963 Baptist Faith and Message Statement with 1998 Amendment

I. The Scriptures

The Holy Bible was written by men divinely inspired and is the record of God's revelation of Himself to man. It is a perfect treasure of divine instruction. It has God

Current Baptist Faith and Message Statement

I. The Scriptures

The Holy Bible was written by men divinely inspired and is God's revelation of Himself to man. It is a perfect treasure of divine instruction. It has God for its author, salvation for its end, and truth, without any error, for its matter; that it reveals the principles by which God will judge us; and therefore is, and will remain to the end of the world, the true center of Christian union, and the supreme standard by which all human conduct, creeds and religious opinions should be tried.

Luke 16:29–31; 2 Tim. 3:15–17; Eph. 2:20; Heb. 1:1; 2 Peter 1:19–21; John 16:13–15; Matt. 22:29–31; Psalm 19:7–10; Psalm 119:1–8.

II. God

There is one and only one living and true God, an intelligent, spiritual, and personal Being, the Creator, Preserver, and Ruler of the universe, infinite in holiness and all

---

for its author, salvation for its end, and truth, without any mixture of error, for its matter. It reveals the principles by which God judges us; and therefore is, and will remain to the end of the world, the true center of Christian union, and the supreme standard by which all human conduct, creeds, and religious opinions should be tried. The criterion by which the Bible is to be interpreted is Jesus Christ.

Ex. 24:4; Deut. 4:1–2; 17:19; Josh. 8:34; Psalms 19:7–10; 119:11,89,105,140; Isa. 34:16; 40:8; Jer. 15:16; 36; Matt. 5:17–18; 22:29; Luke 21:33; 24:44–46; John 5:39; 16:13–15; 17:17; Acts 2:16ff; 17:11; Rom. 15:4; 16:25–26; 2 Tim. 3:15–17; Heb. 1:1–2; 4:12; 1 Peter 1:25; 2 Peter 1:19–21.

II. God

There is one and only one living and true God. He is an intelligent, spiritual, and personal Being, the Creator, Redeemer, Preserver, and Ruler of the universe. God

---

mixture of error, for its matter. Therefore, all Scripture is totally true and trustworthy. It reveals the principles by which God judges us, and therefore is, and will remain to the end of the world, the true center of Christian union, and the supreme standard by which all human conduct, creeds, and religious opinions should be tried. All Scripture is a testimony to Christ, who is Himself the focus of divine revelation.

Exodus 24:4; Deuteronomy 4:1–2; 17:19; Joshua 8:34; Psalms 19:7–10; 119:11,89,105, 140; Isaiah 34:16; 40:8; Jeremiah 15:16; 36:1–32; Matthew 5:17–18; 22:29; Luke 21:33; 24:44–46; John 5:39; 16:13–15; 17:17; Acts 2:16ff; 17:11; Romans 15:4; 16:25–26; 2 Timothy 3:15–17; Hebrews 1:1–2; 4:12; 1 Peter 1:25; 2 Peter 1:19–21.

II. God

There is one and only one living and true God. He is an intelligent, spiritual, and personal Being, the Creator, Redeemer, Preserver, and Ruler of the universe. God is

other perfections, to whom we owe the highest love, reverence, and obedience. He is revealed to us as Father, Son, and Holy Spirit, each with distinct personal attributes, but without division of nature, essence, or being.

Gen. 1:1; 1 Cor. 8:4–6; Deut. 6:4; Jer. 10:10; Isa. 48:12; Deut. 5:7; Ex. 3:14; Heb. 11:6; John 5:26; 1 Tim. 1:17; John 1:14–18; John 15:26; Gal. 4:6; Matt. 28:19.

is infinite in holiness and all other perfections. To him we owe the highest love, reverence, and obedience. The eternal God reveals Himself to us as Father, Son, and Holy Spirit, with distinct personal attributes, but without division of nature, essence, or being.

1. God the Father

God as Father reigns with providential care over His universe, His creatures, and the flow of the stream of human history according to the purposes of His grace. He is all powerful, all loving, and all wise. God is Father in truth to those who become children of God through faith in Jesus Christ. He is fatherly in his attitude toward all men.

Gen. 1:1; 2:7; Ex. 3:14; 6:2–3; 15:11ff; 20:1ff; Levit. 22:2; Deut. 6:4; 32:6; 1 Chron. 29:10; Psalm 19:1–3; Isa. 43:3,15; 64:8; Jer. 10:10; 17:13; Matt. 6:9ff; 7:11; 23:9; 28:19; Mark 1:9–11; John 4:24; 5:26; 14:6–13; 17:1–8; Acts 1:7; Rom. 8:14–15;

infinite in holiness and all other perfections. God is all powerful and all knowing; and His perfect knowledge extends to all things, past, present, and future, including the future decisions of His free creatures. To Him we owe the highest love, reverence, and obedience. The eternal triune God reveals Himself to us as Father, Son, and Holy Spirit, with distinct personal attributes, but without division of nature, essence, or being.

A. God the Father

God as Father reigns with providential care over His universe, His creatures, and the flow of the stream of human history according to the purposes of His grace. He is all powerful, all knowing, all loving, and all wise. God is Father in truth to those who become children of God through faith in Jesus Christ. He is fatherly in His attitude toward all men.

Genesis 1:1; 2:7; Exodus 3:14; 6:2–3; 15:11ff; 20:1ff; Leviticus 22:2; Deuteronomy 6:4; 32:6; 1 Chronicles 29:10;

1 Cor. 8:6; Gal. 4:6; Ephes. 4:6; Col. 1:15; 1 Tim. 1:17; Heb. 11:6; 12:9; 1 Peter 1:17; 1 John 5:7.

2. God the Son

Christ is the eternal Son of God. In His incarnation as Jesus Christ He was conceived of the Holy Spirit and born of the virgin Mary. Jesus perfectly revealed and did the will of God, taking upon Himself the demands and necessities of human nature and identifying Himself completely with mankind yet without sin. He honored the divine law by His personal obedience, and in His death on the cross He made provision for the redemption of men from sin. He was raised from the dead with a glorified body and appeared to His disciples as the person who was with them before His crucifixion. He ascended into heaven and is now exalted at the right hand of God where He is the One Mediator, partaking of the nature of God and of man, and in whose Person is effected the recon-

Psalm 19:1–3; Isaiah 43:3,15; 64:8; Jeremiah 10:10; 17:13; Matthew 6:9ff.; 7:11; 23:9; 28:19; Mark 1:9–11; John 4:24; 5:26; 14:6–13; 17:1–8; Acts 1:7; Romans 8:14–15; 1 Corinthians 8:6; Galatians 4:6; Ephesians 4:6; Colossians 1:15; 1 Timothy 1:17; Hebrews 11:6; 12:9; 1 Peter 1:17; 1 John 5:7.

B. God the Son

Christ is the eternal Son of God. In His incarnation as Jesus Christ He was conceived of the Holy Spirit and born of the virgin Mary. Jesus perfectly revealed and did the will of God, taking upon Himself human nature with its demands and necessities and identifying Himself completely with mankind yet without sin. He honored the divine law by His personal obedience, and in His substitutionary death on the cross He made provision for the redemption of men from sin. He was raised from the dead with a glorified body and appeared to His disciples as the person who was with them before His crucifixion.

ciliation between God and man. He will return in power and glory to judge the world and to consummate His redemptive mission. He now dwells in all believers as the living and ever present Lord.

Gen. 18:1ff.; *Psalms* 2:7ff.; 110:1ff.; *Isa.* 7:14; 53; *Matt.* 1:18–23; 3:17; 8:29; 11:27; 14:33; 16:16,27; 17:5; 27; 28:1–6,19; *Mark* 1:1; 3:11; *Luke* 1:35; 4:41; 22:70; 24:46; *John* 1:1–18,29; 10:30,38; 11:25–27; 12:44–50; 14:7–11; 16:15–16,28; 17:1–5,21–22; 20:1–20,28; *Acts* 1:9; 2:22–24; 7:55–56; 9:4–5,20; *Rom.* 1:3–4; 3:23–26; 5:6–21; 8:1–3,34; 10:4; *1 Cor.* 1:30; 2:2; 8:6; 15:1–8,24–28; *2 Cor.* 5:19–21; 8:9; *Gal.* 4:4–5; *Ephes.* 1:20; 3:11; 4:7–10; *Phil.* 2:5–11; *Col.* 1:13–22; 2:9; *1 Thess.* 4:14–18; *1 Tim.* 2:5–6; 3:16; *Titus* 2:13–14; *Heb.* 1:1–3; 4:14–15; 7:14–28; 9:12–15,24–28; 12:2; 13:8; *1 Peter* 2:21–25; 3:22; *1 John* 1:7–9; 3:2; 4:14–15; 5:9; *2 John* 7–9; *Rev.* 1:13–16; 5:9–14; 12:10–11; 13:8; 19:16.

He ascended into heaven and is now exalted at the right hand of God where He is the One Mediator, fully God, fully man, in whose Person is effected the reconciliation between God and man. He will return in power and glory to judge the world and to consummate His redemptive mission. He now dwells in all believers as the living and ever present Lord.

Genesis 18:1ff.; *Psalms* 2:7ff.; 110:1ff.; *Isaiah* 7:14; 53; *Matthew* 1:18–23; 3:17; 8:29; 11:27; 14:33; 16:16,27; 17:5; 27; 28:1–6,19; *Mark* 1:1; 3:11; *Luke* 1:35; 4:41; 22:70; 24:46; *John* 1:1–18,29; 10:30,38; 11:25–27; 12:44–50; 14:7–11; 16:15–16,28; 17:1–5,21–22; 20:1–20,28; *Acts* 1:9; 2:22–24; 7:55–56; 9:4–5,20; *Romans* 1:3–4; 3:23–26; 5:6–21; 8:1–3,34; 10:4; *1 Corinthians* 1:30; 2:2; 8:6; 15:1–8,24–28; *2 Corinthians* 5:19–21; 8:9; *Galatians* 4:4–5; *Ephesians* 1:20; 3:11; 4:7–10; *Philippians* 2:5–11; *Colossians* 1:13–22; 2:9; *1 Thessalonians* 4:14–18; *1 Timothy* 2:5–6; 3:16; *Titus* 2:13–14; *Hebrews* 1:1–3; 4:14–15; 7:14–28;

3. God the Holy Spirit

The Holy Spirit is the Spirit of God. He inspired holy men of old to write the Scriptures. Through illumination He enables men to understand truth. He exalts Christ. He convicts of sin, of righteousness and of judgment. He calls men to the Saviour, and effects regeneration. He cultivates Christian character, comforts believers, and bestows the spiritual gifts by which they serve God through His church. He seals the believer unto the day of final redemption. His presence in the Christian is the assurance of God to bring the believer into the fulness of the stature of Christ. He enlightens and empowers the believer and the church in worship, evangelism, and service.

Gen. 1:2; Judg. 14:6; Job 26:13; Psalms 51:11; 139:7ff; Isa. 61:1–3; Joel 2:28–32; Matt. 1:18; 3:16; 4:1; 12:28–32; 28:19; Mark 1:10,12; Luke 1:35; 4:1,18–19; 11:13; 12:12; 24:49; John 4:24; 14:16–17,26; 15:26; 16:7–14; Acts 1:8;
9:12–15,24–28; 12:2; 13:8; 1 Peter 2:21–25; 3:22; 1 John 1:7–9; 3:2; 4:14–15; 5:9; 2 John 7–9; Revelation 1:13–16; 5:9–14; 12:10–11; 13:8; 19:16.

C. *God the Holy Spirit*

The Holy Spirit is the Spirit of God, fully divine. He inspired holy men of old to write the Scriptures. Through illumination He enables men to understand truth. He exalts Christ. He convicts men of sin, of righteousness, and of judgment. He calls men to the Saviour, and effects regeneration. At the moment of regeneration He baptizes every believer into the Body of Christ. He cultivates Christian character, comforts believers, and bestows the spiritual gifts by which they serve God through His church. He seals the believer unto the day of final redemption. His presence in the Christian is the guarantee that God will bring the believer into the fullness of the stature of Christ. He enlightens and empowers the believer and the church in worship, evangelism, and service.

III. The Fall of Man

Man was created by the special act of God, as recorded in Genesis. "So God created man in his own image, in the image of God created he him; male and female created he them" (Gen. 1:27). "And the Lord God formed man of the dust of the ground, and breathed into his nostrils the breath of life; and man became a living soul" (Gen. 2:7).

III. Man

Man was created by the special act of God, in His own image, and is the crowning work of His creation. In the beginning man was innocent of sin and was endowed by his Creator with freedom of choice. By his free choice man sinned against God and brought sin into the human race. Through the temptation of Satan man transgressed the command of God, and fell from his

2:1–4,38; 4:31; 5:3; 6:3; 7:55; 8:17,39; 10:44; 13:2; 15:28; 16:6; 19:1–6; Rom. 8:9–11,14–16,26–27; 1 Cor. 2:10–14; 3:16; 12:3–11; Gal. 4:6; Ephes. 1:13–14; 4:30; 5:18; 1 Thess. 5:19; 1 Tim. 3:16; 4:1; 2 Tim. 1:14; 3:16; Heb. 9:8,14; 2 Peter 1:21; 1 John 4:13; 5:6–7; Rev. 1:10; 22:17.

III. Man

Man is the special creation of God, made in His own image. He created them male and female as the crowning work of His creation. The gift of gender is thus part of the goodness of God's creation. In the beginning man was innocent of sin and was endowed by his Creator with freedom of choice. By his free choice man sinned against God and brought sin into the

Genesis 1:2; Judges 14:6; Job 26:13; Psalms 51:11; 139:7ff; Isaiah 61:1–3; Joel 2:28–32; Matthew 1:18; 3:16; 4:1; 12:28–32; 28:19; Mark 1:10,12; Luke 1:35; 4:1,18–19; 11:13; 12:12; 24:49; John 4:24; 14:16–17,26; 15:26; 16:7–14; Acts 1:8; 2:1–4,38; 4:31; 5:3; 6:3; 7:55; 8:17,39; 10:44; 13:2; 15:28; 16:6; 19:1–6; Romans 8:9–11,14–16,26–27; 1 Corinthians 2:10–14; 3:16; 12:3–11,13; Galatians 4:6; Ephesians 1:13–14; 4:30; 5:18; 1 Thessalonians 5:19; 1 Timothy 3:16; 4:1; 2 Timothy 1:14; 3:16; Hebrews 9:8,14; 2 Peter 1:21; 1 John 4:13; 5:6–7; Revelation 1:10; 22:17.

He was created in a state of holiness under the law of his Maker, but, through the temptation of Satan, he transgressed the command of God and fell from his original holiness and righteousness; whereby his posterity inherit a nature corrupt and in bondage to sin, are under condemnation, and as soon as they are capable of moral action, become actual transgressors.

Gen. 1:27; Gen. 2:7; John 1:23; Gen. 3:4-7; Gen. 3:22-24; Rom. 5:12,14,19,21; Rom. 7:23-25; Rom. 11:18,22,32-33; Col. 1:21.

original innocence; whereby his posterity inherit a nature and an environment inclined toward sin, and as soon as they are capable of moral action become transgressors and are under condemnation. Only the grace of God can bring man into His holy fellowship and enable man to fulfil the creative purpose of God. The sacredness of human personality is evident in that God created man in His own image, and in that Christ died for man; therefore every man possesses dignity and is worthy of respect and Christian love.

Gen. 1:26-30; 2:5,7,18-22; 3; 9:6; Psalms 1; 8:3-6; 32:1-5; 51:5; Isa. 6:5; Jer. 17:5; Matt. 16:26; Acts 17:26-31; Rom. 1:19-32; 3:10-18,23; 5:6,12,19; 6:6; 7:14-25; 8:14-18,29; 1 Cor. 1:21-31; 15:19,21-22; Eph. 2:1-22; Col. 1:21-22; 3:9-11.

human race. Through the temptation of Satan man transgressed the command of God, and fell from his original innocence whereby his posterity inherit a nature and an environment inclined toward sin. Therefore, as soon as they are capable of moral action, they become transgressors and are under condemnation. Only the grace of God can bring man into His holy fellowship and enable man to fulfill the creative purpose of God. The sacredness of human personality is evident in that God created man in His own image, and in that Christ died for man; therefore, every person of every race possesses full dignity and is worthy of respect and Christian love.

Genesis 1:26-30; 2:5,7,18-22; 3; 9:6; Psalms 1; 8:3-6; 32:1-5; 51:5; Isaiah 6:5; Jeremiah 17:5; Matthew 16:26; Acts 17:26-31; Romans 1:19-32; 3:10-18,23; 5:6,12,19; 6:6; 7:14-25; 8:14-18,29; 1 Corinthians 1:21-31; 15:19,21-22; Ephesians 2:1-22; Colossians 1:21-22; 3:9-11.

IV. The Way of Salvation

The salvation of sinners is wholly of grace, through the mediatorial office of the Son of God, who by the Holy Spirit was born of the Virgin Mary and took upon him our nature, yet without sin; honored the divine law by his personal obedience and made atonement for our sins by his death. Being risen from the dead, he is now enthroned in Heaven, and, uniting in his person the tenderest sympathies with divine perfections, he is in every way qualified to be a compassionate and all-sufficient Saviour.

Col. 1:21–22; Eph. 1:7–10; Gal. 2:19–20; Gal. 3:13; Rom. 1:4; Eph. 1:20–23; Matt. 1:21–25; Luke 1:35; 2:11; Rom. 3:25.

V. Justification

Justification is God's gracious and full acquittal upon principles of righteousness of all sinners who believe in Christ. This blessing is bestowed, not in consideration of any works of righteousness which we

IV. Salvation

Salvation involves the redemption of the whole man, and is offered freely to all who accept Jesus Christ as Lord and Saviour, who by His own blood obtained eternal redemption for the believer. In its broadest sense salvation includes regeneration, sanctification, and glorification.

1. Regeneration, or the new birth, is a work of God's grace whereby believers become new creatures in Christ Jesus. It is a change of heart wrought by the Holy Spirit through conviction of sin, to which the sinner responds in repentance toward God and faith in the Lord Jesus Christ.

Repentance and faith are inseparable experiences of grace. Repentance is a genuine turning from sin toward God. Faith is the acceptance of Jesus Christ and commitment of the entire personality to Him as Lord and Saviour. Justification is God's gracious and full acquittal upon principles of all

IV. Salvation

Salvation involves the redemption of the whole man, and is offered freely to all who accept Jesus Christ as Lord and Saviour, who by His own blood obtained eternal redemption for the believer. In its broadest sense salvation includes regeneration, justification, sanctification, and glorification. There is no salvation apart from personal faith in Jesus Christ as Lord.

A. Regeneration, or the new birth, is a work of God's grace whereby believers become new creatures in Christ Jesus. It is a change of heart wrought by the Holy Spirit through conviction of sin, to which the sinner responds in repentance toward God and faith in the Lord Jesus Christ. Repentance and faith are inseparable experiences of grace.

Repentance is a genuine turning from sin toward God. Faith is the acceptance of Jesus Christ and commitment of the entire personality to Him as Lord and Saviour.

have done, but through the redemption that is in and through Jesus Christ. It brings us into a state of most blessed peace and favor with God, and secures every other needed blessing.

Rom. 3:24; 4:2; 5:1–2; 8:30; Eph. 1:7; 1 Cor. 1:30–31; 2 Cor. 5:21.

VI. The Freeness of Salvation

The blessings of salvation are made free to all by the gospel. It is the duty of all to accept them by penitent and obedient faith. Nothing prevents the salvation of the greatest sinner except his own voluntary refusal to accept Jesus Christ as teacher, Saviour, and Lord.

Eph. 1:5; 2:4–10; 1 Cor. 1:30–31; Rom. 5:1–9; Rev. 22:17; John 3:16; Mark 16:16.

VII. Regeneration

Regeneration or the new birth is a change of heart wrought by the Holy Spirit,

---

sinners who repent and believe in Christ. Justification brings the believer into a relationship of peace and favor with God.

2. Sanctification is the experience, beginning in regeneration, by which the believer is set apart to God's purposes, and is enabled to progress toward moral and spiritual perfection through the presence and power of the Holy Spirit dwelling in him. Growth in grace should continue throughout the regenerate person's life.

3. Glorification is the culmination of salvation and is the final blessed and abiding state of the redeemed.

Gen. 3:15; Ex. 3:14–17; 6:2–8; Matt. 1:21; 4:17; 16:21–26; 27:22–28:6; Luke 1:68–69; 2:28–32; John 1:11–14,29; 3:3–21,36; 5:24; 10:9,28–29; 15:1–16; 17:17; Acts 2:21; 4:12; 15:11; 16:30–31; 17:30–31; 20:32; Rom. 1:16–18; 2:4; 3:23–25; 4:3ff; 5:8–10; 6:1–23; 8:1–18,29–39; 10:9–10,13; 13:11–14; 1 Cor. 1:18,30; 6:19–20; 15:10; 2 Cor.

B. Justification is God's gracious and full acquittal upon principles of His righteousness of all sinners who repent and believe in Christ. Justification brings the believer unto a relationship of peace and favor with God.

C. Sanctification is the experience, beginning in regeneration, by which the believer is set apart to God's purposes, and is enabled to progress toward moral and spiritual maturity through the presence and power of the Holy Spirit dwelling in him. Growth in grace should continue throughout the regenerate person's life.

D. Glorification is the culmination of salvation and is the final blessed and abiding state of the redeemed.

Genesis 3:15; Exodus 3:14–17; 6:2–8; Matthew 1:21; 4:17; 16:21–26; 27:22–28:6; Luke 1:68–69; 2:28–32; John 1:11–14,29; 3:3–21,36; 5:24; 10:9,28–29; 15:1–16; 17:17; Acts 2:21; 4:12; 15:11; 16:30–31; 17:30–31; 20:32; Romans 1:16–18; 2:4;

whereby we become partakers of the divine nature and a holy disposition is given, leading to the love and practice of righteousness. It is a work of God's free grace conditioned upon faith in Christ and made manifest by the fruit which we bring forth to the glory of God.

John 3:1–8, 1:16–18; Rom. 8:2; Eph. 2:1,5–6,8,10; Eph. 4:30,32; Col. 3:1–11; Titus 3:5.

VIII. Repentance and Faith

We believe that repentance and faith are sacred duties, and also inseparable graces, wrought in our souls by the regenerating Spirit of God; whereby being deeply convinced of our guilt, danger, and helplessness, and of the way of salvation by Christ, we turn to God with unfeigned contrition, confession, and supplication for mercy; at the same time heartily receiving the Lord Jesus Christ as our Prophet, Priest, and King, and relying on him alone as the only and all-sufficient Saviour.

5:17–20; Gal. 2:20; 3:13; 5:22–25; 6:15; Ephes. 1:7; 2:8–22; 4:11–16; Phil. 2:12–13; Col. 1:9–22; 3:1ff.; 1 Thess. 5:23–24; 2 Tim. 1:12; Titus 2:11–14; Heb. 2:1–3; 5:8–9; 9:24–28; 11:1–12:8,14; James 2:14–26; 1 Peter 1:2–23; 1 John 1:6–2:11; Rev. 3:20; 21:1–22:5.

3:23–25; 4:3ff.; 5:8–10; 6:1–23; 8:1–18,29–39; 10:9–10,13; 13:11–14; 1 Corinthians 1:18,30; 6:19–20; 15:10; 2 Corinthians 5:17–20; Galatians 2:20; 3:13; 5:22–25; 6:15; Ephesians 1:7; 2:8–22; 4:11–16; Philippians 2:12–13; Colossians 1:9–22; 3:1ff.; 1 Thessalonians 5:23–24; 2 Timothy 1:12; Titus 2:11–14; Hebrews 2:1–3; 5:8–9; 9:24–28; 11:1–12:8,14; James 2:14–26; 1 Peter 1:2–23; 1 John 1:6–2:11; Revelation 3:20; 21:1–22:5.

Luke 22:31–34; Mark 1:15; 1 Tim. 1:13; Rom. 3:25,27,31; Rom. 4:3,9,12,16–17; John 16:8–11.

IX. Sanctification

Sanctification is the process by which the regenerate gradually attain to moral and spiritual perfection through the presence and power of the Holy Spirit dwelling in their hearts. It continues throughout the earthly life, and is accomplished by the use of all the ordinary means of grace, and particularly by the Word of God.

Acts 20:32; John 17:17; Rom. 6:5–6; Eph. 3:16; Rom. 4:14; Gal. 5:24; Heb. 12:14; Rom. 7:18–25; 2 Cor. 3:18; Gal. 5:16,25–26.

X. God's Purpose of Grace

Election is the gracious purpose of God, according to which he regenerates, sanctifies and saves sinners. It is perfectly consistent with the free agency of man, and

V. God's Purpose of Grace

Election is the gracious purpose of God, according to which He regenerates, sanctifies, and glorifies sinners. It is consistent with the free agency of man and compre-

V. God's Purpose of Grace

Election is the gracious purpose of God, according to which He regenerates, justifies, sanctifies, and glorifies sinners. It is consistent with the free agency of man, comprehends all the means in connection with the end. It is a most glorious display of God's sovereign goodness, and is infinitely wise, holy, and unchangeable. It excludes boasting and promotes humility. It encourages the use of means in the highest degree.

Rom. 8:30; 11:7; Eph. 1:10; Acts 26:18; Eph. 1:17–19; 2 Tim. 1:9; Psalm 110:3; 1 Cor. 2:14; Eph. 2:5; John 6:44–45,65; Rom. 10:12–15.

XI. Perseverance

All real believers endure to the end. Their continuance in well-doing is the mark which distinguishes them from mere professors. A special Providence cares for them, and they are kept by the power of God through faith unto salvation.

John 10:28–29; 2 Tim. 2:19; 1 John 2:19; 1 Cor. 11:32; Rom. 8:30; 9:11,16; Rom. 5:9–10; Matt. 26:70–75.

hends all the means in connection with the end. It is a glorious display of God's sovereign goodness, and is infinitely wise, holy, and unchangeable. It excludes boasting and promotes humility.

All true believers endure to the end. Those whom God has accepted in Christ, and sanctified by His Spirit, will never fall away from the state of grace, but shall persevere to the end. Believers may fall into sin through neglect and temptation, whereby they grieve the Spirit, impair their graces and comforts, bring reproach on the cause of Christ, and temporal judgments on themselves; yet they shall be kept by the power of God through faith unto salvation.

Gen. 12:1–3; Ex. 19:5–8; 1 Sam. 8:4–7,19–22; Isa. 5:1–7; Jer. 31:31ff.; Matt. 16:18–19; 21:28–45; 24:22,31; 25:34; Luke 1:68–79; 2:29–32; 19:41–44; 24:44–48; John 1:12–14; 3:16; 5:24; 6:44–45,65; 10:27–29; 15:16; 17:6,12,17–18; Acts 20:32; Rom. 5:9–10; 8:28–39; 10:12–15; 11:5–7,26–36; 1 Cor.

and comprehends all the means in connection with the end. It is the glorious display of God's sovereign goodness, and is infinitely wise, holy, and unchangeable. It excludes boasting and promotes humility.

All true believers endure to the end. Those whom God has accepted in Christ, and sanctified by His Spirit, will never fall away from the state of grace, but shall persevere to the end. Believers may fall into sin through neglect and temptation, whereby they grieve the Spirit, impair their graces and comforts, and bring reproach on the cause of Christ and temporal judgments on themselves; yet they shall be kept by the power of God through faith unto salvation.

Genesis 12:1–3; Exodus 19:5–8; 1 Samuel 8:4–7,19–22; Isaiah 5:1–7; Jeremiah 31:31ff.; Matthew 16:18–19; 21:28–45; 24:22,31; 25:34; Luke 1:68–79; 2:29–32; 19:41–44; 24:44–48; John 1:12–14; 3:16; 5:24; 6:44–45,65; 10:27–29; 15:16; 17:6, 12,17–18; Acts 20:32; Romans 5:9–10; 8:28–39; 10:12–15; 11:5–7,26–36; 1

XII. The Gospel Church

A church of Christ is a congregation of baptized believers, associated by covenant in the faith and fellowship of the gospel; observing the ordinances of Christ, governed by his laws, and exercising the gifts, rights, and privileges invested in them by his word, and seeking to extend the gospel to the ends of the earth. Its Scriptural officers are bishops, or elders, and deacons.

Matt. 16:18; Matt. 18:15–18; Rom. 1:7; 1 Cor. 1:2; Acts 2:41–42; 5:13–14; 2 Cor. 9:13; Phil. 1:1; 1 Tim. 4:14; Acts 14:23; Acts 6:3,5–6; Heb. 13:17; 1 Cor. 9:6,14.

VI. The Church

A New Testament church of the Lord Jesus Christ is a local body of baptized believers who are associated by covenant in the faith and fellowship of the gospel, observing the two ordinances of Christ, committed to His teachings, exercising the gifts, rights, and privileges invested in them by His Word, and seeking to extend the gospel to the ends of the earth.

This church is an autonomous body, operating through democratic processes under the Lordship of Jesus Christ. In such a congregation, members are equally responsible. Its Scriptural officers are pastors and deacons.

1:1–2; 15:24–28; Ephes. 1:4–23; 2:1–10; 3:1–11; Col. 1:12–14; 2 Thess. 2:13–14; 2 Tim. 1:12; 2:10,19; Heb. 11:39–12:2; 1 Peter 1:2–5,13; 2:4–10; 1 John 1:7–9; 2:19; 3:2.

VI. The Church

A New Testament church of the Lord Jesus Christ is an autonomous local congregation of baptized believers, associated by covenant in the faith and fellowship of the gospel; observing the two ordinances of Christ, governed by His laws, exercising the gifts, rights, and privileges invested in them by His Word, and seeking to extend the gospel to the ends of the earth. Each congregation operates under the Lordship of Christ through democratic processes. In such a congregation each member is responsible and accountable to Christ as Lord. Its scriptural officers are pastors and deacons. While both men and women are gifted for service in the church, the office of pastor is limited to men as qualified by Scripture.

Corinthians 1:1–2; 15:24–28; Ephesians 1:4–23; 2:1–10; 3:1–11; Colossians 1:12–14; 2 Thessalonians 2:13–14; 2 Timothy 1:12; 2:10,19; Hebrews 11:39–12:2; James 1:12; 1 Peter 1:2–5,13; 2:4–10; 1 John 1:7–9; 2:19; 3:2.

The New Testament speaks also of the church as the body of Christ which includes all of the redeemed of all the ages.

Matt. 16:15–19; 18:15–20; Acts 2:41–42,47; 5:11–14; 6:3–6; 13:1–3; 14:23,27; 15:1–30; 16:5; 20:28; Rom. 1:7; 1 Cor. 1:2; 3:16; 5:4–5; 7:17; 9:13–14; 12; Ephes. 1:22–23; 2:19–22; 3:8–11,21; 5:22–32; Phil. 1:1; Col. 1:18; 1 Tim. 3:1–15; 4:14; 1 Peter 5:1–4; Rev. 2–3; 21:2–3.

XIII. Baptism and the Lord's Supper

Christian baptism is the immersion of a believer in water in the name of the Father, the Son, and the Holy Spirit. The act is a symbol of our faith in a crucified, buried and risen Saviour. It is prerequisite to the privileges of a church relation and to the Lord's Supper, in which the

---

The New Testament speaks also of the church as the Body of Christ which includes all of the redeemed of all the ages, believers from every tribe, and tongue, and people, and nation.

Matthew 16:15–19; 18:15–20; Acts 2:41–42,47; 5:11–14; 6:3–6; 13:1–3; 14:23,27; 15:1–30; 16:5; 20:28; Romans 1:7; 1 Corinthians 1:2; 3:16; 5:4–5; 7:17; 9:13–14; 12; Ephesians 1:22–23; 2:19–22; 3:8–11,21; 5:22–32; Philippians 1:1; Colossians 1:18; 1 Timothy 2:9–14; 3:1–15; 4:14; Hebrews 11:39–40; 1 Peter 5:1–4; Revelation 2–3; 21:2–3.

VII. Baptism and the Lord's Supper

Christian baptism is the immersion of a believer in water in the name of the Father, the Son, and the Holy Spirit. It is an act of obedience symbolizing the believer's faith in a crucified, buried, and risen Saviour, the believer's death to sin, the burial of the old life, and the resurrection to walk in

members of the church, by the use of bread and wine, commemorate the dying love of Christ.

Matt. 28:19–20; 1 Cor. 4:1; Rom. 6:3–5; Col. 2:12; Mark 1:4; Matt. 3:16; John 3:23; 1 Cor. 11:23–26; 1 Cor. 10:16–17,21; Matt. 26:26–27; Acts 8:38–39; Mark 1:9–11.

XIV. The Lord's Day

The first day of the week is the Lord's day. It is a Christian institution for regular observance. It commemorates the resurrection of Christ from the dead and

---

to walk in newness of life in Christ Jesus. It is a testimony to his faith in the final resurrection of the dead. Being a church ordinance, it is prerequisite to the privileges of church membership and to the Lord's Supper.

The Lord's Supper is a symbolic act of obedience whereby members of the church, through partaking of the bread and the fruit of the vine, memorialize the death of the Redeemer and anticipate His second coming.

Matt. 3:13–17; 26:26–30; 28:19–20; Mark 1:9–11; 14:22–26; Luke 3:21–22; 22:19–20; John 3:23; Acts 2:41–42; 8:35–39; 16:30–33; Acts 20:7; Rom. 6:3–5; 1 Cor. 10:16,21; 11:23–29; Col. 2:12.

VIII. The Lord's Day

The first day of the week is the Lord's Day. It is a Christian institution for regular observance. It commemorates the resurrection of Christ from the dead and

---

newness of life in Christ Jesus. It is a testimony to his faith in the final resurrection of the dead. Being a church ordinance, it is prerequisite to the privileges of church membership and to the Lord's Supper.

The Lord's Supper is a symbolic act of obedience whereby members of the church, through partaking of the bread and the fruit of the vine, memorialize the death of the Redeemer and anticipate His second coming.

Matthew 3:13–17; 26:26–30; 28:19–20; Mark 1:9–11; 14:22–26; Luke 3:21–22; 22:19–20; John 3:23; Acts 2:41–42; 8:35–39; 16:30–33; 20:7; Romans 6:3–5; 1 Corinthians 10:16,21; 11:23–29; Colossians 2:12.

VIII. The Lord's Day

The first day of the week is the Lord's Day. It is a Christian institution for regular observance. It commemorates the resurrection of Christ from the dead and should be employed in exercises of worship and spiritual devotion, both public and private, and by refraining from worldly amusements, and resting from secular employments, works of necessity and mercy only excepted.

Ex. 20:3–6; Matt. 4:10; Matt. 28:19; 1 Tim. 4:13; Col. 3:16; John 4:21; Ex. 20:8; 1 Cor. 16:1–2; Acts 20:7; Rev. 1:1; Matt. 12:1–13.

XXV. The Kingdom

The Kingdom of God is the reign of God in the heart and life of the individual in every human relationship, and in every form and institution of organized human society. The chief means for promoting the Kingdom of God on earth are preaching the gospel of Christ, and teaching the principles of righteousness contained therein. The Kingdom of God will be complete when every thought and will of man shall be brought into captivity to the will of Christ. And it is the duty of all Christ's

should be employed in exercises of worship and spiritual devotion, both public and private, and by refraining from worldly amusements, and resting from secular employments, work of necessity and mercy only being excepted.

Ex. 20:8–11; Matt. 12:1–12; 28:1ff; Mark 2:27–28; 16:1–7; Luke 24:1–3,33–36; John 4:21–24; 20:1,19–28; Acts 20:7; 1 Cor. 16:1–2; Col. 2:16; 3:16; Rev. 1:10.

IX. The Kingdom

The kingdom of God includes both His general sovereignty over the universe and His particular kingship over men who willfully acknowledge Him as King. Particularly the kingdom is the realm of salvation into which men enter by trustful, childlike commitment to Jesus Christ. Christians ought to pray and to labor that the kingdom may come and God's will be done on earth. The full consummation of the kingdom awaits the return of Jesus Christ and the end of this age.

should include exercises of worship and spiritual devotion, both public and private. Activities on the Lord's Day should be commensurate with the Christian's conscience under the Lordship of Jesus Christ.

Exodus 20:8–11; Matthew 12:1–12; 28:1ff; Mark 2:27–28; 16:1–7; Luke 24:1–3,33–36; John 4:21–24; 20:1,19–28; Acts 20:7; Romans 14:5–10; I Corinthians 16:1–2; Colossians 2:16; 3:16; Revelation 1:10.

IX. The Kingdom

The Kingdom of God includes both His general sovereignty over the universe and His particular kingship over men who willfully acknowledge Him as King. Particularly the Kingdom is the realm of salvation into which men enter by trustful, childlike commitment to Jesus Christ. Christians ought to pray and to labor that the Kingdom may come and God's will be done on earth. The full consummation of the Kingdom awaits the return of Jesus Christ and the end of this age.

people to pray and labor continually that his Kingdom may come and his will be done on earth as it is done in heaven.

Dan. 2:37–44; 7:18; Matt. 4:23; 8:12; 12:25; 13:38,43; 25:34; 26:29; Mark 11:10; Luke 12:32; 22:29; Acts 1:6; 1 Cor. 15:24; Col. 1:13; Heb. 12:28; Rev. 1:9; Luke 4:43; 8:1; 9:2; 17:20–21; John 3:3; John 18:36; Matt. 6:10; Luke 23:42.

X. Last Things

God, in His own time and in His own way, will bring the world to its appropriate end. According to His promise, Jesus Christ will return personally and visibly in glory to the earth; the dead will be raised; and Christ will judge all men in righteousness. The unrighteous will be consigned to hell, the place of everlasting punishment. The righteous in their resurrected and glorified bodies will receive their reward and will dwell forever in heaven with the Lord.

Gen. 1:1; Isa. 9:6–7; Jer. 23:5–6; Matt. 3:2; 4:8–10,23; 12:25–28; 13:1–52; 25:31–46; 26:29; Mark 1:14–15; 9:1; Luke 4:43; 8:1; 9:2; 12:31–32; 17:20–21; 23:42; John 3:3; 18:36; Acts 1:6–7; 17:22–31; Rom. 5:17; 8:19; 1 Cor. 15:24–28; Col. 1:13; Heb. 11:10,16; 12:28; 1 Peter 2:4–10; 4:13; Rev. 1:6,9; 5:10; 11:15; 21–22.

XV. The Righteous and the Wicked

There is a radical and essential difference between the righteous and wicked. Those only who are justified through the name of the Lord Jesus Christ and sanctified by the Holy Spirit are truly righteous in his sight. Those who continue in impenitence and unbelief are in his sight wicked and are under condemnation. This distinction between the righteous and the wicked holds in and after death, and will be made manifest at the judgment when final and everlasting awards are made to all men.

X. Last Things

God, in His own time and in His own way, will bring the world to its appropriate end. According to His promise, Jesus Christ will return personally and visibly in glory to the earth; the dead will be raised; and Christ will judge all men in righteousness. The unrighteous will be consigned to Hell, the place of everlasting punishment. The righteous in their resurrected and glorified bodies will receive their reward and will dwell forever in Heaven with the Lord.

Genesis 1:1; Isaiah 9:6–7; Jeremiah 23:5–6; Matthew 3:2; 4:8–10,23; 12:25–28; 13:1–52; 25:31–46; 26:29; Mark 1:14–15; 9:1; Luke 4:43; 8:1; 9:2; 12:31–32; 17:20–21; 23:42; John 3:3; 18:36; Acts 1:6–7; 17:22–31; Romans 5:17; 1 Corinthians 15:24–28; Colossians 1:13; Hebrews 11:10,16; 12:28; 1 Peter 2:4–10; 4:13; Revelation 1:6,9; 5:10; 11:15; 21–22.

Gen. 3:19; Acts 13:36; Luke 23:43; 2 Cor. 5:1,6,8; Phil. 1:23; 1 Cor. 15:51–52; 1 Thess. 4:17; Phil. 3:21; 1 Cor. 6:3; Matt. 25:32–46; Rom. 9:22–23; Mark 9:48; 1 Thess. 1:7–10; Rev. 22:20.

XVI. The Resurrection

The Scriptures clearly teach that Jesus rose from the dead. His grave was emptied of its contents. He appeared to the disciples after his resurrection in many convincing manifestations. He now exists in his glorified body at God's right hand. There will be a resurrection of the righteous and the wicked. The bodies of the righteous will conform to the glorious spiritual body of Jesus.

1 Cor. 15:1–58; 2 Cor. 5:1–8; 1 Thess. 4:17; John 5:28–29; Phil. 3:21; Acts 24:15; John 20:9; Matt. 28:6.

XVII. The Return of the Lord

The New Testament teaches in many places the visible and personal return of Jesus to

Isa. 2:4; 11:9; Matt. 16:27; 18:8–9; 19:28; 24:27,30,36,44; 25:31–46; 26:64; Mark 8:38; 9:43–48; Luke 12:40,48; 16:19–26; 17:22–37; 21:27–28; John 14:1–3; Acts 1:11; 17:31; Rom. 14:10; 1 Cor. 4:5; 15:24–28,35–58; 2 Cor. 5:10; Phil. 3:20–21; Col. 1:5; 3:4; 1 Thess. 4:14–18; 5:1ff; 2 Thess. 1:7ff; 2; 1 Tim. 6:14; 2 Tim. 4:1,8; Titus 2:13; Heb. 9:27–28; James 5:8; 2 Peter 3:7ff; 1 John 2:28; 3:2; Jude 14; Rev. 1:18; 3:11; 20:1–22:13.

Isaiah 2:4; 11:9; Matthew 16:27; 18:8–9; 19:28; 24:27,30,36,44; 25:31–46; 26:64; Mark 8:38; 9:43–48; Luke 12:40,48; 16:19–26; 17:22–37; 21:27–28; John 14:1–3; Acts 1:11; 17:31; Romans 14:10; 1 Corinthians 4:5; 15:24–28,35–58; 2 Corinthians 5:10; Philippians 3:20–21; Colossians 1:5; 3:4; 1 Thessalonians 4:14–18; 5:1ff; 2 Thessalonians 1:7ff; 2; 1 Timothy 6:14; 2 Timothy 4:1,8; Titus 2:13; Hebrews 9:27–28; James 5:8; 2 Peter 3:7ff; 1 John 2:28; 3:2; Jude 14; Revelation 1:18; 3:11; 20:1–22:13.

this earth. "This same Jesus which is taken up from you into heaven, shall so come in like manner as ye have seen him go into heaven." The time of his coming is not revealed. "Of that day and hour knoweth no one, no, not the angels in heaven, but my Father only" (Matt. 24:36). It is the duty of all believers to live in readiness for his coming and by diligence in good works to make manifest to all men the reality and power of their hope in Christ.

Matt. 24:36, 42–47; Mark 13:32–37; Luke 21:27–28; Acts 1:9–11.

XXIII. Evangelism and Missions

It is the duty of every Christian man and woman, and the duty of every church of Christ to seek to extend the gospel to the ends of the earth. The new birth of man's spirit by God's Holy Spirit means the birth of love for others. Missionary effort on the part of all rests thus upon a spiritual necessity of the regenerate life. It is also expressly and repeatedly commanded in

XI. Evangelism and Missions

It is the duty and privilege of every follower of Christ and of every church of the Lord Jesus Christ to endeavor to make disciples of all nations. The new birth of man's spirit by God's Holy Spirit means the birth of love for others. Missionary effort on the part of all rests thus upon a spiritual necessity of the regenerate life, and is expressly and repeatedly commanded in the

XI. Evangelism and Missions

It is the duty and privilege of every follower of Christ and of every church of the Lord Jesus Christ to endeavor to make disciples of all nations. The new birth of man's spirit by God's Holy Spirit means the birth of love for others. Missionary effort on the part of all rests thus upon a spiritual necessity of the regenerate life, and is expressly and repeatedly commanded in the teachings of Christ.

the teachings of Christ. It is the duty of every child of God to seek constantly to win the lost to Christ by personal effort and by all other methods sanctioned by the gospel of Christ.

Matt. 10:5; 13:18–23; 22:9–10; 28:19–20; Mark 16:15–16; 16:19–20; Luke 24:46–53; Acts 1:5–8; 2:1–2,21,39; 8:26–40; 10:42–48; 13:2,30–33; 1 Thess. 1–8.

XX. Education

Christianity is the religion of enlightenment and intelligence. In Jesus Christ are hidden all the treasures of wisdom and knowledge. All sound learning is therefore a part of our Christian heritage. The new birth opens all

---

child of God to seek constantly to win the lost to Christ by personal effort and by all other methods in harmony with the gospel of Christ.

Gen. 12:1–3; Ex. 19:5–6; Isa. 6:1–8; Matt. 9:37–38; 10:5–15; 13:18–30,37–43; 16:19; 22:9–10; 24:14; 28:18–20; Luke 10:1–18; 24:46–53; John 14:11–12; 15:7–8,16; 17:15; 20:21; Acts 1:8; 2; 8:26–40; 10:42–48; 13:2–3; Rom. 10:13–15; Ephes. 3:1–11; 1 Thess. 1:8; 2 Tim. 4:5; Heb. 2:1–3; 11:39–12:2; 1 Peter 2:4–10; Rev. 22:17.

XII. Education

The cause of education in the kingdom of Christ is co-ordinate with the causes of missions and general benevolence and should receive along with these the liberal

---

The Lord Jesus Christ has commanded the preaching of the gospel to all nations. It is the duty of every child of God to seek constantly to win the lost to Christ by verbal witness undergirded by a Christian lifestyle, and by other methods in harmony with the gospel of Christ.

Genesis 12:1–3; Exodus 19:5–6; Isaiah 6:1–8; Matthew 9:37–38; 10:5–15; 13:18–30,37–43; 16:19; 22:9–10; 24:14; 28:18–20; Luke 10:1–18; 24:46–53; John 14:11–12; 15:7–8,16; 17:15; 20:21; Acts 1:8; 2; 8:26–40; 10:42–48; 13:2–3; Romans 10:13–15; Ephesians 3:1–11; 1 Thessalonians 1:8; 2 Timothy 4:5; Hebrews 2:1–3; 11:39–12:2; 1 Peter 2:4–10; Revelation 22:17.

XII. Education

Christianity is the faith of enlightenment and intelligence. In Jesus Christ abide all the treasures of wisdom and knowledge. All sound learning is, therefore, a part of our Christian heritage. The new birth

human faculties and creates a thirst for knowledge. An adequate system of schools is necessary to a complete spiritual program for Christ's people. The cause of education in the Kingdom of Christ is coordinate with the causes of missions and general benevolence, and should receive along with these the liberal support of the churches.

Deut. 4:1,5,9,13–14; Deut. 6:1,7–10; Psalm 19:7–8; Prov. 4:1–10; Prov. 8:1–7; Matt. 28:20; Col. 2:3; Neh. 8:1–4.

support of the churches. An adequate system of Christian schools is necessary to a complete spiritual program for Christ's people.

In Christian education there should be a proper balance between academic freedom and academic responsibility. Freedom in any orderly relationship of human life is always limited and never absolute. The freedom of a teacher in a Christian school, college, or seminary is limited by the pre-eminence of Jesus Christ, by the authoritative nature of the Scriptures, and by the distinct purpose for which the school exists.

Deut. 4:1,5,9,14; 6:1–10; 31:12–13; Neh. 8:1–8; Job 28:28; Psalms 19:7ff; 119:11; Prov. 3:13ff; 4:1–10; 8:1–7,11; 15:14; Eccl. 7:19; Matt. 5:2; 7:24ff; 28:19–20; Luke 2:40; 1 Cor. 1:18–31; Eph. 4:11–16; Phil. 4:8; Col. 2:3,8–9; 1 Tim. 1:3–7; 2 Tim. 2:15; 3:14–17; Heb. 5:12–6:3; James 1:5; 3:17.

opens all human faculties and creates a thirst for knowledge. Moreover, the cause of education in the Kingdom of Christ is co-ordinate with the causes of missions and general benevolence, and should receive along with these the liberal support of the churches. An adequate system of Christian education is necessary to a complete spiritual program for Christ's people.

In Christian education there should be a proper balance between academic freedom and academic responsibility. Freedom in any orderly relationship of human life is always limited and never absolute. The freedom of a teacher in a Christian school, college, or seminary is limited by the pre-eminence of Jesus Christ, by the authoritative nature of the Scriptures, and by the distinct purpose for which the school exists.

Deuteronomy 4:1,5,9,14; 6:1–10; 31:12–13; Nehemiah 8:1–8; Job 28:28; Psalms 19:7ff; 119:11; Proverbs 3:13ff; 4:1–10; 8:1–7,11; 15:14; Ecclesiastes 7:19; Matthew 5:2;

7:24ff; 28:19–20; Luke 2:40; 1 Corinthians 1:18–31; Ephesians 4:11–16; Philippians 4:8; Colossians 2:3,8–9; 1 Timothy 1:3–7; 2 Timothy 2:15; 3:14–17; Hebrews 5:12–6:3; James 1:5; 3:17.

XIII. Stewardship

God is the source of all blessings, temporal and spiritual; all that we have and are we owe to Him. Christians have a spiritual debtorship to the whole world, a holy trusteeship in the gospel, and a binding stewardship in their possessions. They are therefore under obligation to serve Him with their time, talents, and material possessions; and should recognize all these as entrusted to them to use for the glory of God and for helping others. According to the Scriptures, Christians should contribute of their means cheerfully, regularly, systematically, proportionately, and liberally for the advancement of the Redeemer's cause on earth.

XIII. Stewardship

God is the source of all blessings, temporal and spiritual; all that we have and are we owe to Him. Christians have a spiritual debtorship to the whole world, a holy trusteeship in the gospel, and a binding stewardship in their possessions. They are therefore under obligation to serve Him with their time, talents, and material possessions; and should recognize all these as entrusted to them to use for the glory of God and for helping others. According to the Scriptures, Christians should contribute of their means cheerfully, regularly, systematically, proportionately, and liberally for the advancement of the Redeemer's cause on earth.

XXIV. Stewardship

God is the source of all blessings, temporal and spiritual; all that we have and are we owe to him. We have a spiritual debtorship to the whole world, a holy trusteeship in the gospel, and a binding stewardship in our possessions. We are therefore under obligation to serve him with our time, talents and material possessions; and should recognize all these as entrusted to us to use for the glory of God and helping others. Christians should give cheerfully, regularly, systematically, proportionately, and liberally, contribute of their means to advancing the Redeemer's cause on earth.

Luke 12:42; 16:1–8; Titus 1:7; 1 Peter 4:10; 2 Cor. 8:1–7; 2 Cor. 8:11–19; 2 Cor.

12:1–15; Matt. 25:14–30; Rom. 1:8–15; 1 Cor. 6:20; Acts 2:44–47.

XXII. Co-Operation

Christ's people should, as occasion requires, organize such associations and conventions as may best secure co-operation for the great objects of the Kingdom of God. Such organizations have no authority over each other or over the churches. They are voluntary and advisory bodies designed to elicit, combine, and direct the energies of our people in the most effective manner. Individual members of New Testament churches should co-operate with each other, and the churches themselves should co-operate with each other in carrying forward the missionary, educational, and benevolent program for the extension of

Gen. 14:20; Lev. 27:30–32; Deut. 8:18; Mal. 3:8–12; Matt. 6:1–4,19–21; 19:21; 23:23; 25:14–29; Luke 12:16–21,42; 16:1–13; Acts 2:44–47; 5:1–11; 17:24–25; 20:35; Rom. 6:6–22; 12:1–2; 1 Cor. 4:1–2; 6:19–20; 12; 16:1–4; 2 Cor. 8–9; 12:15; Phil. 4:10–19; 1 Peter 1:18–19.

XIV. Co-Operation

Christ's people should, as occasion requires, organize such associations and conventions as may best secure co-operation for the great objects of the kingdom of God. Such organizations have no authority over one another or over the churches. They are voluntary and advisory bodies designed to elicit, combine, and direct the energies of our people in the most effective manner. Members of New Testament churches should co-operate with one another in carrying forward the missionary, educational, and benevolent ministries for the extension of Christ's kingdom. Christian unity in the New Testament sense is spiritual harmony

Genesis 14:20; Leviticus 27:30–32; Deuteronomy 8:18; Malachi 3:8–12; Matthew 6:1–4,19–21; 19:21; 23:23; 25:14–29; Luke 12:16–21,42; 16:1–13; Acts 2:44–47; 5:1–11; 17:24–25; 20:35; Romans 6:6–22; 12:1–2; 1 Corinthians 4:1–2; 6:19–20; 12; 16:1–4; 2 Corinthians 8–9; 12:15; Philippians 4:10–19; 1 Peter 1:18–19.

XIV. Cooperation

Christ's people should, as occasion requires, organize such associations and conventions as may best secure cooperation for the great objects of the Kingdom of God. Such organizations have no authority over one another or over the churches. They are voluntary and advisory bodies designed to elicit, combine, and direct the energies of our people in the most effective manner. Members of New Testament churches should cooperate with one another in carrying forward the missionary, educational, and benevolent ministries for the extension of Christ's Kingdom. Christian unity in the New Testament sense is

Christ's Kingdom. Christian unity in the New Testament sense is spiritual harmony and voluntary co-operation for common ends by various groups of Christ's people. It is permissable and desirable as between the various Christian denominations, when the end to be attained is itself justified, and when such co-operation involves no violation of conscience or compromise of loyalty to Christ and his Word as revealed in the New Testament.

Ezra 1:3–4; 2:68–69; 5:14–15; Neh. 4:4–6; 8:1–4; Mal. 3:10; Matt. 10:5–15; 22:1–10; Acts 1:13–14; 1:21–26; 2:1, 41–47; 1 Cor. 1:10–17; 12:11–12; 13; 14:33–34, 40; 16:2; 2 Cor. 9:1–15; Eph. 4:1–16; 3 John 1:5–8.

XXI. Social Service

Every Christian is under obligation to seek to make the will of Christ regnant in his own life and in human society to oppose in the spirit of Christ every form of greed, selfishness, and vice; to provide for the

---

and voluntary co-operation for common ends by various groups of Christ's people. Co-operation is desirable between the various Christian denominations, when the end to be attained is itself justified, and when such co-operation involves no violation of conscience or compromise of loyalty to Christ and his Word as revealed in the New Testament.

Ex. 17:12; 18:17ff; Judg. 7:21; Ezra 1:3–4; 2:68–69; 5:14–15; Neh. 4; 8:1–5; Matt. 10:5–15; 20:1–16; 22:1–10; 28:19–20; Mark 2:3; Luke 10:1ff; Acts 1:13–14; 2:1ff; 4:31–37; 13:2–3; 15:1–35; 1 Cor. 1:10–17; 3:5–15; 12; 2 Cor. 8–9; Gal. 1:6–10; Eph. 4:1–16; Phil. 1:15–18.

XV. The Christian and the Social Order

Every Christian is under obligation to seek to make the will of Christ supreme in his own life and in human society. Means and methods used for the improvement of

---

spiritual harmony and voluntary cooperation for common ends by various groups of Christ's people. Cooperation is desirable between the various Christian denominations, when the end to be attained is itself justified, and when such cooperation involves no violation of conscience or compromise of loyalty to Christ and His Word as revealed in the New Testament.

Exodus 17:12; 18:17ff; Judges 7:21; Ezra 1:3–4; 2:68–69; 5:14–15; Nehemiah 4; 8:1–5; Matthew 10:5–15; 20:1–16; 22:1–10; 28:19–20; Mark 2:3; Luke 10:1ff; Acts 1:13–14; 2:1ff; 4:31–37; 13:2–3; 15:1–35; 1 Corinthians 1:10–17; 3:5–15; 12; 2 Corinthians 8–9; Galatians 1:6–10; Ephesians 4:1–16; Philippians 1:15–18.

XV. The Christian and the Social Order

All Christians are under obligation to seek to make the will of Christ supreme in our own lives and in human society. Means and methods used for the improvement of

orphaned, the aged, the helpless, and the sick; to seek to bring industry, government, and society as a whole under the sway of the principles of righteousness, truth and brotherly love; to promote these ends Christians should be ready to work with all men of good will in any good cause, always being careful to act in the spirit of love without compromising their loyalty to Christ and his truth. All means and methods used in social service for the amelioration of society and the establishment of righteousness among men must finally depend on the regeneration of the individual by the saving grace of God in Christ Jesus.

Luke 10:25–37; Ex. 22:10,14; Lev. 6:2; Deut. 4:42; Deut. 15:2; Deut. 20:10; 27:17; Psalm 101:5; Ezek. 18:6; Heb. 2:15; Zech. 8:16; Ex. 20:16; James 2:8; Rom. 12–14; Col. 3:12–17.

society and the establishment of righteousness among men can be truly and permanently helpful only when they are rooted in the regeneration of the individual by the saving grace of God in Christ Jesus. The Christian should oppose in the spirit of Christ every form of greed, selfishness, and vice. He should work to provide for the orphaned, the needy, the aged, the helpless, and the sick. Every Christian should seek to bring industry, government, and society as a whole under the sway of the principles of righteousness, truth, and brotherly love. In order to promote these ends Christians should be ready to work with all men of good will in any good cause, always being careful to act in the spirit of love without compromising their loyalty to Christ and his truth.

Ex. 20:3–17; Lev. 6:2–5; Deut. 10:12; 27:17; Psalm 101:5; Micah 6:8; Zech. 8:16; Matt. 5:13–16, 43–48; 22:36–40; 25:35; Mark 1:29–34; 2:3ff.; 10:21; Luke 4:18–21; 10:27–37; 20:25; John 15:12;

society and the establishment of righteousness among men can be truly and permanently helpful only when they are rooted in the regeneration of the individual by the saving grace of God in Jesus Christ. In the spirit of Christ, Christians should oppose racism, every form of greed, selfishness, and vice, and all forms of sexual immorality, including adultery, homosexuality, and pornography. We should work to provide for the orphaned, the needy, the abused, the aged, the helpless, and the sick. We should speak on behalf of the unborn and contend for the sanctity of all human life from conception to natural death. Every Christian should seek to bring industry, government, and society as a whole under the sway of the principles of righteousness, truth, and brotherly love. In order to promote these ends Christians should be ready to work with all men of good will in any good cause, always being careful to act in the spirit of love without compromising their loyalty to Christ and His truth.

XIX. Peace and War

It is the duty of Christians to seek peace with all men on principles of righteousness. In accordance with the spirit and teachings of Christ they should do all in their power to put an end to war.

The true remedy for the war spirit is the pure gospel of our Lord. The supreme need of the world is the acceptance of his teachings in all the affairs of men and nations, and the practical application of his law of love.

17:15; Rom. 12–14; 1 Cor. 5:9–10; 6:1–7; 7:20–24; 10:23–11:1; Gal. 3:26–28; Eph. 6:5–9; Col. 3:12–17; 1 Thess. 3:12; Philemon; James 1:27; 2:8.

XVI. Peace and War

It is the duty of Christians to seek peace with all men on principles of righteousness. In accordance with the spirit and teachings of Christ they should do all in their power to put an end to war.

The true remedy for the war spirit is the gospel of our Lord. The supreme need of the world is the acceptance of His teachings in all the affairs of men and nations, and the practical application of His law of love.

Exodus 20:3–17; Leviticus 6:2–5; Deuteronomy 10:12; 27:17; Psalm 101:5; Micah 6:8; Zechariah 8:16; Matthew 5:13–16,43–48; 22:36–40; 25:35; Mark 1:29–34; 2:3ff; 10:21; Luke 4:18–21; 10:27–37; 20:25; John 15:12; 17:15; Romans 12–14; 1 Corinthians 5:9–10; 6:1–7; 7:20–24; 10:23–11:1; Galatians 3:26–28; Ephesians 6:5–9; Colossians 3:12–17; 1 Thessalonians 3:12; Philemon; James 1:27; 2:8.

XVI. Peace and War

It is the duty of Christians to seek peace with all men on principles of righteousness. In accordance with the spirit and teachings of Christ they should do all in their power to put an end to war.

The true remedy for the war spirit is the gospel of our Lord. The supreme need of the world is the acceptance of His teachings in all the affairs of men and nations, and the practical application of His law of love. Christian people throughout the

We urge Christian people throughout the world to pray for the reign of the Prince of Peace, and to oppose everything likely to provoke war.

Matt. 5:9,13–14,43–46; Heb. 12:14; James 4:1; Matt. 6:33; Rom. 14:17,19.

XVIII. Religious Liberty

God alone is Lord of the conscience, and he has left it free from the doctrines and commandments of men which are contrary to his Word or not contained in it. Church and state should be separate. The state owes to the church protection and full freedom in the pursuit of its spiritual ends. In providing for such freedom no ecclesiastical group or denomination should be favored by the state more than others. Civil government being ordained of God, it is the duty of Christians to render loyal obedience thereto in all things not contrary to the revealed will of God. The church should not resort to the civil power to carry on its work. The gospel of

Isa. 2:4; Matt. 5:9,38–48; 6:33; 26:52; Luke 22:36,38; Rom. 12:18–19; 13:1–7; 14:19; Heb. 12:14; James 4:1–2.

XVII. Religious Liberty

God alone is Lord of the conscience, and He has left it free from the doctrines and commandments of men which are contrary to His Word or not contained in it. Church and state should be separate. The state owes to every church protection and full freedom in the pursuit of its spiritual ends. In providing for such freedom no ecclesiastical group or denomination should be favored by the state more than others. Civil government being ordained of God, it is the duty of Christians to render loyal obedience thereto in all things not contrary to the revealed will of God. The church should not resort to the civil power to carry on its work. The gospel of

world should pray for the reign of the Prince of Peace.

Isaiah 2:4; Matthew 5:9,38–48; 6:33; 26:52; Luke 22:36,38; Romans 12:18–19; 13:1–7; 14:19; Hebrews 12:14; James 4:1–2.

XVII. Religious Liberty

God alone is Lord of the conscience, and He has left it free from the doctrines and commandments of men which are contrary to His Word or not contained in it. Church and state should be separate. The state owes to every church protection and full freedom in the pursuit of its spiritual ends. In providing for such freedom no ecclesiastical group or denomination should be favored by the state more than others. Civil government being ordained of God, it is the duty of Christians to render loyal obedience thereto in all things not contrary to the revealed will of God. The church should not resort to the civil power to carry on its work. The gospel of

Christ contemplates spiritual means alone for the pursuit of its ends. The state has no right to impose penalties for religious opinions of any kind. The state has no right to impose taxes for the support of any form of religion. A free church in a free state is the Christian ideal, and this implies the right of free and unhindered access to God on the part of all men, and the right to form and propagate opinions in the sphere of religion without interference by the civil power.

Rom. 13:1–7; 1 Peter 2:17; 1 Tim. 2:1–2; Gal. 3:9–14; John 7:38–39; James 4:12; Gal. 5:13; 2 Peter 2:18–21; 1 Cor. 3:5; Rom. 6:1–2; Matt. 22:21; Mark 12:17.

XVIII. The Family
(1998 Amendment)

God has ordained the family as the foundational institution of human society. It is composed of persons related to one another by marriage, blood, or adoption.

Christ contemplates spiritual means alone for the pursuit of its ends. The state has no right to impose penalties for religious opinions of any kind. The state has no right to impose taxes for the support of any form of religion. A free church in a free state is the Christian ideal, and this implies the right of free and unhindered access to God on the part of all men and the right to form and propagate opinions in the sphere of religion without interference by the civil power.

Gen. 1:27; 2:7; Matt. 6:6–7; 24; 16:26; 22:21; John 8:36; Acts 4:19–20; Rom. 6:1–2; 13:1–7; Gal. 5:1,13; Phil. 3:20; 1 Tim. 2:1–2; James 4:12; 1 Peter 2:12–17; 3:11–17; 4:12–19.

XVIII. The Family

God has ordained the family as the foundational institution of human society. It is composed of persons related to one another by marriage, blood, or adoption.

Christ contemplates spiritual means alone for the pursuit of its ends. The state has no right to impose penalties for religious opinions of any kind. The state has no right to impose taxes for the support of any form of religion. A free church in a free state is the Christian ideal, and this implies the right of free and unhindered access to God on the part of all men, and the right to form and propagate opinions in the sphere of religion without interference by the civil power.

Genesis 1:27; 2:7; Matthew 6:6–7, 24; 16:26; 22:21; John 8:36; Acts 4:19–20; Romans 6:1–2; 13:1–7; Galatians 5:1,13; Philippians 3:20; 1 Timothy 2:1–2; James 4:12; 1 Peter 2:12–17; 3:11–17; 4:12–19.

XVIII. The Family

God has ordained the family as the foundational institution of human society. It is composed of persons related to one another by marriage, blood, or adoption.

Marriage is the uniting of one man and one woman in covenant commitment for a lifetime. It is God's unique gift to reveal the union between Christ and His church and to provide for the man and the woman in marriage the framework for intimate companionship, the channel of sexual expression according to biblical standards, and the means for procreation of the human race.

The husband and wife are of equal worth before God, since both are created in God's image. The marriage relationship models the way God relates to His people. A husband is to love his wife as Christ loved the church. He has the God-given responsibility to provide for, to protect, and to lead his family. A wife is to submit herself graciously to the servant leadership of her husband even as the church willingly submits to the headship of Christ. She, being in the image of God as is her husband and thus equal to him, has the God-given responsibility to respect her husband and to serve as his helper in managing the household and nurturing the next generation.

Marriage is the uniting of one man and one woman in covenant commitment for a lifetime. It is God's unique gift to provide for the man and the woman in marriage the framework for intimate companionship, the channel for sexual expression according to biblical standards, and the means for procreation of the human race.

The husband and wife are of equal worth before God, since both are created in God's image. The marriage relationship models the way God relates to His people. A husband is to love his wife as Christ loved the church. He has the God-given responsibility to provide for, to protect, and to lead his family. A wife is to submit herself graciously to the servant leadership of her husband even as the church willingly submits to the headship of Christ. She, being in the image of God as is her husband and thus equal to him, has the God-given responsibility to respect her husband and to serve as his helper in managing the household and nurturing the next generation.

Children, from the moment of conception, are a blessing and heritage from the Lord. Parents are to demonstrate to their children God's pattern for marriage. Parents are to teach their children spiritual and moral values and to lead them, through consistent lifestyle example and loving discipline, to make choices based on biblical truth. Children are to honor and obey their parents.

Genesis 1:26–28; 2:15–25; 3:1–20; Exodus 20:12; Deuteronomy 6:4–9; Joshua 24:15; 1 Samuel 1:26–28; Psalms 51:5; 78:1–8; 127; 128; 139:13–16; Proverbs 1:8; 5:15–20; 6:20–22; 12:4; 13:24; 14:1; 17:6; 18:22; 22:6,15; 23:13–14; 24:3; 29:15,17; 31:10–31; Ecclesiastes 4:9–12; 9:9; Malachi 2:14–16; Matthew 5:31–32; 18:2–5; 19:3–9; Mark 10:6–12; Romans 1:18–32; 1 Corinthians 7:1–16; Ephesians 5:21–33; 6:1–4; Colossians 3:18–21; 1 Timothy 5:8,14; 2 Timothy 1:3–5; Titus 2:3–5; Hebrews 13:4; 1 Peter 3:1–7.

Children, from the moment of conception, are a blessing and heritage from the Lord. Parents are to demonstrate to their children God's pattern for marriage. Parents are to teach their children spiritual and moral values and to lead them, through consistent lifestyle example and loving discipline, to make choices based on biblical truth. Children are to honor and obey their parents.

Gen. 1:26–28; 2:18–25; 3:1–20; Ex. 20:12; Deut. 6:4–9; Josh. 24:15; 1 Sam. 1:26–28; Ps. 51:5; 78:1–8; 127; 128; 139:13–16; Prov. 1:8; 5:15–20; 6:20–22; 12:4; 13:24; 14:1; 17:6; 18:22; 22:6,15; 23:13–14; 24:3; 29:15,17; 31:10–31; Eccl. 4:9–12; 9:9; Mal. 2:14–16; Matt. 5:31–32; 18:2–5; 19:3–9; Mark 10:6–12; Rom. 1:18–32; 1 Cor. 7:1–16; Eph. 5:21–33; 6:1–4; Col. 3:18–21; 1 Tim. 5:8,14; 2 Tim. 1:3–5; Titus 2:3–5; Heb. 13:4; 1 Pet. 3:1–7.

About the Contributors

Daniel L. Akin (Ph.D., University of Texas at Arlington) is president and professor of Preaching and Theology at Southeastern Baptist Theological Seminary.

Douglas K. Blount (Ph.D., University of Notre Dame) is associate professor of Philosophy of Religion; assistant dean for Ethics and Philosophical Studies; and managing editor, *Southwestern Journal of Theology*, at Southwestern Baptist Theological Seminary.

Chad Owen Brand (Ph.D., Southwestern Baptist Theological Seminary) is professor of Christian Theology at Southern Baptist Theological Seminary; and associate dean for Biblical and Theological Studies, Boyce College.

E. David Cook (Ph.D., New College, Edinburgh University) is Holmes Professor of Faith and Learning at Wheaton College; fellow, Green College, Oxford; and Distinguished Professor of Christian Ethics at Southern Baptist Theological Seminary.

Barry K. Creamer (Ph.D., University of Texas at Arlington) is associate professor of Humanities at Criswell College; and adjunct professor of Philosophy at Texas Woman's University and the University of Texas at Arlington.

Keith E. Eitel (D.Theol., University of South Africa; D.Miss., Trinity Evangelical Divinity School) is dean and professor of Missions at the Roy Fish School of Evangelism and Missions, Southwestern Baptist Theological Seminary.

John S. Hammett (Ph.D., Southern Baptist Theological Seminary) is professor of Systematic Theology at Southeastern Baptist Theological Seminary.

Susie Hawkins (M.A., Criswell College) has served as director of women's ministries in local churches and leads Bible studies. Her interests are in encouraging ministry wives and researching women in church history.

Jerry A. Johnson (Ph.D., Southern Baptist Theological Seminary) is president and professor of Theology and Ethics at Criswell College; and hosts *Jerry Johnson Live*, a daily syndicated radio talk show.

Steve W. Lemke (Ph.D., Southwestern Baptist Theological Seminary) is provost and professor of Philosophy and Ethics at New Orleans Baptist Theological Seminary; director of the Baptist Center for Theology and Ministry; executive editor of the *Journal for Baptist Theology and Ministry*; and a founding fellow of the Research Institute of the Ethics and Religious Liberty Commission of the Southern Baptist Convention.

C. Ben Mitchell (Ph.D., University of Tennessee at Knoxville) is director of the Center for Bioethics and Human Dignity; associate professor of Bioethics and Contemporary Culture at Trinity Evangelical Divinity School; and consultant on biomedical and life issues for the Ethics and Religious Liberty Commission of the Southern Baptist Convention.

R. Albert Mohler Jr. (Ph.D., Southern Baptist Theological Seminary) is president and James Emerson Brown Professor of Christian Theology at Southern Baptist Theological Seminary; he also hosts a daily radio program for the Salem Radio Network, and writes a popular daily commentary on moral, cultural, and theological issues (www.albertmohler.com).

Russell D. Moore (Ph.D., Southern Baptist Theological Seminary) is senior vice president for Academic Administration and dean of the School of Theology at Southern Baptist Theological Seminary.

Tom J. Nettles (Ph.D., Southwestern Baptist Theological Seminary) is professor of Historical Theology at Southern Baptist Theological Seminary.

Dorothy Kelley Patterson (D.Theol., University of South Africa; D.Min., Luther Rice Seminary) is a homemaker and wife of Paige Patterson (president of Southwestern Baptist Theological Seminary); professor of Theology in Women's Studies at Southwestern Baptist Theological Seminary, and author and lecturer on topics relating to the family and Biblical Womanhood.

Paige Patterson (Ph.D., New Orleans Baptist Theological Seminary) is president of Southwestern Baptist Theological Seminary.

Robert B. Stewart (Ph.D., Southwestern Baptist Theological Seminary) is associate professor of Philosophy and Theology, and Greer-Heard Professor of Faith and Culture at New Orleans Baptist Theological Seminary.

Joseph D. Wooddell (Ph.D., Southwestern Baptist Theological Seminary) is assistant professor of Philosophy at Criswell College.

Malcolm B. Yarnell III (D.Phil., Oxford University) is director of the Center for Theological Research, director of the Oxford Studies Program, assistant dean (Theological Studies Division), and associate professor of Systematic Theology at Southwestern Baptist Theological Seminary; and managing editor of www.BaptistTheology.org.

Breinigsville, PA USA
11 November 2010
249117BV00001B/3/P